Heaven or Halakah

Heaven or Halakah

Walking with Jesus in John 14

Andrea L. Robinson

WIPF & STOCK · Eugene, Oregon

HEAVEN OR *HALAKAH*
Walking with Jesus in John 14

Copyright © 2024 Andrea L. Robinson. All rights reserved. Except for brief quotations in critical publications or reviews, no part of this book may be reproduced in any manner without prior written permission from the publisher. Write: Permissions, Wipf and Stock Publishers, 199 W. 8th Ave., Suite 3, Eugene, OR 97401.

Wipf & Stock
An Imprint of Wipf and Stock Publishers
199 W. 8th Ave., Suite 3
Eugene, OR 97401

www.wipfandstock.com

PAPERBACK ISBN: 979-8-3852-0184-6
HARDCOVER ISBN: 979-8-3852-0185-3
EBOOK ISBN: 979-8-3852-0186-0

VERSION NUMBER 10/03/24

Scripture quotations taken from the (NASB®) New American Standard Bible®, Copyright © 1960, 1971, 1977, 1995, 2020 by The Lockman Foundation. Used by permission. All rights reserved. lockman.org

New Revised Standard Version Bible, copyright 1989, Division of Christian Education of the National Council of the Churches of Christ in the United States of America. Used by permission. All rights reserved.

For Asher and Abel

May you walk with Jesus all your days.

Contents

Preface | ix
Abbreviations | xi

Introduction | xvii
    Heaven or *Halakah* | xix
    A New Way of Life | xx
    The Ways of the Past | xxii
    Foundations for the Road Ahead (Academic Prolegomena) | xxiii
    A Road Map | xxiv

1. A History of "Heaven" | 1
    Conceptions of the Afterlife in the Ancient Near East and Hebrew Bible | 2
    Jewish Conceptions of the Afterlife in the Intertestamental Period | 5
    Hellenistic Conceptions of the Afterlife | 8
    Interlude I: Synthesis and Summary | 11
    Afterlife Philosophy at the Turn of the Millennium | 12
    Pharisees, Sadducees, and Qumran | 14
    After the Fall | 16
    The Church Fathers and Beyond | 19
    Interlude II: Synthesis and Summary | 22
    Afterlife in the New Testament | 23
    Past, Present, and Future | 32

2. Mansions in the Sky: Abiding and "Many Rooms" | 34
    The Path Ahead | 35
    Supporting Concept: The Hebrew Bible and the Gospel of John | 35
    Supporting Concept: The Farewell Discourse | 40
    Supporting Concept: Faith, Truth, and Knowledge | 42
    Abiding in the Gospel of John | 44

3. A Very, Very, Very Fine House: The Temple and Household of the Father | 55
   The Path Ahead | 56
   Supporting Concept: Sacred Space | 56
   Supporting Concept: The Temple as God's House | 59
   Sacred Space in the Gospel of John | 63

4. Walk This Way: The *Halakah* of Jesus | 76
   The Path Ahead | 77
   Supporting Concept: *Halakah* | 77
   Halakah in the Gospel of John | 79

5. Paradise Lost and Found: Prepared Place and Promised Land | 93
   The Path Ahead | 94
   Passover and Atonement in the Gospel of John | 95
   Supporting Concept: The Accessibility of Sacred Space | 106
   The Accessibility of Sacred Space in the Gospel of John | 108
   Supporting Concept: A Prepared Place | 113
   A Prepared Place in the Gospel of John | 115
   Atonement, Sacred Space, and Prepared Place in John 14 | 117

6. Coming and Going: The Return of Christ as Spirit-Paraclete | 119
   The Path Ahead | 120
   Supporting Concept: Spirit and Water | 120
   Spirit and Water in the Gospel of John | 123
   Spirit and Paraclete in the Farewell Discourse | 134
   Converging Streams | 141

7. The End of the Road | 144
   Is Heaven for Real? | 145
   Downward Mobility | 147
   United Nations | 151
   Walking with Jesus | 153

Bibliography | 155
Subject Index | 163
Greek and Hebrew Terms Index | 167
Ancient Document Index | 169

Preface

WITH EACH BOOK I'VE written, the process is a bit like bearing a child. The work of research and writing is always more laborious than I expect, but also enormously rewarding when the final manuscript is birthed. Throughout the process, I feel anxious and uncomfortable, yet also hopeful and excited. Because the gestation period for this particular book was nearly a decade, I may have even shed a few tears when the manuscript was complete.

The inception of the project took place in a PhD seminar on the Gospels at New Orleans Baptist Theological Seminary (NOBTS). I am thankful for the robust discussion and feedback from my professor Craig Price and my fellow 'Terps (those in my biblical interpretation cohort). Shortly thereafter, the paper was accepted for presentation at the annual meeting of the Evangelical Theological Society, my first presentation at a national meeting. It was a productive experience, and I am ever thankful for the ongoing dialogue with my fellow ETS members.

Over the years, I continued meditating on John 14 and teaching on the passage. In academic settings, my interpretation was largely accepted. In church settings, however, my ideas about John 14 were typically met with stunned silence, if not open antagonism. So, I couldn't simply let the subject drop. I am, thus, indebted to Adam Harwood, Tommy Doughty, and the *Journal for Baptist Theology and Ministry* for publishing my article "Heaven or *Halakah*: John 14:1–3 Reexamined."[1] Since publishing the article and in the process of writing this book, however, I have refined my views. Most notably, I originally equated "the Father's house" with Jesus himself, the incarnate temple and presence of God. While I still believe this to be correct, my understanding has expanded to include the

---

1. Robinson, "Heaven or *Halakah*."

Father's house as a household. In other words, Jesus is the temple of God *through* which believers enter the family of God.

I would also like to express sincere gratitude to Jeff Griffin and the staff of the John T. Christian Library at NOBTS. Thank you for supporting my research by making a wealth of resources available to me. I echo the words of noteworthy Johannine scholar Francis J. Moloney and offer my interpretation of John's Gospel "within the rich results of [centuries] of critical scholarship to which I am the privileged heir."[2]

On a more personal note, I am thankful for the dear family and friends with whom God has blessed me. To my mentor, Gerald Stevens, thank you for continuing to pour wisdom and encouragement into my life. To my faith family, Asbury Methodist Church, and my pastor Tommy Gray, thank you for creating a life-giving space in which I can continue to pursue my calling. To my family, thank you for putting up with my periods of writing-related self-isolation. To my husband, Wesley, thank you for continuing to be a faithful beta reader and first-stage editor. I'm always grateful for your feedback, even when I don't like it. To my mom, Debra, thank you for reading everything I write and telling me it is fantastic. Your encouragement means more than you know.

Finally, thank you to my Savior, Jesus Christ. Writing this book hasn't simply been an analytical endeavor but a spiritually edifying journey. Through the Gospel of John, the Lord has called me into a deeper abiding with him and a more meaningful walk. To my readers, I hope you likewise experience Jesus' call to "follow" in a more profound manner than ever before.

---

2. Moloney, *Belief in the Word*, x.

Abbreviations

AB	Anchor Bible
AYBD	*Anchor Yale Bible Dictionary.* Edited by David Noel Freedman. 6 vols. New Haven: Yale University Press, 2008
AThRSup	*Anglican Theological Review Supplement Series*
BBR	*Bulletin for Biblical Research*
BDAG	Danker, Frederick W., Walter Bauer, William F. Arndt, and F. Wilbur Gingrich. *Greek-English Lexicon of the New Testament and Other Early Christian Literature* 3rd ed. Chicago: University of Chicago Press, 2000
BECNT	Baker Exegetical Commentary on the New Testament
Bib	*Biblica*
BJS	Brown Judaic Studies
BSac	*Bibliotheca Sacra*
CBQ	*Catholic Biblical Quarterly*
ConcJ	*Concordia Journal*
FR	*Fides Reformata*
HTR	*Harvard Theological Review*
ICC	International Critical Commentary
IEJ	*Israel Exploration Journal*
Int	*Interpretation*
IVPNTC	IVP New Testament Commentary
JBL	*Journal of Biblical Literature*
JBPR	*Journal of Biblical and Pneumatological Research*
JBTM	*Journal for Baptist Theology and Ministry*
JETS	*Journal of the Evangelical Theological Society*
JR	*Journal of Religion*
JSNT	*Journal for the Study of the New Testament*

JSNTSS	Journal for the Study of the New Testament Supplement Series
JTSA	*Journal of Theology for Southern Africa*
L&N	Louw, Johannes P., and Eugene A. Nida, eds. *Greek-English Lexicon of the New Testament: Based on Semantic Domains*. 2nd ed. New York: United Bible Societies, 1989
LCL	Loeb Classical Library
LNTS	Library of New Testament Studies
NAC	New American Commentary
NASB	New American Standard Bible
Neot	*Neotestamentica*
NICNT	New International Commentary on the New Testament
NIDNTT	*New International Dictionary of New Testament Theology*
NIGTC	New International Greek Testament Commentary
NovT	*Novum Testamentum*
NT	New Testament
NTL	New Testament Library
NTS	*New Testament Studies*
OT	Old Testament
OTL	Old Testament Library
PBM	Paternoster Biblical Monographs
PNTC	Pillar New Testament Commentary
PresB	*Presbyterion*
RB	*Revue biblique*
RevExp	*Review and Expositor*
Sal	*Salesianum*
SJT	*Scottish Journal of Theology*
SNTSMS	Society for New Testament Studies Monograph Series
SP	*Sacra Pagina*
SVTQ	*St. Vladimir's Theological Quarterly*
TBT	*The Bible Today*
TDNT	*Theological Dictionary of the New Testament*
TJ	*Trinity Journal*
TOTE	Through Old Testament Eyes
TWOT	*Theological Wordbook of the Old Testament*
TynBul	*Tyndale Bulletin*
VT	*Vetus Testamentum*
WisC	Wisdom Commentary
WBC	Word Biblical Commentary

WUNT	Wissenschaftliche Untersuchungen zum Neuen Testament		
ZNW	*Zeitschrift für die neutestamentliche Wissenschaft und die Kunde der älteren Kirche*		

Primary Sources

Old Testament

Gen	Genesis	Jer	Jeremiah
Exod	Exodus	Lam	Lamentations
Lev	Leviticus	Ezek	Ezekiel
Num	Numbers	Dan	Daniel
Deut	Deuteronomy	Hos	Hosea
Josh	Joshua	Obad	Obadiah
1–2 Sam	1–2 Samuel	Mic	Micah
1–2 Kgs	1–2 Kings	Nah	Nahum
1–2 Chr	1–2 Chronicles	Hab	Habakkuk
Neh	Nehemiah	Zeph	Zephaniah
Esth	Esther	Hag	Haggai
Ps/Pss	Psalms	Zech	Zechariah
Song	Song of Songs	LXX	Septuagint
Isa	Isaiah		

New Testament

Matt	Matthew	Heb	Hebrews
1–2 Cor	1–2 Corinthians	1–2 Pet	1–2 Peter
Gal	Galatians	Rev	Revelation
Eph	Ephesians		

Apocrypha

Tob	Tobit	1–2 Macc	1–2 Maccabees
Jdt	Judith	1 Esd	1 Esdras
Wis	Wisdom of Solomon	2 Esd	2 Esdras
Sir	Sirach	4 Macc	4 Maccabees
Bar	Baruch		

Pseudepigrapha

Apoc. Ab.	Apocalypse of Abraham
2 Bar.	2 Baruch
3 Bar.	3 Baruch
1 En.	1 Enoch
Jub.	Jubilees
LAB	Liber antiquitatum biblicarum (Pseudo-Philo)
Let. Aris.	Letter of Aristeas
Sib. Or.	Sibylline Oracles
T. 12 Patr.	Testaments of the Twelve Patriarchs
T. Levi	Testament of Levi
T. Mos.	Testament of Moses
T. Sol.	Testament of Solomon
T. Zeb.	Testament of Zebulun

Dead Sea Scrolls

CD	Cairo Genizah copy of the Damascus Document
1QH	*Hodayot* or Thanksgiving Hymns
1QM	War Scroll
1QS	Rule of the Community
4QShirŠabb	Songs of the Sabbath Sacrifice
11QT^a	Temple Scroll^a

Rabbinic Literature

b.	Babylonian Talmud
B. Meṣ	Baba Meṣiʿa
Gen. Rab.	Rabbah Genesis
Kelim	Kelim
Ketub.	Ketubbot
m.	Mishnah
Mek. Pisha	Mekilta Pisha
Mid.	Middot
Midr. Ps.	Midrash on the Psalms
Miqw.	Miqwaʾot
Nid.	Niddah

Pesiq. Rab.	Pesiqta Rabbati
Šabb.	Šabbat
Sanh.	Sanhedrin
Sukkah	Sukkah
Tg. Neof.	Targum Neofiti
Tg. Yer.	Targum Yerušalmi I

Josephus

Ant.	*Jewish Antiquities*
J.W.	*Jewish War*

Introduction

I'M A COUNTRY GIRL through and through. I was born and raised in Alabama, and I still reside there. I exist in a distinct southern culture through which my perspective on life tends to filter. I try, however, to experience as much of the world as possible, to learn about different belief systems, and to develop a broader view of God's creation. I travel to the extent that my bank account allows, and I learn about the world through books and other forms of media.

I especially love to learn about the cultures of the Bible. I have, in fact, devoted my life to studying God's word and the societies from which it arose. Imagine for a moment, however, that instead of learning about the world of the ancient Near East and the Greco-Roman Empire, I imported my own southern culture into the Bible. I might suppose that the meal of the Last Supper consisted of fried chicken, buttermilk biscuits, and mashed potatoes instead of matzah and bitter herbs. I might imagine that when Jesus knelt to wash his disciples feet, they were stained with red Alabama clay instead of fine, powdery Judean dirt.

Although such imagery is ridiculous, we regularly import our own cultural norms into Scripture. Instead of reading God's word through the lens of its own background, we interpret it through the filter of twenty-first century thought. Instead of understanding Jesus as a Jewish man living in the Greco-Roman Empire, we understand his life and words through the filter of our own Western culture. We typically make such mistakes unknowingly, but our innocence does not rectify the interpretive errors. When we read Scripture anachronistically and anaculturally,[1]

---

1. Whereas "anachronism" refers to a custom, event, or way of life attributed to the wrong time period, "anaculturalism" refers to a custom, event, or way of life attributed to the wrong culture.

we distort God's message . . . at best. At worst, we risk distorting the very fabric of the gospel message.

I believe John 14, especially vv. 1–3, is one such passage that modern Christendom has grossly distorted. The prominent passage narrates Jesus' encouraging words to the disciples just prior to his crucifixion:

> Do not let your hearts be troubled; believe in God, believe also in me. In my Father's house are many rooms; unless it were so, would I say to you that I go to prepare a place for you? And if I should go and prepare a place for you, I will come again and receive you to myself, that where I am also you will be. (John 14:1–3)[2]

A staple of Christian funerals, the passage is typically interpreted as Jesus' promise to usher believers, upon death, into "heaven." However, John 14 has much more to say about how we live than what happens when we die. Johannine scholar Francis Moloney writes, "There can be no gainsaying John's conviction that the believer enjoys favorable judgment, eternal life, and an intense belonging to God through faith and love of Jesus *on this side of death*."[3] Rather than describing an event that takes place solely in the future, in John 14:1–3, Jesus calls believers to follow his pattern of cruciform obedience.

Along such lines, I will argue that the popular understanding of John 14 disregards the context of the Fourth Gospel and misses the deep theological significance of Jesus' words. Like expecting fried chicken at a Passover meal, we've imposed upon John 14:1–3 ideas that are foreign to the original context. Instead of understanding Jesus' words as a call to abide in the presence of God and live according to his will, we've transmuted them into an escape clause. In short, we've created a stunted gospel in which belief in Jesus amounts to little more than escaping hell and earning a pass into a disembodied afterlife paradise.

Because such thinking pervades the church more so than the academy, I have aimed this book toward a broad audience. I hope that any serious student of Scripture, including educated churchgoers, will benefit from this work. I have endeavored to minimize scholarly jargon and explain concepts that might be unfamiliar to general readers. At the same time, I hope this monograph will contribute to the field of Johannine

---

2. All Scripture quotations are translated by the author unless otherwise noted.

3. Moloney, "God," 205 (emphasis original). Cf. Jeffrey Gibbs, "Already Dwelling," 13.

studies such that the academic community will benefit as well. To balance the needs of such a broad audience, I have provided robust footnotes. For a general audience, I use footnotes to define terms and concepts that might be confusing or unfamiliar. For more academically oriented readers, I have endeavored to provide a detailed trail of sources, both primary and secondary, for those who might desire further study.

Heaven or *Halakah*

In recent decades, the idea of "heaven" as the eternal dwelling place of the redeemed has come under increasing scrutiny. Most evangelical scholars do not dispute the idea that some type of intermediate paradise exists, but most are beginning to doubt whether the redeemed will spend eternity there. In fact, the notion of "heaven" is more a matter of tradition than biblical exegesis as the overarching narrative of Scripture points to the resurrection of God's people and the restoration of creation. In the meantime, believers are called to implement God's will upon the earth, bringing it ever closer to his created intent.

I'm not the first to suggest that our understanding of the gospel message and the nature of heaven has become skewed.[4] The distinctive contribution of this monograph, however, is in the contextual analysis of John 14. The Fourth Gospel is steeped in imagery from the Hebrew Bible, especially that of the exodus and Passover. As such, a contextual analysis of John 14 reveals that "the Father's house" is not a designation for heaven, but a reference to the temple, the archetypal place of God's presence, which is extended to the household of faith. Similarly, the "prepared place" is a reconceptualization of exodus imagery. Jesus, through his cruciform work as Passover lamb, makes the presence of God accessible for all believers and leads them into a new promised land.

In addition, as Christ walks in obedience to the Father, he models a new *way* of living based on personal, relational faith, the true fulfillment of the Mosaic law. Such a mode of faithful obedience is defined by the Jewish concept of *halakah*. Though obscured somewhat by the transition from Hebrew to Greek terminology and again by translation into English, *halakah* describes both God's law and the *way* in which one walks in obedience. As such, those who follow Jesus are called to follow in his cruciform footsteps by bringing about the will of the Father—not

---

4. See especially Middleton, *New Heaven*; Wright, *Surprised by Hope*.

in a future heavenly paradise but right now. In order to equip believers to carry out such a high calling, Jesus will "come again," receiving believers to himself and equipping them through the indwelling presence of the Spirit-Paraclete.

A New Way of Life

Richard Middleton stresses that "eschatology is inevitably connected to ethics."[5] In other words, our afterlife theology will inform the way we live. If we believe that God's material creation is irreparably damaged and destined for destruction, we become less motivated to work for its healing. If our greatest hope is to escape the earth, we become less sensitive to earthly needs. If we believe that salvation entails escape from hell, we become less determined to live in sacrificial service to others.

Instead, understanding the earthly aspects of the gospel and the kingdom of God should motivate believers to embody the mission of Christ and work for the betterment of the world. Again, Middleton writes, "The creator has not given up on creation and is working to salvage and restore the world (human and nonhuman) to the fullness of shalom and flourishing intended from the beginning. And redeemed human beings, renewed in God's image, are to work toward and embody this vision in their daily lives."[6]

At the same time, re-centering traditional notions of heaven is not a purely material endeavor. God himself and our faith in him should remain the central motivating force behind our mission in this world. The hope of a more intimate walk with God both now and in the afterlife should impact the way we live every day, *even if* we already have assurance of salvation.[7] Such a focus on our place in God's kingdom and our relationship with the Father should engender a complete reorientation of self that takes place at the moment of salvation and continues throughout one's earthly walk.

The Gospel of John has often been accused of being a "spiritual" Gospel that offers little real-world application. Whereas the Synoptics offer specific ethical teachings (i.e., the Sermon on the Mount), John's Gospel is often thought to say more about faith than practice, more "about

---

5. Middleton, *New Heaven*, 23. Cf. Allen, *Grounded in Heaven*, 125.
6. Middleton, *New Heaven*, 27.
7. Allen, *Grounded in Heaven*, 47.

believing than doing."[8] To the contrary, such assumptions disregard John's portrayal of true belief, which is not simply an inner disposition but is a transformative phenomenon resulting in productive action. John's Gospel addresses "the deepest issues of God's relation to the world and the human race, and of the human response to God and to one another."[9] The dualism so often observed in the Fourth Gospel is not a dichotomy of material versus spiritual. Rather, John contrasts the kingdom "above," i.e., the material *and* spiritual aspects of God's kingdom, with the kingdom of this world, i.e., the material *and* spiritual domain enslaved to the devil (John 8:23–44; 18:36). As a result, those who choose to believe in Jesus and accept the gift of salvation also accept the responsibility to contribute meaningfully to the execution of God's will upon the earth.

It is true that the Fourth Gospel offers few direct ethical commands. According to Christopher Skinner, "If we approach the Johannine literature looking for an ethics that consists of explicit references to moral conduct, the observation of a set of rules, or the development of a series of virtues, there is a good chance that we will come away from our search disappointed. There is an equally good chance of our concluding that John has nothing to contribute to a conversation about New Testament ethics."[10] John does, however, prescribe one commandment that encompasses all the others: love.[11] And as Jesus asserts in Matt 22:40, the entirety of the Law and Prophets hang upon such a command.

More than a law code, John's ethos of love should motivate believers to sacrificial service. This ethos elevates obedience to God above a set of rules to a relationship-oriented loyalty that results in the good of others.[12] Though love was always the greatest command (Lev 19:18; Matt 22:36–40), God's people were unable to live it out due to their enslavement to the kingdom of this world. Only through the sacrificial model of Christ and subsequent empowerment of the Holy Spirit are God's people able to walk in his perfect will.

---

8. Kanagaraj, "Implied Ethics," 33.

9. Rensberger, *Johannine Faith*, 137.

10. Skinner, "Introduction," xx.

11. John 3:16, 19, 35; 5:20, 42; 8:42; 10:17; 11:3, 5, 36; 12:25, 43; 13:1, 23, 34, 35; 14:15, 21–24; 15:9, 10, 12, 13, 17, 19; 16:27; 17:23, 24, 26; 19:26; 20:2; 21:7, 15–17, 20.

12. Van der Watt, "Ethics and Ethos," 166.

The Ways of the Past

Two contexts dominate the Fourth Gospel: the Jewish context of Judea and the Hellenistic context of first-century Rome. Because the authors of Scripture wrote to their immediate audience, they assumed a shared cultural background. Yet, first-century Mediterranean cultures were largely agrarian and communal, the polar opposite to the modern Western world, which is industrialized and individualistic. According to Malina and Rohrbaugh, our "understanding of the self, of others, of nature and time and space, and perhaps even God" has shifted from that of the biblical authors and audiences.[13] Such a cultural gap had hindered the ability of modern Western readers to understand and apply God's word.

Where the authors of Scripture leave information gaps or fail to provide detailed definitions, modern readers unwittingly fill in such gaps with assumptions from their own culture. Even familiar terms such as "love" and "belief" bear a different nuance than they did in the context of the first-century Mediterranean world. Along such lines, meaning expressed via language doesn't arise from *words*, but from the *social system* in which the communication is embedded.[14] Specifically with regard to the Fourth Gospel, Malina and Rohrbaugh explain, "John speaks of 'believing *into* Jesus.' And to express this reality, he has recourse to terms such as: *following* him, *abiding* in him, *loving* him, *keeping* his word, *receiving* him, *having* him, or *seeing* him. While for us all these verbs express different facets of behavior, not so in John. All these words describe 'believing into Jesus.'"[15]

An additional layer that challenges modern believers is the use of the OT in the NT, as many OT themes are woven throughout the NT without explanation. John, in particular, utilizes a variety of themes and sources, often combining them in unique ways, to present a portrait of the Messiah that is in continuity with the OT, but also transcends it.[16] One primary goal of this monograph, therefore, is to bring such cultural and Scriptural backgrounds to the forefront so that readers can more closely appropriate the message of the Fourth Gospel. Although we can never step into the mind of the author and apprehend his communicative

---

13. Malina and Rohrbaugh, *John*, 2.
14. Malina and Rohrbaugh, *John*, 3.
15. Malina and Rohrbaugh, *John*, 4.
16. Carey, "Lamb of God," 108–10.

intent with certainty, by situating the Gospel in its original context, we can hear his voice more clearly.

Foundations for the Road Ahead (Academic Prolegomena)

For over a century, John has been viewed largely as a sectarian document. In recent decades, however, many Johannine scholars have begun to challenge the notion that the Fourth Gospel was written for a specific community. Stanley Porter posits that "the Gospel of John was written with the intention of being a public and widespread declaratory statement and witness to the work of God through Jesus Christ, and it was composed in a way that declared this intention openly."[17] Indeed, the cosmic, multicultural emphasis of the Fourth Gospel seems to shape a message that is universal and directed toward "whosoever might believe" (John 3:16). As I will argue, John portrays Jesus as a Savior who invites all peoples into the spacious presence of the Father.

I will not, however, engage in an extended discussion of John's intended audience. Such arguments serve little constructive purpose for the current monograph. Yet, I do believe that the trend away from viewing the Fourth Gospel as a sectarian document takes Johannine scholarship in the right direction. Likewise, a discussion of Johannine authorship yields little benefit for the current work. I will simply refer to the author of the Fourth Gospel as "John" and trust that academic readers will seek out trustworthy commentaries for such discussions.[18]

The cultural and scriptural backgrounds already mentioned offer more productive and fruitful avenues of exploration. Thus, my primary methodology will be literary-historical analysis, relying especially upon socio-scientific research for historical foundations. As Stanley Porter has noted, utilizing literary analysis alongside traditional exegetical methods yields much interpretive fruit.[19] Thus, I will examine the narrative flow

---

17. Porter, *John*, 42. Cf. Bauckham, "John for Readers of Mark," 153–61; Klink, *Sheep of the Fold*; Skinner, "Love One Another," 26.

18. Staples in the field include Brown, *Gospel according to John*; Morris, *Gospel according to John*; Carson, *Gospel according to John*. Noteworthy recent commentaries include Keener, *The Gospel of John*; Thompson, *John*; Coloe, *John*; Jobes, *John through Old Testament Eyes*.

19. Porter, "Traditional Exegesis."

and thematic development of the final form of John's Gospel in addition to the historical, cultural, and scriptural background from which it evolved.

In particular, I will examine the OT sources upon which the Gospel author so often draws. My purpose is not to undertake an exhaustive analysis of *which* OT passages John draws upon, but *how* John's OT source material informs and contributes to specific themes and motifs. As such, I will not offer a full intertextual analysis. Many of John's references to the OT are well recognized quotations, echoes, and allusions, which are sufficiently strong to establish with near certainty that John's Gospel is permeated with OT tradition. Determining the precise nature of each citation does little to advance my argument. Finally, as I examine the Jewish background of the Fourth Gospel, I am not denying the presence of Hellenistic influences. I'm simply focusing on the manner in which John used his OT sources.

More specifically, John repeatedly presents Jesus as a newer and truer version of OT rituals and institutions. Supersession, a common theological term used to describe the manner in which Jesus replaces the institutions and rituals of Israel, might be used to describe some of my points. However, I want to be clear that Jesus' new covenant work is in continuity with God's work throughout the history of Israel. Neither the idea of replacement nor the idea of fulfillment alone describes the manner in which Jesus completes God's mission. While Jesus does do away with incomplete and inferior modes of relating to God, the idea of replacement alone gives the impression that OT institutions are simply discarded. Keeping replacement closely connected to fulfillment communicates both continuity and discontinuity as Jesus brings the promises of God to fruition.[20]

A Road Map

Our journey through John 14 will proceed along several avenues. First, we will seek to clear away obstacles in our path with a history of heaven. Our survey will not be exhaustive; rather, we will examine the major ideologies of OT and NT, as well as conceptions about heaven in the cultures in which early Jewish people and Christians were embedded. As we examine documents from different periods of history, we will see how ideas evolved and developed over time. We will conclude that modern ideas

---

20. Hoskins, *Jesus as the Fulfillment*, 189.

about an otherworldly heaven arose more from Hellenistic culture than scriptural teaching. Although our interaction with John 14 will be minimal, the discussion will provide clarity as we move into subsequent chapters. Equipped with an understanding of what the Bible actually teaches about "heaven," we may examine our focal passage without centuries of extra-biblical baggage.

In subsequent chapters, I will argue that specific themes throughout the Gospel provide an interpretive matrix for Jesus' teaching in chapter 14. In other words, we will allow John to interpret his own Gospel. Understanding how John uses specific imagery and terminology throughout equips us to understand corresponding imagery and terminology in John 14. In addition, each chapter will feature "supporting concepts." These sections provide additional background from Greco-Roman culture, Jewish culture, and/or Scripture that helps us interpret John's narrative.

We will begin our study of John's Gospel with the key concept of abiding in chapter 2 ("Mansions in the Sky"). The concepts of truth, relationship, and obedience come together in the Fourth Gospel to formulate the notion of a close, interpersonal communion between God, Christ, and his people. Such a concept is crucial to understanding the entirety of John and especially the "rooms" in chapter 14. In 14:2, Jesus says to his disciples, "In my Father's house are many rooms," a phrase often understood to refer to living quarters in heaven. The broader concept of John's Gospel, however, indicates that Jesus is referring to intimacy in the presence of God, not a heavenly dwelling place. Through Christ's work on the cross, his followers are empowered to abide in the Father, not move into a heavenly apartment upon death.

In chapter 3 ("A Very, Very, Very Fine House"), we will discuss the imagery of the Father's house and the supporting concept of sacred space. Just as the "rooms" in the Father's house represent the intimate relationship between God and his children, the "house" represents the presence of God and, by extension, the household of God, comprised of those who believe into Christ and abide in the Father's presence. As members of the Father's household, Christ's followers are unbound from imperfect institutions of the past, yet still called to meet the high holy standards of abiding in God's presence. As Christ's people seek to live in the light of such an intimate relationship—in the Father's house—they become mobile incarnations of the temple, spreading God's sacred presence throughout the earth, not seeking an escape to heaven.

In chapter 4 ("Walk This Way"), we will turn to the concept of *halakah* and the sacrificial model that Christ provides through his life, ministry, death, and resurrection. The focus of John 14 is not Jesus' journey to heaven but to the cross. In his cruciform work, he both opens the door to God's presence and provides the perfect model of obedience. Likewise, those who place faith in Christ aren't being transported to a heavenly dwelling but being called to follow Jesus' sacrificial model and carry out God's mission in the world.

In chapter 5 ("Paradise Lost and Found"), we will survey John's use of Exodus imagery with a special focus on Christ as Passover lamb and atoning sacrifice. Through dying as the perfect Passover lamb, Jesus leads his people out of slavery to sin and into the household of God. Prior to Christ, access to God was highly regulated, but the atoning work of Christ renders the presence of God available to all of humanity. Indeed, there are "many rooms" in the Father's house—plenty of space for whosoever would believe, whether Jew or gentile, male or female.

The chapter will conclude with an examination of the place prepared by Jesus, imagery that is closely associated with the promised land. As Jesus leads his people out of slavery, he simultaneously leads them into the place he prepares, a new promised land in the presence of the Father. Unlike the original promised land, the place Jesus prepares isn't just for hereditary Israel but for anyone who would place faith in him. And the prepared place isn't simply a geographical space (the land of Israel), an architectural structure (the tabernacle/temple), or a heavenly mansion but the space in which God's people experience the culmination of the Father's love and consummation of his promises.

In chapter 6 ("Coming and Going"), we will examine language and themes surrounding the Holy Spirit. Water, in particular, is a symbol upon which John draws to convey the manifold work of the Spirit in the life of the believer. However, the theme of water fades into the background in the Farewell Discourse as Jesus says, "And if I should go and prepare a place for you, *I will come again* and receive you to myself, that where I am also you will be" (John 14:3; emphasis mine). This coming again is not Christ's return to individual believers to transport them to heaven when they die. Rather, Jesus tells his followers exactly what form his return will take: the Paraclete. As such, Jesus' return through the Spirit empowers believers to continue Jesus' own work in the world.

Though Christ's return as Spirit-Paraclete is dominant in John 14, the larger setting of the Gospel anticipates a broader work of the Spirit.

Thus, the immediate return of Christ as Spirit-Paraclete anticipates an end-time return of Christ in which he will complete the process of redemption and restoration. As such, the return of Christ through the Spirit fulfills the cosmic scope and OT focus of John. The same spirit who hovered over the waters in Genesis brings new life to creation as the incarnation, death, and resurrection of Christ inaugurates the final era of history. The Spirit, anticipated by the Jewish prophets, would now begin to pour out the living water that renews and restores all of creation.

Finally, in chapter 7 ("The End of the Road"), we will return to where we began and examine several passages that inform our understanding of the afterlife while also supporting our interpretation of John 14. Christianity is and has always been a resurrection movement. From its birth out of Judaism onward, the promise of life after death has consisted of an embodied existence in a restored creation in the presence of God. As such, John directs the attention of his readers not to the heavenly realm but to the Father himself. The great hope in the Gospel of John, and in the Christian faith, is not "heaven" but eternity in the presence of the Lord.

1.

A History of "Heaven"

There was once a wealthy man who had worked hard and achieved great success during his life. As the day of his death approached, he desperately wanted to keep some of the fortune for which he had labored. So, the man diligently petitioned God and was finally given permission to take one suitcase to heaven. Overjoyed, the man procured the largest suitcase he could find and filled it with gold bars.

Shortly thereafter, the man passed away and took his suitcase to the pearly gates of heaven. Saint Peter stopped the man before he could enter and told him the suitcase wouldn't be allowed inside. The man quickly explained that he had received special permission from God. So, Peter verified the story with the Lord, found the man's claim to be true, and told him he could enter. First, however, Peter would need to inspect the contents of the suitcase. Proudly, the man unzipped the bag and revealed his treasure. Saint Peter, though, was perplexed and asked, "Why did you bring dirt?"

Theologically speaking, this joke is inaccurate in every possible way. Yet, the silly punch line does reveal one important truth about the afterlife. For those who belong to Christ, eternity will be better than we can imagine. The greatest treasures of our earthly existence will be less valuable than the dirt beneath our feet.

Virtually all Christians believe that eternity with God will be markedly different and better than our current existence. However, ideas about what the afterlife will look like have drifted from the actual teachings of Scripture. *In fact, the notion of "going to heaven" for eternity isn't a biblical concept at all.*

If such a statement is new or upsetting to you, let me offer a few words of reassurance. Eternity will be better than you imagined—it just won't be in "heaven." Holding onto our ideas about a paradise in the clouds, complete with harps, angels, and golden streets, is like carrying around a suitcase full of dirt. Such images are a "truncated and distorted version" of the greatest of all biblical expectations: resurrection.[1] From Genesis to Revelation, Scripture moves toward a restoration of the earthly garden that was lost as biblical authors describe a reconciliation between God, humanity, and the natural world. The overarching narrative of Scripture points to the redemption of creation, not an escape from it. So, God's people will, indeed, spend eternity with him, but we will do it in a redeemed creation and a restored Eden, not an otherworldly heaven.

To clarify the trajectory by which modern Western culture arrived at our current beliefs about the afterlife, we will now embark upon a history of heaven. Our survey will not be exhaustive; rather, we will examine the major ideologies of the OT and NT, as well as conceptions about heaven in the cultures in which the early Jewish and Christian believers were embedded. In order to do so, we will examine many ancient texts that are not in the canon of Scripture. Such texts help us determine how people of the day interpreted God's word and how they understood certain concepts, like the afterlife. As we examine documents from different periods of history, we can also see how ideas evolved and developed over time.

Although our interaction with John 14 will be minimal, the discussion will provide clarity as we move into subsequent chapters. Equipped with an understanding of what the Bible actually teaches about "heaven," we may examine our focal passage without centuries of extra-biblical baggage.

Conceptions of the Afterlife in the Ancient Near East and Hebrew Bible

In order to understand ancient Semitic beliefs about the afterlife, we must first understand their conception of the cosmos. For ancient peoples of the Near East, the universe was comprised of three tiers: the upper realm, which housed the gods (heaven); the middle realm, which was occupied by humans (the earth); and the lowest realm, which housed chthonic, or underworld, deities along with the dead (Sheol/Hades). The upper realm of the gods was separated from the earthly realm by the "firmament," a

---

1. Wright, *Surprised by Hope*, 19.

hard covering that was supported by pillars and had windows through which rain could fall.[2]

Upon death, every person, whether good or evil, transitioned to Sheol. A dark, quiet cavity under the earth, Sheol was not the equivalent of hell but a place where the dead existed as diminished, shadowy versions of themselves. And though Sheol is mentioned in the OT, biblical authors never offer any explicit teaching on the subject.

Early Semitic peoples, including the Jewish people, held out virtually no hope for a blissful afterlife. Everyone simply drifted to Sheol upon death. Although God abided in heaven, humans never expected to join him there.

From his heavenly seat God could look down and watch over events upon the earth.[3] Although he could deign to visit the earth, his supreme dwelling place remained in heaven. Further, as heaven was the domain of God, the term was also used to refer to God himself.[4] As time passed, heaven became an increasingly common appellation for God since Jewish people avoided using God's personal name, YHWH.[5]

More broadly, although the "heavens" were the realm of the gods, the term was also used to refer to everything above the earth.[6] In fact, "heaven" served as a synonym for "sky" in ancient Hebrew and Greek, a nuance that will be discussed shortly.

Despite the ubiquitous belief that every human ended up in Sheol, the hope of a joyful life after death eventually began to emerge among the Jewish people. According to N. T. Wright, "At some point (nobody knows when; dating of developments in such matters is notoriously difficult) some pious Israelites came to regard the love and power of YHWH as so strong that the relationship they enjoyed with him in the present could not be broken even by death."[7] Wright suggests that by the era of Moses such beliefs began to emerge in nascent form. As Moses offers the choice between life and death to his people, he expresses hope in a future in

---

2. H. Bietenhard, "*Ouranos*," *NIDNTT*, 2:188–89; McDannell and Lang, *Heaven*, 3; Reddish, "Heaven," 90. See Gen 1:6–8; 7:11; Job 26:11.

3. Isa 40:22; Ps 102:18.

4. Reddish, "Heaven," 91. See Gen 49:25; Deut 33:13.

5. H. Bietenhard, "*Ouranos*," *NIDNTT*, 2:191.

6. Reddish, "Heaven," 90. See Exod 9:22–35; Job 37:9; 38:22; Ps 135:7; Jer 10:30; Isa 55:10; Josh 10:11; Rev 11:19.

7. Wright, *Resurrection*, 86.

which repentance will lead to a restored relationship with God, a renewal of human hearts, and a return to the "promised land."[8]

G. K. Beale locates the first biblical conceptions of resurrection even further back in Scripture—right in the beginning.[9] He notes that God's plan always entailed an earthly existence. When Adam and Eve failed to fulfill their calling, God didn't dispose of his plan for creation, he "raised up other Adam-like figures," first through the line of Abraham and ultimately culminating in the last Adam, Christ.[10]

The promises to Israel renew and reaffirm the vision presented in Gen 1–2. But, as Beale explains, "after the events of Israel's rebellious attitude in Egypt and at the event of the golden calf, it becomes clear that the promise is not consummated in the first generation of Israel."[11] Thus, the Hebrew Scriptures anticipate a return to Edenic conditions in the future. These hopes increasingly prefigure eschatological[12] rewards, especially by the time of the prophets, as "salvation history advances towards a kind of paradise regained."[13]

The idea of resurrection began to emerge more overtly in the period of the exile (nearly a millennia after the time of Moses). Since, outside of Christians and the Jewish people, the only ancient sect to anticipate an embodied resurrection were the Zoroastrians, many scholars have attributed Jewish resurrection beliefs to Persian influence.[14] However, Wright argues that when the belief in resurrection (re)emerged, it did so as a (re) expression of ancient Hebrew views.[15] He explains, "We may add that the thrust of resurrection, emerging around the time of the exile . . . was upon Israel's status as the unique chosen people of the one creator god. To express this by borrowing a key idea from the very people who were causing

---

8. See Deut 30; Wright, *Resurrection*, 92–93.

9. For a detailed analysis of the concept of resurrection throughout Scripture, see Beale, *Union*.

10. Beale, *Union*, 25.

11. Beale, *Union*, 28.

12. Eschatology is the study of the "end-times," including death, judgment, and the afterlife.

13. McCaffrey, *House*, 55. See Hos 2:14–23; Isa 11:6–9; 51:3; 65:25; Ezek 36:35; 47:7–12; Joel 3:18.

14. Ferguson, *Backgrounds of Early Christianity*, 250.

15. Wright, *Resurrection*, 87.

the problem [the Persians] . . . does no justice to the much subtler process of reflection, devotion, and vision that seems to have taken place."[16]

Regardless of origin, resurrection theology had clearly emerged by the exilic period. As the Jewish people dealt with the loss of their temple and land, they hoped for a better future. Along such lines, salvation and resurrection were more political than personal.[17] Although addressed in only a few passages, the future hope involved a day in which God would resurrect the Jewish people, remove hardship, and restore Israel to national prominence.[18]

Prophetic texts such as Ezek 37 and Isa 25–26 relay eschatological hopes for an embodied future. Indeed, "the expectation is manifestly this-worldly, meant to guarantee for the faithful the earthly promises of shalom that death has cut short."[19] Additionally, national restoration and bodily resurrection are so closely related that making a distinction between the two ideas is nearly impossible. But, according to Wright, "That is part of the point. The intertwining adds to the robustness of the emerging belief."[20] Resurrection was the very reversal of death, a miracle in which God would remake his creation along with his people.[21]

Jewish Conceptions of the Afterlife in the Intertestamental Period

Ideas surrounding resurrection gained prominence during the intertestamental period. As the Hebrew Scriptures were translated into Greek (ca. 250 BCE), translators made vague references to resurrection more pronounced. Wright explains, "Many passages which might have been at most ambiguous became clear, and some which seemed to have nothing to do with resurrection might suddenly give a hint, or more than a hint, in that direction."[22]

In the early Jewish resurrection theology we have discussed thus far, individual salvation and personal righteousness have virtually no place.

---

16. Wright, *Resurrection*, 125.
17. Himmelfarb, "Afterlife," 549.
18. Martin-Achard, "Resurrection," 681; McDannell and Lang, *Heaven*, 2.
19. Middleton, *New Heaven*, 26.
20. Wright, *Resurrection*, 124. Cf. Beale, *Union*, 67.
21. Wright, *Resurrection*, 127–28.
22. Wright, *Resurrection*, 147.

The idea of rewards for righteous individuals and punishment for wicked individuals only begins to emerge as the Maccabean period approaches. The most relevant and noteworthy passage in the canonical Scriptures from this period is Dan 12:[23]

> Many of those who sleep in the dust of the ground will awaken, some to eternal life, but others to disgrace and to eternal abhorrence. Those who have insight will shine like the brilliance of the expanse of heaven, and those who lead the many to righteousness, like the stars forever and ever. (Dan 12:2–3)

The passage indicates that many of those "who sleep"—those who have died—will awaken either to everlasting life or everlasting contempt. Clearly, individuals who have lived wisely will be rewarded and those who have failed to meet such a standard will experience everlasting disgrace.

Much about the passage, however, is ambiguous. The author states only that "some"—not all—who sleep will reawaken. As Daniel is highly apocalyptic, scholars are also divided about how to interpret the language of shining "like the stars." Yet, clearly, Daniel does not envision a return to the conditions of the past; he articulates the hope of a better life in the future.[24] Though the passage doesn't explicitly state that resurrection includes both body and soul, most interpreters regard Dan 12:2 as the most overt statement of bodily resurrection in the Hebrew Bible.[25]

Daniel's apocalyptic and eschatological theology was far from standard, as beliefs about the afterlife were in a state of transition. Some texts of the time period continued to offer a more ancient portrayal of the afterlife. The deuterocanonical[26] books of Sirach and Tobit, for example, reflect the older perspective that, upon death, all people enter into a shadowy existence in the underworld (Sheol/Hades).[27]

Likely contemporaneous with Daniel, Sirach, and Tobit, 1 Enoch represents a major step in the development of afterlife beliefs, being the first Jewish text to offer a clear teaching on resurrection (at least the first of which we are aware). In visionary form, the author indicates that

---

23. Although the narrative setting of Daniel is the Babylonian/Persian period (ca. 500 BCE), the majority of biblical scholars believe it came to final form in the second century BCE.

24. Martin-Achard, "Resurrection," 683.

25. Miller, *Daniel*, 318.

26. Deuterocanonical works are books accepted as Holy Scripture by the Catholic Church, but not by Protestants.

27. Sir 14:16–19; 17:25–32; 38:16–23; 41:3–4; 48:4–5; 51:5–6; Tob 3:10, 4:19.

resurrection is the means of recompense for the tenor of one's earthly life.[28] In chapters 14–36, Enoch is taken on a tour of the heavens and underworld. His angelic guide shows him the chambers beneath the earth in which the wicked dead and fallen angels have been confined. A separate chamber, however, is reserved for the souls of the righteous, who enjoy a "bright spring of water" while all souls await final judgment. On the final day of judgment, the righteous will be raised, while the evil will be forever bound in the underworld.[29]

As the passage makes clear, Sheol/Hades was increasingly regarded as the abode of, and punishment for, the wicked.[30] Thus, by the late third/early second century BCE, at least some Jewish people had begun to believe that "the survival of the soul after death [was] an opportunity to reward the righteous and punish the wicked."[31]

Such expectations are overt in the intertestamental book of 2 Maccabees (ca. 150–100 BCE). Preserved in chapter 7 is the story of the mother and seven sons who are martyred by Antiochus IV. The sons, with the encouragement of their mother, refuse to eat swine and, in doing so, defy the king. As sons (and mother) are tortured and killed, they remain steadfast through their faith in God's promise of resurrection. According to the author, "The mother was especially admirable and worthy of honorable memory. Although she saw her seven sons perish within a single day, she bore it with good courage because of her hope in the Lord. . . . [She said to them,] 'The Creator of the world, who shaped the beginning of humankind and devised the origin of all things, will in his mercy give life and breath back to you again, since you now forget yourselves for the sake of his laws'" (2 Macc 7:20, 23 NRSV). Shortly thereafter, the final son continues to defy Antiochus as he dies: "For our brothers after enduring a brief suffering have drunk of ever-flowing life, under God's covenant; but you, by the judgment of God, will receive just punishment for your arrogance" (2 Macc 7:36 NRSV). Thus, the author of 2 Maccabees offers a clear statement that the righteous will be rewarded with bodily resurrection, while the wicked will suffer posthumously.

Beliefs surrounding resurrection would continue to grow, evolve, and fragment as the turn of the millennium approached. A myriad of

---

28. Himmelfarb, "Afterlife," 549.
29. See 1 En. 21–22.
30. Ferguson, *Backgrounds of Early Christianity*, 555.
31. Himmelfarb, "Afterlife," 550.

Jewish works reveal intensified curiosity about the afterlife. We should note, however, that to this point in history, no extant Jewish works offer any teaching about a heavenly afterlife in which disembodied souls spend eternity. The idea of dualism between body and soul was just beginning to emerge in Jewish thought. To discover the origins of such a development, we must go backward in history to explore prominent Hellenistic philosophies.

Hellenistic Conceptions of the Afterlife

The oldest known Greek conceptions of the afterlife are reflected in the works of Homer, whose influence on Greek thought was similar to that of the Hebrew Bible on Jewish and Christian theology.[32] In the *Iliad* and *Odyssey*, written in the seventh or eighth century BCE, most souls drift to Hades, the Greek equivalent of Sheol. Death meant passing into a shadowy, numb, disembodied existence.[33] For example, when Odysseus visits his deceased mother in Hades, he desires to embrace her, but is unable:

> Then in my heart I wanted to embrace the spirit of my mother. She was dead, and I did not know how. Three times I tried, longing to touch her. But three times her ghost flew from my arms, like shadows or like dreams.... [She responds,] "This is the rule for mortals when we die. Our muscles cease to hold the flesh and skeleton together; as soon as life departs from our white bones, the force of blazing fire destroys the corpse. The spirit flies away and soon is gone, just like a dream."[34]

Thus, upon death, the body dies and the immaterial soul transitions to the underworld.

Rather than a disembodied existence, however, exceptionally righteous and brave individuals are allowed to go to Elysium—a refreshing land of gentle breezes at the end of the earth.[35] Yet, humans don't go there at death; they are translated to Elysium in embodied form. Since only a select few are allowed into Elysium, it was not a major component of

---

32. Ferguson, *Backgrounds of Early Christianity*, 47–48; Wright, *Resurrection*, 47–48.

33. Homer, *Iliad* 1.1–3; 3.320–22; 6.486–89; 23.99–107; *Odyssey* 3.409; 11.208–22; 11.475–77.

34. Homer, *Odyssey* 11.205–9, 219–25.

35. Homer, *Odyssey* 4.562–69.

Hellenistic theology and, in this early stage, no other conception of afterlife rewards (or punishments) seem to have existed.[36]

As time progressed, the Homeric epics influenced various strands of Greek thought, and afterlife philosophy branched in a number of directions. As we continue our survey, we will focus only upon the most prominent philosophies and those that influenced Judeo-Christian theology.

A philosophy that emerged in the sixth century BCE, Orphism was a collection of thoughts on the origins of the universe, proper ritual, and ethical conduct. Orphism innovated upon traditional Greek thought in regard to the nature of the afterlife and, for the first time, defined a clear body-soul dualism. More specifically, Orphic philosophy taught that the soul preexisted the body. Once the physical body—the tomb of the soul—died, the liberated soul continued to exist. As the body was viewed in a negative light, those who adhered to the philosophy utilized asceticism to liberate the soul from the flesh. Ferguson explains, "Whereas in Homer the living body was the person and the soul had no prehistory and only a shadowy repetition in the afterlife, in this literature the soul is the real 'you' liable to a reincarnation and in the afterlife paying for sins or being rewarded for virtues."[37] As we have seen with Elysium, the belief in afterlife rewards already existed; the idea of Hades as a place of punishment, though, was new.

Orphic ideas continued to spread during the Hellenistic period, often in connection with Pythagorean thought.[38] Little is known about the historical Pythagoras (sixth century BCE) aside from his brilliant mathematics. Yet, his followers became a close-knit pseudo-religious group that lived according to such ascetic principles that they had almost disappeared by the fifth century BCE. The literature they produced, however, had a lasting impact on Hellenistic culture.

In Pythagorean philosophy, the body-soul dualism of Orphism merged with astral thought to create a new "map" of the celestial world. No longer was the heavenly sphere reserved for the gods; righteous souls, once freed from their bodies, could enjoy immortality among the sun, moon, and stars. The remainder of the dead resided in a place akin to Hades, but one that occupied a lower celestial sphere rather than a cavern below the earth. Somewhat later in history, a compromise with the more

---

36. Ferguson, *Backgrounds of Early Christianity*, 157.
37. Ferguson, *Backgrounds of Early Christianity*, 163.
38. Ferguson, *Backgrounds of Early Christianity*, 164.

traditional view was reached, such that the heavenly sphere was reserved for the righteous dead and the underworld was again viewed as the domain of the wicked.[39]

Orphic and Pythagorean philosophies served as an important source for the teaching of Plato, one of the most influential Western thinkers of all time (along with his mentor Socrates and his student Aristotle).[40] Influenced by dualistic thought, Plato (ca. 428–348 BCE) postulated two distinct realities: the physical realm of the body and the nonmaterial realm of the soul. Ferguson explains, "The familiar dichotomy in Western thought between body and soul is a product of the Platonic tradition. Thus in the modern world the clumsy word *psychosomatic* (from *psychē*, 'soul,' and *sōma*, 'body') had to be coined in order to put back together two things that from the biblical perspective never should have been separated."[41]

Nonetheless, Plato taught that the soul is an independent, immortal entity, diametrically opposed to the corrupted body. Physical senses are inaccurate because the body deceives the soul. Thus, the enlightened philosopher should despise food, drink, fine clothing, and personal adornments. Only through pure reason and by abstaining from bodily desires can absolute reality, justice, beauty, and goodness become clear. Death entails the separation of soul and body, which is akin to being freed from fetters. Further, one who fears death is a base human who is ruled by pleasures.[42] Accordingly, not only the body, but the entire material universe is inferior to the immaterial realm of the soul.[43]

Plato's student Aristotle (ca. 384–22 BCE) carried on his philosophy. While Aristotle came to view the body and soul as a unified, inseparable entity, he maintained the dualism between the inferior material realm and the superior immaterial reality.[44] His thoughts on the afterlife are unclear, but since the material realm was viewed as corrupt, the thought of

---

39. Ferguson, *Backgrounds of Early Christianity*, 239, 250.

40. Middleton, *New Heaven*, 31; Ferguson, *Backgrounds of Early Christianity*, 249.

41. Ferguson, *Backgrounds of Early Christianity*, 334–35. See also Bavinck, *Reformed Dogmatics*, 695; Middleton, *New Heaven*, 31.

42. Plato, *Phaedo* 64c–69a.

43. Although Plato always maintains the dualism between the spiritual and material world, he does relax his position somewhat in later teachings. See *Timaeus* 29e–31b; Middleton, *New Heaven*, 31.

44. Wright, *Resurrection*, 52–53; Middleton, *New Heaven*, 32.

an embodied resurrection would have been difficult for Aristotle, Plato, or subsequent Hellenistic thinkers to accept.[45]

Although the influence of Plato and Aristotle on Western thought is immeasurable, their impact was scattered during the Hellenistic period.[46] The idea of an enlightened immaterial realm or an afterlife in the celestial sphere was far from universal in the centuries following their teaching. Nonetheless, Platonic philosophy remained a constant, if sometimes subtle, influence during the coming centuries.

Interlude I: Synthesis and Summary

Before proceeding to the turn of the millennium, let us pause to consider the evolution of afterlife philosophies thus far. Both early Jewish and Hellenistic beliefs consisted of a singular and simple conception of the afterlife. Upon death, the individual was reduced to a shadowy existence in a dark cavern—Sheol/Hades—beneath the surface of the earth. This underworld was not equivalent to hell, and it was not a punishment for the wicked. Every individual went to Sheol/Hades, as there was not, as yet, any belief in a paradisal afterlife for the righteous. Heaven was the abode of the gods, not a destination for deceased souls.

The only exception to the straightforward Sheol/Hades paradigm was the Homeric Elysium. A reward for individuals who were extraordinarily brave and righteous, being transported to this embodied paradise was rare. Certainly, the idea of Elysium bears great similarity to biblical teachings on resurrected believers inhabiting a renewed creation in the eschaton.[47] However, the concept of an embodied afterlife failed to gain traction in Hellenistic thought, which moved in quite the opposite direction.

With the advent of Orphism, Pythagoreanism, and especially Platonic thought, the idea of a dualism between body and soul emerged. The body was conceived as a base vessel from which the human soul desired to flee. Upon death, righteous souls would be liberated to enjoy

---

45. Ferguson, *Backgrounds of Early Christianity*, 609.

46. Ferguson, *Backgrounds of Early Christianity*, 335; Middleton, *New Heaven*, 32.

47. The eschaton refers to the period of time after the current age. It is the final stage of history that encompasses the hopes of God's people and extends into eternity. Though specifics can vary based on one's theological orientation, for Christ followers, the eschaton is the time period that follows the resurrection of the saints and the return of Christ.

an afterlife in the celestial realm, while the wicked were consigned to the underworld.

Shortly prior to the time of Plato, the idea of resurrection began to coalesce in Jewish thought. Upon death, an individual would sleep until the day all Jewish people would be raised bodily. This event was national and political in nature, and individual righteousness played little part in whether an individual was raised.

As time passed, however, the idea of rewards for the righteous and punishment for the wicked began to emerge. It is possible that this development took place in Jewish culture under the influence of Greek philosophy, but it is also possible that the idea developed in parallel as a natural progression of thought. Either way, the idea of rewards and punishment upon death was firmly enmeshed in both Greek and Jewish thought by the turn of the millennium. One key divergence, however, was the nature of the afterlife. Among Hellenistic philosophers, the afterlife was largely viewed as a disembodied, spiritual experience, whereas in Judaism, the afterlife remained firmly enfleshed. In fact, it seems that, outside of Judaism, no ancient cultures adhered to the idea of a bodily resurrection.[48]

We should note that such philosophical and theological innovations were taking place among the great thinkers and scholars of both cultures. The extent to which such beliefs were assimilated by the general populace is impossible to know. However, the explosion of literature around the turn of the millennium reveals that the afterlife continued to be a deep well of lively speculation and dialogue.

Afterlife Philosophy at the Turn of the Millennium

By the first century CE, Jewish theology on the afterlife had begun to branch in a number of directions. Evolving beliefs on resurrection prompted further reflection on the status of God's people at death. As most Jewish people had been immersed in Greek culture since the reign of Alexander the Great in the fourth century BCE, Hellenistic language about the soul offered a ready source of ideas.[49]

Wisdom of Solomon, a Jewish work from around the turn of the millennium, reflects an overt Hellenistic viewpoint regarding the immortality of the soul. The text presumes afterlife judgment and body/soul

---

48. Wright, *Resurrection*, 35.
49. Wright, *Resurrection*, 175.

dualism as a matter of fact: righteous souls enjoy rewards in the presence and protection of the Lord, while the wicked go to Hades.[50] Yet this is not the Hades with which we are familiar. The bodies of the wicked perish *and* their spirits dissolve, but they somehow still suffer dread and anguish in the afterlife.[51]

Likely composed around the same time, 4 Maccabees presents a similar viewpoint. Utilizing Greek rhetoric to promote the logic and virtue of obedience to torah, the book consists largely of a retelling of 2 Macc 7, the narrative of the mother and seven sons martyred by Antiochus IV. Unlike the author of 2 Maccabees, however, the author of 4 Maccabees makes no mention of resurrection, focusing only on the blissful immortality of righteous souls.[52] According to Wright, "Assuming, as we must, that the writer knew and was using 2 Maccabees, we may state confidently that for this book at least there was a conscious redactional decision to delete all mention of bodily resurrection and substitute a version of the doctrine of the immortal soul, or at least of souls that could become immortal through the pursuit of wisdom."[53] We should note, in addition, that neither Wisdom of Solomon nor 4 Maccabees describe immortality as an inherent quality of the soul—as does Platonism. Rather, eternal life is granted to the soul only as a reward for virtuous living.[54]

The thoroughly Hellenistic yet Jewish philosopher Philo (ca. 20 BCE-45 CE) expressed similar ideas. The scholar drew upon Plato and Aristotle, as well as Neopythagorean writers, to propagate the idea that the body is a tomb from which the soul must escape. Despite his Jewish heritage, his teaching held no place for bodily resurrection. Philo was primarily concerned with the nature of the soul and the spiritual realm.[55]

Whereas Wisdom of Solomon and 4 Maccabees both accept the immortality of the *righteous* soul as a given, Philo developed the idea further. Building upon the philosophy of Plato, Philo believed that the soul was immortal. The following passage from his work *On the Giants* is worth quoting at length:

---

50. Wis 3:1–4; 4:7; 5:1, 15–16.
51. Wis 1:14—2:3; 4:18–20; 5:3.
52. 4 Macc 7:18–20; 9:8–9, 22; 10:15; 14:5; 16:13, 25; 17:5, 12, 18; 18:3–5, 17, 23.
53. Wright, *Resurrection*, 143.
54. Ferguson, *Backgrounds of Early Christianity*, 554.
55. McDannell and Lang, *Heaven*, 17; Wright, *Resurrection*, 140–45.

> And [some souls] having descended into the body as into a river, at one time are carried away and swallowed up by the voracity of a most violent whirlpool; and, at another time, striving with all their power to resist its impetuosity, they at first swim on the top of it, and afterwards fly back to the place from which they started. These, then, are the souls of those who have been taught some kind of sublime philosophy, meditating, from beginning to end, on dying as to the life of the body, in order to obtain an inheritance of the incorporeal and imperishable life, which is to be enjoyed in the presence of the uncreated and everlasting God. But those, which are swallowed up in the whirlpool, are the souls of those other men who have disregarded wisdom, giving themselves up to the pursuit of unstable things regulated by fortune alone, not one of which is referred to the most excellent portion of us, the soul or the mind; but all rather to the dead corpse connected with us, that is to the body.[56]

In other words, the physical body is nothing more than a "dead corpse," even while inhabited by the soul, which exists in the spiritual realm prior to one's physical birth. The souls of worldly individuals, once embodied, lose their way and perish in the material world. The souls of enlightened philosophers, however, return to their higher, incorporeal existence upon death.

While such teachings don't necessarily align with modern beliefs about the afterlife, Philo's unique blend of Platonic philosophy and biblical tradition became highly influential for later Christian theologians.[57] We will discuss those theologians shortly, but first we must discuss other prominent Jewish theologies of the first century CE.

Pharisees, Sadducees, and Qumran

The most noteworthy Jewish theologies regarding the afterlife in the first century are represented by the Pharisees and Sadducees. Although we encounter these groups in the NT, we learn most about them from the Jewish historian Josephus. In *Antiquities of the Jews*, written near the end of the first century CE, Josephus explains that the Pharisees believe in the immortality of the soul. Upon death, the soul receives either rewards or punishments in the underworld. The souls of the virtuous, however,

---

56. Philo, *On the Giants* 13–15.
57. McDannell and Lang, *Heaven*, 17.

would eventually experience bodily resurrection, while the souls of those who had lived viciously would "be detained in an everlasting prison."[58]

Such an idea of rewards and punishments upon death, along with bodily resurrection, seems to have become the majority belief among first-century Jewish people.[59] The Mishnah, a compendium of Jewish tradition, indicates that "all Israelites have a share in the world to come" with the exception of those who engage in forbidden beliefs and practices, such as saying "that there is no resurrection of the dead."[60] Himmelfarb explains, "The embrace of these ideas about the afterlife by [Jewish people] in the late Second Temple period and the early rabbinic era helps to explain why the New Testament takes them for granted."[61]

The views of the Sadducees, who believed that both soul and body perished upon death, stood in stark contrast to the beliefs of the majority of Jewish people. Members of this small group gave little attention to the spiritual side of human existence, being more concerned with political power and philosophy.[62] Had the viewpoint of the sect not been preserved in the works of Josephus and the Bible, it would have had little enduring impact.

One further group should be mentioned before moving on. The Dead Sea Sect at Qumran (ca. 200 BCE–70 CE) was a hub of thriving theological praxis, study, and dialogue. Although determining a precise trajectory of beliefs on the afterlife is difficult, the sectarians seemed to adhere to a belief in the immortality of the soul and some form of afterlife reward for the righteous.[63] Whether they believed in an embodied resurrection is unclear since sect members didn't draw a stark distinction between physical and spiritual realities. As members offered service to God in the physical realm, they believed that they served simultaneously in the heavenly temple.[64]

---

58. Josephus, *Ant.* 18.1.3. See also Wright, *Resurrection*, 129–33, 147, 190–206; Ferguson, *Backgrounds of Early Christianity*, 516.

59. Josephus, *Ant.* 18.1.3; Wright, *Resurrection*, 147; Himmelfarb, "Afterlife," 550.

60. M. Sanh. 10.1–6. Although the Mishnah was completed in the fourth century CE, the text preserves traditions that developed much earlier.

61. Himmelfarb, "Afterlife," 550.

62. Josephus, *Ant.* 18.1.4; Himmelfarb, "Afterlife," 549; Ferguson, *Backgrounds of Early Christianity*, 519–20; Wright, *Resurrection*, 131–35.

63. Josephus, *Ant.* 18.1.5.

64. 4QShirŠabb; 1QH XVI, 5–26; 1QS VIII, 5–10; Robinson, *Temple of Presence*, 64–71.

Sect members rejected the nihilism of the Sadducees as well as the materialistic notions of the Pharisees. "Placing the spiritual over the material, they preferred lifestyles that separated them from too much involvement with the world."[65] Nonetheless, the community seems to have anticipated an imminent final battle between their forces of light and the forces of darkness, after which they believed that the earth would be restored to God's perfect design.[66]

After the Fall

Although we are at the point in our survey where a discussion of the NT would be chronologically appropriate, we must briefly skip over the Christian Scriptures to conclude our analysis of extra-biblical texts.

The fall of the Jerusalem temple in 70 CE was an event of apocalyptic proportions. Jewish people and Christians alike anticipated an imminent end to the current world order. Such end-time speculation reinvigorated the afterlife dialogue that was already taking place.

The idea of rewards and punishment upon death had become standard, and as discussed above, most Jewish people anticipated some form of bodily resurrection. The idea of a disembodied heavenly existence, however, seems to have become the expectation of a Hellenistic Jewish minority.

A prominent Jewish text written in response to the fall of the temple, 4 Ezra, reflects an intense interest in the afterlife. The current world, which is "full of sadness and infirmities" (4 Ezra 4:27), is contrasted with the "world to come," which is characterized by goodness, rest, and wisdom (4 Ezra 8:52).[67] As 4 Ezra is an apocalyptic work, and therefore highly symbolic, debate exists over whether the description of the world to come is literal or figurative. However, "It should be recalled that for authors of the age of 4 Ezra, heavenly objects were no less real than earthly ones, so that opposed categories 'material' and 'spiritual' seem irrelevant."[68] Therefore, much like the Qumran sectarians, the author of 4 Ezra blurred the distinction between material and spiritual.

---

65. McDannell and Lang, *Heaven*, 21.
66. 1QM I, 5–13; XVIII.
67. Stone, *Fourth Ezra*, 286.
68. Stone, *Fourth Ezra*, 286.

In 4 Ezra, the spirit of each person leaves the body at death and returns to God. One who has not "kept the way of the Most High" will immediately begin to wander around in torment, confusion, shame, and fear. The soul will continue to roam until the dawning of the new age, at which time he or she will be judged and consigned to thirst and torment in the furnace of hell.[69] Alternately, those who have kept the law of God shall, upon death, see his glory and experience great joy. These righteous souls are gathered into chambers where they are guarded by angels as they enjoy peaceful rest while waiting upon the dawning of the new age.[70] Thus, the viewpoint presented by 4 Ezra is in close alignment with the Pharisaic belief in the resurrection of the righteous. The major innovation of 4 Ezra, however, is the detailed description of the intermediate state.

The Syriac Apocalypse of Baruch (2 Baruch), a contemporaneous work, offers a slightly different approach to the afterlife. Whereas 4 Ezra offers hope for a better future through a blessed future age in which spiritual realities merge with material ones, 2 Baruch makes a greater distinction between the two. As in the works of Plato and Aristotle, the author of 2 Baruch views the present world as inherently corrupt.[71] His focus remains largely upon the heavenly realm as the righteous eagerly anticipate the coming age/world.[72] As in 4 Ezra, the souls of the dead spend the intermediate state in Sheol, which will be sealed upon the dawning of the new age.[73] At that time, the unrighteous will be trapped inside and waste away while the righteous souls are set free to experience "the expanses of Paradise."[74] Whether such souls receive a new body is unclear, although some passages do seem to anticipate a renewed material creation.[75] The ambiguity does not seem to bother the author, as his purpose is to offer hope, not formulate a coherent theology of the afterlife.[76]

The Greek Apocalypse of Baruch (3 Baruch) is similar in style yet much shorter. The titular figure, Baruch, is taken on a tour of the heavens. In the third heaven, Baruch and his angelic guide encounter Hades, a

---

69. 4 Ezra 7:36, 78–87; 8:59.
70. 4 Ezra 4:35; 7:88–99.
71. 2 Bar. 21:19–25; 44:9–10.
72. Robinson, *Temple of Presence*, 85.
73. 2 Bar. 21:23–24; 30:1–4.
74. 2 Bar. 51:11; c.f. 2 Bar. 30:1–5; 44:15.
75. 2 Bar. 32:4–6; 49:2—51:3.
76. Murphy, *Second Baruch*, 89.

dark, evil serpent who eats the bodies of the wicked (3 Bar. 4:3–6). Next, in the fourth heaven, Baruch sees the souls of the righteous, who dwell in the midst of a great plain with a pool that waters the earth (3 Bar. 10:1–10). Whether this afterlife is embodied is unclear, yet the location of the heavens in the celestial sphere seems to indicate that the righteous enjoy a spiritual rather than a material afterlife. Thus, the authors of both 2 and 3 Baruch appear to blend traditional Jewish theology with more Hellenistic, Platonic thought in which the material creation is a corrupted realm from which righteous souls desire to escape.

Indeed, Platonic, Neoplatonic, and Neopythagorean thought continued to spread and mutate as philosophers speculated on the spiritual realm and the afterlife. Ultimately, these philosophies seem to be a key source of "the general pessimism about the world that began to spread in the second century A.D."[77]

Epictetus (ca. 50–135 CE), an influential Roman stoic, drew heavily upon Plato and Plato's mentor, Socrates. As "one of our best witnesses to what was pondered and believed at a fairly popular level towards the end of the first century AD," Epictetus taught that death was a welcome transition back to one's natural, disembodied state.[78] More specifically, the philosopher described the physical body as a corpse that the soul was burdened with carrying around.[79]

Gnosticism, a prominent movement whose origins are obscure, was a natural development of Platonism and Neopythagoreanism. Arthur Nock, an expert on the Hellenistic backgrounds of early Christianity, went so far as to call it "Platonism run wild."[80] According to gnostic thought, righteous souls needed to be freed from mortal bodies in order to reenter the celestial realm. Since the immortal soul was imprisoned in an unsuitable body, it often forgot its origin. Thus, individuals required a spark of knowledge, or *gnosis*, to remind them of their heavenly origin and empower them to return to the divine realm upon death.[81] Unlike Judaism and Christianity, gnostic thought did not include the hope of a collective paradise in the eschaton, and eternal life wasn't achieved through righteousness. The celestial afterlife was of a personal nature, it

---

77. Ferguson, *Backgrounds of Early Christianity*, 383.
78. Wright, *Resurrection*, 53.
79. Wright, *Resurrection*, 54.
80. Nock, "Gnosticism," 267.
81. Wright, *Resurrection*, 52.

took place immediately upon death, and it was achieved through proper knowledge.[82]

Although not considered gnostic, Roman/Egyptian philosopher Plotinus (ca. 205–70 CE) also emphasized the enlightenment of the soul through knowledge. Plotinus taught that the highest part of the soul was a mind connected to the divine reality—the Spirit or Logos. Unlike many previous philosophers, however, Plotinus did not regard the material realm as evil or corrupt. Rather, matter is the furthest "emanation" from the divine source to which the soul longs to return.[83] As a result, salvation of the soul was achieved through contemplation and wisdom. Plotinus was, thus, one of the first Western thinkers to explicitly link union with God to a process of inner transformation.

The Church Fathers and Beyond

Most Christian theologians of the first and second century, such as Irenaeus, Tertullian, Clement, Ignatius of Antioch, Polycarp, and Papias, avoided Hellenistic philosophies and remained close to the biblical teaching of a bodily resurrection.[84] Wright explains that "the early Christian future hope centered firmly on resurrection. . . . They virtually never spoke simply of going to heaven when they died."[85] In other words, the afterlife did not consist of a postmortem experience in a glorious heavenly realm, but "coming to bodily life again after bodily death."[86]

Nonetheless, Platonic philosophy, along with Philo's theological adaptations of it, became highly influential for certain Christian thinkers.[87] In addition, the philosophies of Plotinus initiated "a Western form of mysticism that has reverberated throughout the church in the Middle Ages and even into the modern period."[88] As early Christian theologians attempted to situate the gospel within their own culture, many turned to a synthesis of the Christian Scriptures and Greek philosophy, inducing "a

---

82. Ferguson, *Backgrounds of Early Christianity*, 307–11.

83. Cross and Livingstone, "Plotinus," *Oxford Dictionary of the Christian Church*, 1310; Ferguson, *Backgrounds of Early Christianity*, 391–92.

84. Middleton, *New Heaven*, 284; Wright, *Resurrection*, 481–526.

85. Wright, *Surprised by Hope*, 41.

86. Wright, *Surprised by Hope*, 45.

87. McDannell and Lang, *Heaven*, 17; Ferguson, *Backgrounds of Early Christianity*, 335.

88. Middleton, *New Heaven*, 33.

transformation of Christian eschatology beyond anything that the writers of the New Testament would have envisioned."[89]

Origen of Alexandria (ca. 185–254 CE), under overt Platonic influence, proposed a final blessed state in the heavenly realm. He taught that, upon death, the bodily substance of the exceptionally righteous would be transformed into a pure ethereal state. Yet, Origen also attempted to harmonize biblical conceptions of the afterlife with Greek philosophies. Thus, he theorized that individuals of average piety would inhabit a good earthly land until they proved themselves worthy of a higher existence.[90] Though Origen's eschatology was far from mainstream at the time, by locating the afterlife in "heaven," he contributed to the increasing belief in a disembodied afterlife.[91]

As Christianity transitioned from a fringe sect to the official religion of the Roman Empire in 313 CE, beliefs in the afterlife continued to slide further from the teachings of the NT. Augustine (ca. 354–430 CE), one of the greatest sources of our modern ideas about heaven, was heavily influenced by gnostic and Neoplatonic thought.[92] The theologian posited two realms of reality—one transcendent and one earthly—as he consistently devalued the body in favor of the soul.[93] Drawing directly upon the work of Plotinus, Augustine taught that spiritual union with God was achieved as one moved increasingly toward the interior of the soul, through which God could eventually be reached.[94]

By the Middle Ages (ca. 500–1500 CE), the idea of a physical resurrection and renewed creation had almost completely disappeared from Christian thought. Whereas the earliest Christians had anticipated an embodied eternity in a restored creation, medieval Christians believed that God's kingdom occupied a distant space and time.[95]

Thomas Aquinas (ca. 1225–1274 CE), one of the most noteworthy medieval theologians, built upon the work of Augustine and the Platonic philosophers. On the surface, Aquinas seemed to teach the resurrection of the body and the renewal of the cosmos, yet he simply redefined

---

89. Middleton, *New Heaven*, 34.
90. Origen, *De Principiis* 2.3.7.
91. Middleton, *New Heaven*, 285.
92. Ferguson, *Backgrounds of Early Christianity*, 391; McDannell and Lang, *Heaven*, 47, 57.
93. Middleton, *New Heaven*, 292.
94. McDannell and Lang, *Heaven*, 57.
95. Bynum, *Resurrection*, 14; Middleton, *New Heaven*, 294.

familiar terms along Hellenistic lines. The theologian held firmly to a Platonic view of the soul, as he emphasized that the resurrection "body" would be spiritual in nature. He also continued to promote the notion that contemplation and knowledge are the means by which humans could draw closer to God and experience his presence. Therefore, upon death, the truly righteous would immediately enjoy the beatific vision of God in a noncorporeal paradise.[96]

Like Aquinas, John Calvin (ca. 1509–1564 CE) also seemed to teach a bodily resurrection, but he likewise redefined concepts. He affirmed that immediately upon death, the souls of the righteous would depart from their bodies and join Christ in paradise.[97] Upon the final return of Christ, the spirits waiting in paradise would receive new bodies. Calvin even goes so far as to affirm that believers can confidently expect the "resurrection of our flesh."[98] Yet, he immediately clarifies his stance as he explains that the human authors of Scripture only describe our future spiritual blessedness in physical terms because they cannot find adequate words to describe it. Calvin, thus, concludes that souls approach the celestial presence of God through meditation upon Scripture and contemplation of God. The godliness achieved in this world will, thus, be completed as the righteous individual achieves "glory in heaven."[99]

Although Calvin's conception of the afterlife was closer to the actual teaching of Scripture than many of his predecessors, fellow Protestant Reformer Martin Luther (ca. 1483–1546 CE) offered a much-needed corrective to the centuries of Hellenistically-infused afterlife theology. Whereas Calvin implied that the righteous saint could approach a near-divine state upon death, Luther taught that each individual deserved damnation and could only achieve salvation through divine grace and mercy. Further, he anticipated an embodied eternity in a material creation. At the final judgment, God would cleanse the earth and banish evil to hell. The renewed creation—complete with vegetation, animals, and insects—would function as a renewed Eden and a fitting home for the resurrected saints.[100]

---

96. Aquinas, *Summa Theologica* 1.102; McDannell and Lang, *Heaven*, 91; Middleton, *New Heaven*, 294.

97. Calvin, *Institutes*, 3.25.6.

98. Calvin, *Institutes*, 3.25.8.

99. Calvin, *Institutes*, 3.25.10.

100. McDannell and Lang, *Heaven*, 152–53.

Interlude II: Synthesis and Summary

Before proceeding to our final section, let us pause once more to reflect upon the results of our survey. As we established at the start, ancient Jewish and Hellenistic beliefs consisted of a singular and simple conception of the afterlife: upon death, humans entered Sheol/Hades. While "heaven" did exist, it was the abode of the gods, not a posthumous reward for deceased saints.

By the sixth century BCE, however, Jewish and Hellenistic afterlife beliefs began to diverge. In Greek thought, the idea of body/soul dualism emerged, such that the body was considered a corrupted vessel. Upon death, sufficiently enlightened or righteous souls could be liberated to the celestial realm. Around the same time, the idea of resurrection began to coalesce in Jewish thought. Initially, resurrection was conceived of as national and political in nature, as individual righteousness had little bearing on one's afterlife.

As time passed, however, belief in afterlife rewards and punishment began to develop, becoming firmly enmeshed in both Greek and Jewish thought by the turn of the millennium. One key difference, however, was the nature of the afterlife. Among Hellenistic philosophers, the afterlife was largely viewed as a disembodied, spiritual experience, whereas in Judaism, the afterlife remained firmly enfleshed.

By the time of the first century CE, Jewish afterlife theology had branched in a number of directions as Hellenism increasingly influenced Judaism. The Jewish philosopher Philo drew directly upon Plato and Aristotle to promulgate the idea that the body is a tomb from which the soul must escape. Despite his Jewish heritage, his teaching held no place for a bodily resurrection. Likewise, numerous texts of the period, such as Wisdom of Solomon and 4 Maccabees, departed from the clear concept of resurrection, seemingly teaching eternal life for righteous souls.

Other sects remained somewhat immune to Hellenistic philosophy. The Sadducees eschewed both Greek and Jewish ideas with their belief in total annihilation; the Pharisees remained faithful to the biblical view of resurrection; and the Qumran sect adopted a more unique view in which spiritual and material realities overlap in the present and future. However, the afterlife beliefs of the Qumran sectarians had little lasting impact as their sect was destroyed by Rome in the revolt of 70 CE. The views of the small Saducean minority likewise died out, as their sect ceased to exist after they fell from power during the same conflict.

The Pharisaic philosophy of bodily resurrection, thus, became the majority belief among the first-century rabbis and Jewish populace. Nonetheless, the destruction of Jerusalem and the temple in 70 CE prompted a fresh wave of interest in the afterlife as Jewish philosophers struggled to make sense of the devastating events. In the process, Hellenistic dualism became increasingly intertwined with traditional Jewish theology. Texts that blend traditional Jewish theology with Platonic thought, such as 2 and 3 Baruch, however, seem to represent only a minority group.

Early Christian theologians largely managed to avoid Hellenistic ideas and stay close to the biblical teaching of a bodily resurrection. Yet, by the end of the second century CE, Platonism, Gnosticism, and other Greek philosophies increasingly began to make their way into the teachings of influential church leaders. As theologians attempted to situate the gospel within their own cultures, many turned to a synthesis of the Christian scriptures and Greek philosophy. Scholars such as Origen and Augustine promoted Platonic dualism, in addition to the idea that one's spiritual life is more important that one's embodied existence.

By the time of the Middle Ages, the idea of a physical resurrection and a renewed creation had almost completely disappeared from the teaching of the church. Whereas the earliest Christians had anticipated an embodied eternity in a restored earth, medieval Christians believed that God's coming kingdom existed in a completely different space-time. Although the Protestant Reformers sought to correct course by teaching an embodied resurrection, too much damage had already been done. Hellenistic ideas about body/soul dualism, along with the hope of a disembodied afterlife in "heaven," had been so firmly entrenched in Christian thought that they persist into the modern day.[101] Though many Christians claim to believe in resurrection and a renewed creation, "going to heaven" remains a fundamental hope for Christians of the twenty-first century.

Afterlife in the New Testament

With nearly two millennia of history in place, we may now proceed to the NT. With a more accurate awareness of the origin of modern ideas about heaven, we will strive to examine the biblical text without importing non-Scriptural ideas into it.[102]

---

101. Ferguson, *Backgrounds of Early Christianity*, 555.
102. For a detailed analysis of the concept of resurrection throughout Scripture,

Pharisaic/rabbinic conceptions of resurrection, derived directly from the Hebrew Scriptures, form the backdrop for NT teachings on the afterlife.[103] While Hellenistic philosophies have become part of modern Christian thought, the idea of a disembodied afterlife is not found in Scripture. To anticipate the results of our forthcoming survey, Reformed scholar Herman Bavinck summarizes succinctly:

> While Christian theology may find some of the traditional arguments for the immortality of the soul useful at points, Scripture is more restrained. In fact, while the immortality of the soul may seem to be of the greatest importance for religion and life, Scripture never explicitly mentions it. In the face of death the immortality of the soul is no real comfort. . . . The Bible affirms and celebrates God's gift of life as a blessing; death is a punishment for sin. The victory of Christ over sin and death means that believers enjoy the first fruits of Christ's kingly reign now and, immediately after death, a provisional bliss with Christ in heaven, while unbelievers enter a state of torment. . . . For those who are in Christ Jesus, death is no longer death but a passage into eternal life, and the grave is a place of sanctified rest until the day of resurrection.[104]

In short, the NT reflects a pervasive expectation for the reversal of death—an eternal, embodied, life for God's people.[105] Jesus provides the paradigm for those who believe in him: just as he died, ascended to the Father, and was resurrected, his followers will experience the same. Consistent with Jewish expectation, even the righteous saints of the OT are included in the promise of resurrection.[106]

Texts which *seem* to teach that the final destiny of the saints is "in heaven" are almost always apocalyptic texts, which should be interpreted symbolically rather than literally.[107] Indeed, many of our ideas surrounding "heaven" come from the book of Revelation, with imagery of pearly

---

see Beale, *Union*.

103. Wright, *Resurrection*, 447; McDannell and Lang, *Heaven*, 2.

104. Bavinck, *Reformed Dogmatics*, 697, 707.

105. Matt 27:51–53; 28:2–7; Mark 9:42–48; 16:5–19; Luke 24:6–7, 38–40; John 5:24–28; 6:39–54; 11:25–26; 12:23–26; Rom 6:8–11, 22–23; 8:18–25; 1 Cor 15:20–23; 1 Pet 1:3; Rev 1:5–6; etc.

106. Tabor, "Heaven, Ascent to," 92–93. See Heb 11.

107. See 1 Thess 4:13–18; Rev 7:9–17; 21:1—22:5.

gates and golden streets.[108] With his awesome imagery, however, John symbolically conveys that the new creation will be stunningly beautiful, pure, safe, and holy. To view the imagery in a literal fashion disregards and diminishes the message John is actually communicating. Likewise, the notion that righteous saints will join God in a heaven somewhere *above* the earth is no more literal than the idea that the wicked will die and go to hell in the actual core of the earth.

Lest we get ahead of ourselves, however, we should pause to examine the language surrounding "heaven" in the NT.

What and Where Is "Heaven"?

In both the OT and NT, the word for "heaven" is the same term translated as "sky." *Shamayim*, from Hebrew, is rendered "heaven" in roughly 70 percent of uses and as "sky" in 30 percent. In the NT Greek, *ouranos* is translated "heaven" over 90 percent of the time, and "sky" just under 10 percent. Typically, when translators use "heaven" they are referring to the abode of God and/or his angels. However, because the sky *is* the realm of the gods, determining whether *shamayim/ouranos* should be translated "heaven" or "sky" in any given instance is tricky. For example, when the pagans of Gen 11 sought to build a "tower whose top would reach into the *shamayim*," was their intent to build a tower that would reach into the realm of the gods or a tower that would reach high into the sky?

While we, as modern readers, might feel frustrated by such ambiguity, original readers likely felt no need to distinguish between the two concepts. The sky *was* the dwelling place of the gods, a place where physical and spiritual realities overlapped. Thus, attempting to determine whether a particular usage of *ouranos* or *shamayim* refers to the realm of God *or* to the sky is to make an artificial distinction not typically found in the text itself.

Along such lines, the usage of words like "above" and "below" do not necessarily denote spatial directions. As already discussed, ancient peoples of the near east believed that the universe was comprised of three tiers: the upper realm of the gods (heaven), the middle realm of the earth, and the lower realm of the underworld. Although such conceptions faded

---

108. For a thorough analysis of John's vision of the afterlife, see my published dissertation, *Temple of Presence*.

somewhat over time, the authors of the NT were influenced by such cosmic geography—as we are still today.

Scriptural authors used the language, philosophy, and theology available to them to describe cosmic realities beyond the scope of comprehension. The exact relationship between the realm of God and the realm of humanity simply is not defined by the biblical text. According to Rodney Whitacre, "The idea that someone could reach heaven in a spaceship misunderstands the language of Scripture."[109] Rather, "heaven" is more a person than a place since the defining trait of heaven is God himself.

Thus, "heaven"—the locus of God's presence—might more accurately be described as an alternate reality.[110] Wright explains that Jesus will not return "like a spaceman from the sky," nor will he simply reappear. When heaven and earth are joined in the eschaton, Jesus will appear to his people and we will appear to him in the new creation.[111] In fact, Jesus, the first fruits of our redemption, already bestrides heaven and earth. Even when he is on earth he is in "heaven" because he is the embodiment of God's presence.[112] What Scripture asks believers to grasp in the light of Christ's work is that God's space is no longer separated from ours. The veil that separated God from his people was ripped away (Matt 27:51). Beale explains that, through Christ, "the coming new creation penetrated back into this world through the resurrected, new-creational body of Jesus."[113] Although God's space, for the moment, remains distinct from the physical dwelling of his people, the future return of Christ will fuse the two domains fully.

The Intermediate State

In any discussion of resurrection or heaven, the intermediate state is always a topic of interest. Though the fate of righteous souls who die prior to the resurrection is not clear, the NT offers two possible options. First, passages from both Paul and the Gospels seem to indicate that those who have died are in a state of "sleep." Paul says to the Thessalonian church, "But we do not want you to be uninformed, brothers and sisters, about

---

109. Whitacre, *John*, 349.
110. Whitacre, *John*, 348–49.
111. Wright, *Surprised by Hope*, 134–35. See 1 John 2:28; 3:2.
112. Black, "Johannine Rhetoric," 228–29.
113. Beale, *Union*, 70.

the ones who are asleep, so that you should not be grieved like the rest, those having no hope. For if we believe Jesus died and rose again, God will also, thus, through Christ bring with him those who have fallen asleep" (1 Thess 4:13-14).[114] This idea that the dead await the resurrection in a state of unconsciousness, sometimes called "soul sleep," is also in line with OT expectations in which death was equated to sleeping.[115]

Numerous other passages, however, seem to indicate that saints will be consciously in the presence of God immediately upon death. The first verse that comes to mind for most people is 2 Cor 5:8, Paul's statement that "to be absent from the body [is] to be present with the Lord."[116] Revelation 6:9-11, similarly, offers a description of fully conscious souls surrounding God's throne as they await the final judgment. Luke 16:19-31, the familiar parable of the rich man and the beggar, likewise provides a portrait of individuals consciously inhabiting a pre-resurrection afterlife. However, as the passage takes the form of a parable, it should be regarded as a moralistic story rather than an accurate statement of afterlife theology.

Perhaps the clearest statement about the intermediate state comes from Jesus himself. In Luke 23:43, Christ says to the criminal on the cross beside him, "Today you will be with me in paradise." Thus, "paradise," at least in this passage, appears to be a resting place where the dead await resurrection in the presence of God.[117]

The Greek term "paradise," *paradeisos*, is used only three times in the NT, the first of which is in the aforementioned passage. The second usage is in 2 Cor 12:4. In this puzzling passage, Paul describes what seems to be his own temporary journey into God's presence in heaven/paradise. In the final passage, Rev 2:7, we learn that righteous saints are granted the right to eat from the tree of life in paradise. Clearly, this eventuality takes place after death, but whether in the intermediate state or the new creation is unclear. If such an intermediate paradise exists, therefore, we should clarify that it is a temporary dwelling, not the final destiny of God's people.

In sum, we must conclude with less specificity than we desire. There is simply no uniform NT statement on the status of the believer

---

114. Cf. 1 Thess 5:10; 1 Cor 15:18-20; Eph 5:14; Gospels: John 11:11-12; Mark 5:39; Matt 9:24; 27:52; Luke 8:52.

115. Pss 13:3; 90:5; Dan 12:2; Jer 51:39.

116. Cf. Phil 1:21-24.

117. Wright, *Surprised by Hope*, 150.

between the time of death and resurrection.[118] Wright, however, does bring a measure of accord to the two seemingly contrasting options of waiting in paradise or "sleeping" until the resurrection. He proposes that the NT language of sleeping may simply be a useful way of describing a stage of temporary inactivity or tranquil rest as opposed to complete unconsciousness.[119]

Heaven and Resurrection in Pauline Literature

To say that we have defined our terms and concepts clearly may be an overstatement. Hopefully though, our understanding of heaven is becoming less murky, such that we are equipped to examine specific NT passages with greater expertise. We will first examine Pauline literature then move to the Gospels.

In his epistles, Paul uses the term *ouranos* twenty-five times. In every passage except two, Paul uses the term to denote the sky or the place where God/Christ resides. And more importantly, Paul never articulates a belief that God's people will *go to heaven*.[120]

In regard to the two unusual usages of *ouranos*, we've already seen that one, 2 Cor 12:2–10, describes Paul's journey into paradise, a place akin to the intermediate state. Though the journey is otherworldly, and possibly even disembodied, the heaven Paul visits is not presented as the final destiny of God's people. In the second passage, 2 Cor 5:1–5, Paul contrasts our "earthly tent" with our "heavenly dwelling." At a surface level, the apostle seems to reference a future dwelling place, i.e., heaven. Upon closer inspection of the surrounding context, however, we see that Paul is metaphorically referring to the human body, as he contrasts perishable mortal bodies with immortal future ones. In the chapter just prior, Paul had described our "earthen vessels," i.e., our perishable human bodies, which are weak and afflicted as we reflect the sufferings of Christ in our "mortal flesh." At the same time, we also bear the "surpassing greatness" of God's power as the life of Jesus is manifested in our *bodies* (2 Cor 4:7–11). As a result, believers can have confidence that when

---

118. Tabor, "Heaven, Ascent to," 93.

119. Wright, *Resurrection*, 216; Wright, *Surprised by Hope*, 150.

120. Although 1 Thess 4:17 is often interpreted as a teaching about a "rapture" to "heaven," Paul is actually referring to believers greeting Christ on the day of his return to the earth. For further discussion, see the section "Downward Mobility" in ch. 7.

the "earthly tent" perishes, the imperishable life of Christ will animate our resurrected "heavenly" bodies. Further confirmation that Paul isn't contrasting heaven and earth, but rather, the earthly body with the resurrected body, is the mention of clothing in 2 Cor 5:3–4. At the resurrection, those who place faith in Christ will not be naked and ashamed but clothed in the glory of Christ.

Under the influence of the Jewish Scriptures and interpretive traditions, Paul holds firmly to a belief in the resurrection and the renewal of creation.[121] Unlike Platonic and gnostic views, Paul did not anticipate an escape from creation, but a redemption of it. Christ came into the world to reconcile the material realm with the spiritual.[122] As such, Paul remains firmly in line with the mainstream Jewish view, though through a more refined Christological lens. According to Wright, "Perhaps the most striking development from within the Jewish tradition is the sheer volume and frequent reference of resurrection in Paul's thought. . . . Even among those Jewish writings which speak of, and indeed celebrate, resurrection, at no point do we find this belief woven into the fabric of anyone's thought, informing and undergirding one topic after another, in the way it is in Paul."[123]

Heaven and Resurrection in the Synoptic Gospels

Our familiar term *ouranos* is used roughly 190 times in the Synoptic Gospels (Matthew, Mark, and Luke). As usual, the vast majority of instances refer to the sky or the place God resides. While several passages do indicate that righteous believers can store rewards or treasures "in heaven," none of the usages indicate that believers go there upon death.[124] Instead, the Synoptics point to a two-stage resurrection in which Christ rises bodily from the dead, and believers later follow.[125] Like Paul but to an even greater extent, the Gospel authors draw upon Jewish resurrection expectations

---

121. Rom 6:8–11, 22–23; 8:18–25; 1 Cor 6:14; 15:20–23; Phil 3:10–11; 1 Thess 4:14; etc.

122. See, for example, Eph 1:10; Rom 8:20–23; Col 1:15–23; H. Bietenhard, "*Ouranos*," NIDNTT, 2:195.

123. Wright, *Resurrection*, 273–74. For a discussion of additional Pauline passages, see the section "Downward Mobility" in ch. 7.

124. Matt 5:12; 6:20; 19:21; Mark 10:21; Luke 6:33; 12:33; 18:22; 20:34–38.

125. Matt 19:28–29; 27:51–53; 28:1–10; Mark 12:25–27; 16:1–8; Luke 22:28–30; 24:1–44.

and present them through a Christological lens.[126] For example, of those who provide food to the needy, Christ promises, "You will be blessed, since they do not have *the means* to repay you; for you will be repaid at the resurrection of the righteous" (Luke 14:14 NASB, emphasis original).

One additional usage of *ouranos* is distinctive in the Gospel of Matthew: the "kingdom of heaven."[127] Also sometimes called the "kingdom of God," this domain isn't equivalent to a place one goes upon death or any geographical space at all. In the OT, the kingdom of God generally refers to the reign of God, in glory and power, over his people.[128] In the Synoptics, however, the kingdom of God/heaven describes the new community and way of life inaugurated by Christ, as opposed to the systems of this world.[129] Sverre Aalen explains, "The gospels neither tell us that the kingdom of God will be 'established', nor that it already, through the presence of Jesus, has been established or set up. They simply say that the kingdom is 'coming'; it will come, and has already come."[130] More specifically, we know from the Lord's prayer, that the kingdom of God is closely associated with the will of God.[131] Thus, the kingdom consists of the people of God doing the will of God in the creation of God. It is a present reality that will be expressed more fully in the future.[132] Such a concept accords well with the notion of heaven discussed above, in which we defined "heaven" as the locus of God's presence and the resurrected afterlife as a merging of God's space with our own.

Heaven and Resurrection in the Gospel of John

Hopefully by now you will not be surprised to learn that each of the eighteen occurrences of *ouranos* in John refer to the sky or the abode of God rather than a place believers go upon death. Nonetheless, the Fourth Gospel is often viewed as being more "spiritual" than the Synoptics.

---

126. Wright, *Resurrection*, 438–39.

127. The "kingdom of heaven" [*ouranos*] is referred to thirty-one times in Matt: 3:2; 4:17; 5:3, 10, 19, 20; 7:21; 8:11; 10:7, 11, 12; 13:11, 24, 31, 33, 44, 45, 47, 52; 16:19; 18:1, 3, 4, 23; 19:12, 14, 23; 20:1; 22:2; 23:13; 25:1.

128. Aalen, "'Reign' and 'House,'" 215–16.

129. Hart, *Woman*, 57.

130. Aalen, "'Reign' and 'House,'" 219.

131. Matt 6:9–13.

132. Aalen, "'Reign' and 'House,'" 222, 232.

In the early twentieth century, John was even accused of reflecting a form of Gnosticism as some scholars sought to uncover Hellenistic sources behind the Fourth Gospel.[133] Such connections, however, were largely overstated, as seeing gnostic thought in John was "in no small degree due to a scholarly minimizing of the Jewish relations that it exhibits."[134] Instead, similarities between the Gospel of John and gnostic literature are likely the result of exposure to the same source material—Jewish wisdom literature. Further, the idea that the Fourth Gospel exhibited heavy gnostic influence was largely dismissed after the discovery of the Dead Sea Scrolls, which reveal that John is thoroughly saturated in the Jewish theology and philosophy of the era.

The Gospel of John does exhibit a heavy emphasis upon eternal life, but not the sort of disembodied spiritual existence often imagined. While casual readers often equate eternal life to immortality in heaven, John's conception is fully in line with resurrection theology.[135] According to John, eternal life in the present anticipates future resurrection for those who believe in Christ. Wright explains, "Those who believe are given a real, new identity in the present, a life which now will never die; in other words . . . the believer now possesses, already, a divinely given immortal life which will survive death and be re-embodied in the final resurrection."[136]

Starting in the prologue, John begins constructing the road to the resurrection. From the bodily incarnation of Christ (1:14), to the feeding of the hungry (6:1–12), to the healing of the sick (5:1–9) and blind (9:1–7), John reveals a pointed interest in restoring God's material creation. With the raising of Lazarus (11:38–41), John foreshadows the resurrection of Christ as well as the new reality the incarnation and resurrection would reveal (20:1–31).[137] Furthermore, Jesus specifically teaches the doctrine of resurrection in John 6:39, 44, and 54, and, in 5:24–28, references the prominent OT resurrection passage Dan 12. To view the teaching of John as nothing more than a flimsy, ethereal spirituality is to miss the most vital aspect of this rich Gospel. John vividly depicts "God's special presence

---

133. Most notably Rudolf Bultmann.
134. DeSilva, *New Testament*, 415.
135. John 11:25–26; 12:23–26.
136. Wright, *Resurrection*, 444.
137. Jobes, *John*, 196; Beale, *Union*, 70, 112. See also John 14:19.

amidst creation[,] . . . not only the divine life but also the eternal reality turned into the creaturely realm in grace and mercy."[138]

John's portrayal of Jesus' heavenly origin also stands in stark contrast to the extra-biblical texts of the day, many of which we surveyed above. In such—often Hellenistically influenced—texts, revelations about the afterlife and the eschatological future often take the form of visionary journeys, in which an angelic guide takes a human figure on a tour of the heavens.[139] In John, however, Jesus "is not a 'sightseer' who glimpses a few secrets on a short visit, but is the one who has dwelt there from the beginning (1.1–3; 17.4–5). Nor does Jesus bring descriptions of the heavenly world, an eschatological timetable, interpretations of past history, or accounts of fleeting or dazzling glimpses of divine hair or garments. Rather Jesus the *logos* is the revelation (10.30; 14.9)."[140] John, thus, directs the attention of his readers, not to the heavenly realm, but to Jesus himself. The great hope in the Gospel of John, and the Christian faith, is not heaven but the presence of God in Christ.

Past, Present, and Future

Christianity is and has always been a resurrection movement. From its birth out of Judaism and onward, the promise of life after death has consisted of an embodied existence in a restored creation. This theological tenant not only yields hope for the future but should shape life in the present.[141]

Under the lasting legacy of Platonism and Hellenistic philosophy, however, humanity has been distanced from this great promise.[142] "Thoughts of 'life after death' still conjure up for most people some notion of a disembodied soul flying, rather forlornly, through pearly gates and golden streets. Preachers and theologians (especially Protestants) pride themselves on avoiding soul-body dualism, but pious talk at funerals is usually of the departed person surviving as a vague, benign spirit or as a thought in the memories of others."[143]

138. Allen, *Grounded in Heaven*, 92.
139. See 1 En., T. Levi, 4 Ezra, 2 Bar., 3 Bar., Apoc. Abr.
140. Carter, "Prologue," 45.
141. Wright, *Resurrection*, 210.
142. Bauckham and Hart, *Hope against Hope*, 128.
143. Bynum, *Resurrection*, 15.

One passage has been especially abused in this regard. John 14, used ubiquitously at funerals and wakes, has brought comfort to many mourners. The idea that Jesus comes to guide a deceased loved one to God's heavenly home certainly brings peace to the grieving soul. However, we should be well equipped to see that such an interpretation is foreign to the narrative of Scripture. Thus, with our history of heaven complete, we may now focus our full attention upon the Gospel of John and our focal passage, John 14.

2.

Mansions in the Sky
Abiding and "Many Rooms"

When I was a little girl, I loved my stuffed animals. My brown bear, my Pound Puppies, and my Glo Worm were among my favorites. As I chatted with them and played pretend, I desperately wished they could come to life. I longed for them to reciprocate my affection and respond to my playful banter.

As an adult, my miniature schnauzers have fulfilled the desire for playful companions beyond my childhood expectations. They are affectionate (to a fault), they are protective (to a fault), and they are ready to play any time of the day or night. They even "talk" to me with comical warblings. In the light of my dogs' lively companionship, the lifeless stuffed animals of my past have become nothing more than a shadowy memory.

If you'll allow me to draw an imperfect analogy, Christ fulfilled the OT law in a comparable manner. Like my stuffed animals, the ancient Jewish law codes were a blessing in their time. Yet, they foreshadowed something better to come. The Mosaic law provided useful guidelines for living as God's people, but in Christ they were replaced by the true substance to which they pointed. Instead of following lifeless statutes, Jesus opened the door for people to embark upon a whole new way of life. Instead of approaching God through priests or temple, Jesus made a way for people to live in the very presence of God. Choosing the law over Christ himself would be like clinging to my stuffed animals so tightly that I didn't realize that real animals exist. Yet this is how so many characters in John's Gospel respond to Jesus.

The Path Ahead

In this chapter and beyond we will examine the purpose of Christ's work in conjunction with John's portrayal of Christ as the completion of the OT. We will begin by examining the OT background of John and illuminating specific ways the OT informs our understanding of the Fourth Gospel and the afterlife. We will then situate John 14 within the larger context of the Gospel and establish its purpose within the narrative—namely that Christ's followers are called to carry on his redemptive mission in the world. Along similar lines, we will examine how the concepts of faith, knowledge, and truth inform our relationship with Christ and our response to his work.

As discussed in the introduction, specific themes throughout the Gospel provide an interpretive matrix for Jesus' teaching in chapter 14. Understanding how John uses specific imagery and terminology throughout his Gospel equips us to understand corresponding imagery and terminology in John 14. So, the concept of abiding will be the first theme examined, initially in the larger context of the Gospel and then with greater scrutiny in John 14:1–6. Throughout, we will argue that Jesus' promise of a dwelling in the Father's house does not refer to a room in heaven but a place in the presence of God.

Supporting Concept: The Hebrew Bible and the Gospel of John

To a markedly greater degree than the Synoptic Gospels, John is saturated in the OT. In fact, the Gospel of John cannot be understood properly without recognizing its dependence upon the OT.[1] DeSilva explains, "John has brought together a vast amount of material . . . aimed at helping readers see Jesus as the embodiment, fulfillment, and point of connection with the sum total of the Jewish religious heritage."[2]

Major themes from the OT are present at every important juncture in John, as the author assumes his readers are familiar with Hebrew Scriptures.[3] Throughout the Gospel, John refers to passages from each

---

1. Morgan, "Fulfillment," 165; Jobes, *John*, 16; DeSilva, *New Testament*, 420–21.

2. DeSilva, *New Testament*, 427. Cf. Porter, "Traditional Exegesis," 403; Evans, *Word and Glory*, 174.

3. Morgan, "Fulfillment," 156; Coloe, "Temple Imagery," 368.

book of the Pentateuch, in addition to Daniel, Malachi, Zechariah, Isaiah, and the Psalms. In the opening chapter of John alone, at least twenty-five direct connections to the OT can be identified. With such a preponderance of OT quotations, allusions, and echoes at the outset of his narrative, John is directing his readers to interpret the remainder of his Gospel in the light of the Hebrew Scriptures.[4]

Although we will not deal with the mechanics of intertextuality here, one point is of vital importance. The frequent *recurrence* of OT imagery and language indicates that the history of Israel is a fundamental aspect of the Johannine narrative.[5] More specifically, the repeated allusions to the exodus, Passover, and Jewish cult[6] indicate that the author intends his readers to understand the life and work of Christ within the framework of the OT legal system.[7] With the phrase "behold, the Lamb of God" (1:29), "John introduces the reader gently but firmly to symbolism without which it is impossible to understand the Fourth Gospel."[8] From the first chapter onward, the author presents a sustained build through which the lamb of God will become the perfect Passover sacrifice (John 19). According to Merrill Tenney,

> The spiritual significance of the Hebrew ritual is perfected in Christ. In His person the various elements of ceremonial worship are unified and integrated. He is the Lamb of God, or the sacrifice on the altar (1:29), the bread of life that excels the shewbread (6:51), the light of the world that outshines the golden candelabrum (8:12), the medium of intercession through whom more effectual prayer can be offered at the golden altar, and the final revelation of God, in whom divine law and divine life become more accessible to men than they were through the ark of the covenant (1:18).[9]

---

4. Bauckham, *Gospel of Glory*, 50; Jobes, *John*, 196.

5. For Hayes's seven criteria for intertextuality see *Echoes*, 30–33.

6. Biblical scholars commonly refer to the OT temple system as the "cult." Such usage is a convenient way to encapsulate the priestly duties and ritual practices of ancient Israel. It does not carry the modern nuance of religious fanatics who drink poisoned Kool-Aid.

7. DeSilva, *New Testament*, 415; Evans, *Word and Glory*, 174; Porter, "Traditional Exegesis," 403.

8. Collins, *Studies on the Fourth Gospel*, 49. Cf. Mouton, "Torah Reimag(in)ed," 103.

9. Tenney, "Old Testament," 306.

In sum, to understand the identity and purpose of Jesus, readers must remain attentive to the ways that John connects his narrative to the images, metaphors, and motifs of the OT, specifically those of the Mosaic era.[10]

The First Adam and the Last Adam

Although not as overt as the Passover theme, John's portrayal of Christ as true Israel is important to our discussion of the afterlife. To understand this aspect of Christ's identity, in addition to why it matters for our study of the afterlife, we must go all the way back to Genesis. In the beginning, Adam was commissioned to be fruitful and multiply, to subdue the earth, and to rule over creation (Gen 1:26–28). "Just as God, during his initial work of creation, subdued the chaos, ruled over it, and, further, created and filled the earth will all kinds of animate life, so Adam and Eve, in their garden abode, were to reflect God's activities."[11] In addition, Adam represented and ruled on behalf of all humanity, or if you'll allow me to use a bit of theological jargon, he exercised corporate headship.[12]

As Adam ruled over creation on behalf of humanity, knowing the will of God and obeying it were crucial to carrying out God's commission upon the earth. But, as we know, Adam failed, and because of his headship, all humanity fell with him. But, fortunately, God had a plan, and though the "first Adam" was unable to carry out his commission, God continued to raise up Adam-like figures until the "last Adam" came in Christ.[13]

Thus, the mantle of Adam was first passed on to Noah and later to Abraham.[14] Through Abraham the mantle was passed on to Israel, a new "firstborn" called to subdue evil and shine God's light to the nations.[15] Echoes of the original commission to Adam can be observed in passages about the promised land, the tabernacle, and the temple, which are replete with Edenic imagery.[16] Such imagery implies that if Israel had been

---

10. Jobes, *John*, 16.
11. Beale, *Union*, 23.
12. Middleton, *Liberating Image*, 121; Beale, *Union*, 22–23.
13. Rom 5:12–21.
14. Gen 5:1–3; 17:1–8.
15. Exod 4:22; 19:5–6; Isa 42:6. See also Mouton, "Torah Reimag(in)ed," 98–99.
16. 1 Kgs 6:29–35; 7:18–20; Ezek 28:13–17; 47:1–12. For a detailed discussion see Beale, *Union*, 198–99.

successful in its commission, God's covenant people could have ushered in a return to the blessed state God intended from the beginning. Yet, Israel—a corporate Adam—failed to cultivate its own "garden of Eden."[17]

Such theology is important to the current study for a couple of reasons. First, God's ultimate plan for humanity has never been "going to heaven." If the first Adam had been successful, his obedience would have led to eternal, embodied blessings. Humanity would have reflected God's glory upon the earth and brought creation to its fullest potential.

Second, Scripture gives no indication that when Adam failed, God abandoned his original plan for humanity and for creation. To the contrary, God already had a plan in place for restoration. Jesus, therefore, is the culmination of God's redemptive plan. By adopting the mantle of Adam, Christ came to set right what every human had done wrong. According to Beale, "[Jesus] was coming to obey successfully, in contrast to Israel's former disobedience, as well as, ultimately, that of Israel's progenitors, Adam, and Noah."[18] Because Jesus succeeded where others had failed, he could become the "firstborn" of the new creation and the "last Adam."[19] Just as sin entered humanity through Adam's corporate headship, righteousness was imputed to all humanity through Christ. And as such, all who are in Christ take on the mission of Christ—that of the original Adam—which is to bring creation to its fullest potential and fill the earth with the glory of God.

True Israel

The traditions and institutions of the law were unable to bring about God's ultimate plan because the people who upheld them were fatally flawed. The Gospel of John, however, reveals "Jesus being and doing what the first Adam and Israel should have been and should have done."[20] As the true Israel and the reality to which the OT institutions pointed, Christ is the corporate head, or King, of Israel, and as such, his followers can likewise be regarded as Israelites.

Throughout John's Gospel, "Israel(ite)" (*Israēlitē*) occurs only five times, while references to "the Judeans" (*Ioudaios*) occur approximately

---

17. Beale, *Union*, 112.
18. Beale, *Union*, 111.
19. Rom 5:14; 8:29; 1 Cor 15:45–47; Col 1:15–19; etc.
20. Beale, *Union*, 107.

seventy times.[21] While *Ioudaios* is sometimes used in a neutral sense in reference to the ethnic group, the term more often is used pejoratively in reference to the community that opposes Jesus and his followers. More specifically, "the Judeans" serve as a symbol of "the world," i.e., the domain that is antithetical to the kingdom of God.[22] *Israēlitē*, on the other hand, is always used in a positive sense. Whereas *Ioudaios* bears national, political, and territorial associations, *Israēl* is an honorific title for the people of God. The term does not exclude Jewish people but, rather, *includes* all who place faith in Jesus.

As John the Baptist announces the messiah in 1:31, he proclaims that his own purpose has been to make the Lamb of God manifest to *Israēl*. In other words, John was sent by God not to reveal Jesus to the *Ioudaios* but to *Israēl*. This concept is made apparent narratively as the obstinate Jewish leaders (1:19–28) stand in stark contrast to Nathaniel, a "true Israelite" who acknowledges Jesus as the Son of God and proclaims Christ "the King of Israel" (1:47–49). Pancaro explains, "[Nathaniel] recognizes Jesus as the one about whom Moses wrote in the Law. This detail is important. It marks the continuity between the Israel of old and the new Israel. . . . Those who believe in Moses should believe in Jesus (John 5.46); those who believe in Jesus are the true followers of the Mosaic tradition—true Israelites!"[23]

The next usage of *Israēl* occurs in John 3:10. Under the cover of darkness, Nicodemus approaches Jesus to question his identity and mission. When the Pharisee continually misunderstands, Jesus offers a gentle rebuke: "Are you the teacher of Israel, yet do not understand these things?" (3:10). In other words, a true Israelite should understand the identity of Christ and the kingdom he has come to inaugurate.

The final usage of *Israēl* in John is found in 12:13. When Jesus enters Jerusalem prior to his crucifixion, the people wave palm branches and proclaim him "King of Israel." Jesus, for his part, seems to accept the title. In contrast, however, when Pilate asks Jesus if he is "King of the Judeans" (18:33), Jesus rejects the designation and declares, "My kingdom is not of this world" (18:36). Further, the repeated accusation that Jesus is "King of the Judeans" throughout the crucifixion narrative (John 19) seems to imply that the title is at odds with Jesus' true identity and purpose. Sherri

---

21. John 1:31, 47, 49; 3:10; 12:13.
22. Fortna, "Theological Use of Locale," 93.
23. Pancaro, "Relationship of the Church to Israel," 399.

Brown explains, "Jesus is not, it turns out, a political messiah who revels in victory; rather, the evangelists teach that he is a covenantal messiah whose kingdom *is not* of this earth, who *is* the gift of truth that fulfills the promises of God's prior covenants and puts in place a new covenant open to all humankind."[24] As King of Israel, Christ rules over a kingdom much greater than Judea; his kingdom spans the entire creation.

Supporting Concept: The Farewell Discourse

After a lengthy prelude we are finally prepared to introduce John 14, our focal passage. The chapter is part of the larger grouping of chapters 14–17, often termed the "Farewell Discourse." Johannine scholar Raymond Brown identifies the unit as "one of the greatest compositions in religious literature."[25] He exhorts interpreters to approach the important chapters with an attitude of prayerful meditation but also admits that 14:2–3 is "extraordinarily difficult" to interpret.[26]

To understand the material in John 14, discerning the nature of the larger discourse is helpful. Overall, chapters 14–17 seem to follow the pattern of the testament genre common around the turn of the millennium. Farewell discourses, similar in some ways to a "last will and testament," are typically patterned after Moses' speech in Deut 31–33 as well as other parting speeches from the OT.[27] Blomberg points out that "themes of announcing one's approaching death, predicting other future events, reflecting upon one's past ministry, 'passing the torch' to one's followers, commissioning their ministry, and promising God's future presence" lead us to identify these chapters as Jesus' last testament to his disciples.[28]

In John 14, Jesus seeks to assuage the anxiety of his followers in the face of his departure.[29] Jesus is already on his way to the Father, yet his greatest concern is the welfare of those who believe in him—those

---

24. Brown, "Believing," 22. Cf. John 1:12–18; 3:16–17; 18:33–38.

25. Brown, *John XIII–XXI*, 582.

26. Brown, *John XIII–XXI*, 625.

27. See, in addition, the farewell speech of Jacob in Gen 49, as well as examples in intertestamental literature: T. 12 Patr., T. Adam, T. Isaac, T. Mos., T. Sol, etc. Cf. Blomberg, *Historical Reliability*, 195.

28. Blomberg, *Historical Reliability*, 195–97. Cf. Moloney, *Glory Not Dishonor*, 4–7. The exhortation not to fear was also a common feature of the testament; see 1 En. 92:2; T. Zeb. 10:1–2; Jub. 22:23.

29. Keener, *John*, 2:930; Köstenberger, *Encountering John*, 152.

who must remain behind.[30] Jesus' words were uttered to "disciples who under substantial emotional pressure were on the brink of catastrophic failure."[31] A key purpose of chapter 14 is, therefore, Jesus' reassurance that his death would not end the fellowship between himself and his followers but enhance it.[32]

Jesus' exhortation, "Do not let your hearts be troubled (*tarassō*)," may reflect OT usages, where God's followers are told not to fear prior to a great reward or victory.[33] In Moses' speech just prior to his death, he exhorts his people, "Be strong and courageous, do not be afraid and do not tremble before them, for the Lord your God—he is the one who goes with you" (Deut 31:6); and just before entering the promised land, Joshua likewise exhorts, "Be strong and courageous! Do not tremble and do not be dismayed, for the Lord your God is with you everywhere you go" (Josh 1:9).[34]

More than encouraging words, however, Jesus also provides the example of trusting the Father in the face of distress. Jesus' instructions in 14:1 delineate the way by which the disciples may calm their hearts: "Believe in God, and believe in me." Such faith, which is modeled by Jesus, "denotes personal relational trust."[35] Moreover, the comforting words of Jesus don't simply direct the disciples toward mental assent, but the more specific sense of trusting in the truth of his identity and participating in his mission.

Along such lines, the promises of chapter 14 are made *only* to those who love and believe Jesus.[36] The ever-deepening faith of Christ's followers parallels Jesus' work in drawing believers into deeper union with himself *and* God the Father. If the disciples will actualize the experience of knowing Jesus, they will know the Father as well.[37] In other words,

---

30. Brown, *John XIII–XXI*, 581–82.

31. Carson, *John*, 487.

32. Jobes, *John*, 26; Moloney, *Glory Not Dishonor*, 34; Stagg, "Farewell Discourses," 459–72.

33. In addition to the topical similarity, a semitism in the use of "heart" (*kardia*) may also support the OT connection. The singular form preferred throughout John's Gospel follows the Semitic preference for a distributive singular rather than the Greek/Latin preference for the plural. Brown, *John XIII–XXI*, 618.

34. Cf. Gen 26:24; Deut 1:21, 29; 20:1, 3; Josh 1:9; 2 Kgs 25:24; Isa 10:24; Jer 1:8.

35. Köstenberger, *Encountering John*, 425.

36. Segovia, "Structure," 486.

37. Whitacre, *John*, 347; McCaffrey, *House*, 218; Reese, "Literary Structure," 325.

"Jesus' demand that they have faith in him is more than a request for a vote of confidence."[38] The faith of the disciples will bring the redemptive, new-creational mission of Jesus increasingly toward fruition.

Further, a verbal link between 14:1 and 12:27 (*tarassō*) also serves to remind John's audience that when Jesus' heart was troubled, he focused on accomplishing the Father's will through obedience. In John 12:27, Jesus prays, "Now my soul has become troubled, and what should I say? 'Father, deliver me from this hour?' To the contrary, for this purpose I came to this hour." By following Jesus' injunction to have faith, the disciples engage in the same battle as Jesus himself. Jesus' faithful obedience to the point of death is central to his victory over the world (12:31, 16:33).[39] And, at the risk of becoming repetitive, the outcome of such victory is not a trip to heaven but the resumption of God's original plan for humanity and for creation.

Supporting Concept: Faith, Truth, and Knowledge

We have already noted that individuals become part of Christ's kingdom, part of true Israel, and part of Christ's redemptive mission through placing faith in Jesus. Yet, we should pause to clarify the nature of faith and truth, especially the manner in which the concepts are portrayed in the Fourth Gospel.

In John 18:38 Pilate poses the question "What is truth?"—a question John has already answered in 1:10–14. Jesus is the embodiment of the Father and the locus of all that is true. Christ is the light who illuminates the entire world with the truth, will, and identity of God.

Neither the Hebrew nor the Greek term for truth (*emet* and *alēthia*, respectively) implies a simple factual veracity. The truth of God is a relational concept, denoting his trustworthiness, reliability, and fidelity to his people.[40] Porter explains, "As a whole, the Gospel indicates that truth originates in the tripartite relationship of Father-Son-Spirit, and it is realized in truthful relations between the Son and human beings."[41] Yet, because the Father dwells in the realm "above" and humanity is confined

---

38. Brown, *John XIII–XXI*, 624.
39. Whitacre, *John*, 347.
40. Kanagaraj, "Implied Ethics," 56.
41. Porter, *John*, 175. Cf. Peterson, "Union with Christ," 15–16.

to the realm "below," a mediator is required. Jesus, therefore, becomes the embodiment of truth, enabling the world to experience God's truth and come to know him.[42] In other words, knowing the truth entails placing faith in the incarnational nature of the Son.[43]

Moreover, knowing the truth of God in Christ implies a deep personal relationship that results in action. In the Gospel of John, as well as the larger canon of Scripture and Greco-Roman culture, terms like "knowing" and "believing" weren't simply internal dispositions or emotions but actions.[44] Thus, knowing the Father entailed living and acting in accordance with the truth as revealed through the Son.

Ironically, many people in John's narrative claim to know Jesus but fail to recognize his true identity.[45] Yet, Jesus clearly states that those who fail to recognize his divine origin do not know the Father: "I have not come of Myself, but the one who sent Me is true, whom you do not know" (John 7:28b). Carson explains that Jesus' opponents don't doubt the existence of God but, rather, that God is the one who sent Jesus.[46] Thus, in failing to recognize Jesus, they also fail to know God himself. Even worse, those who do not accept the truth are children of Satan and, instead of doing God's will, do the will of the father of lies.[47]

Returning momentarily to John 1:10–14, an OT current runs beneath our discussion of the truth. By identifying Christ as the grace and truth who dwells (*skenoō*) among us, John likely references the exodus narrative in which God dwells (*skenoō*) among his people and describes himself as "compassionate and gracious, slow to anger, and abounding in lovingkindness and truth" (Exod 34:6). Confirming the OT reference, in 1:16–17 John compares the grace and truth of Christ with the law of Moses, implying that Jesus is the fullness of God's grace and the truth to which the law pointed. Other passages throughout the Gospel likewise indicate that the law of Moses was fulfilled by Christ.[48] According to Kanagaraj, "The commandments that were given by Moses pointed to human failure, whereas love and faith, representing the grace and truth

---

42. Porter, *John*, 180–97.
43. Neyrey, *John*, 204.
44. Kanagaraj, "Implied Ethics," 57; Milgrom, *Leviticus*, 1403; Mouton, "Torah Reimag(in)ed," 105; Porter, *John*, 176; Rad, *Genesis*, 81.
45. John 1:46; 6:42; 7:27, 41, 52.
46. Carson, *John*, 318. Cf. Porter, *John*, 179.
47. Porter, *John*, 193; Kanagaraj, "Implied Ethics," 56. See John 8:42–55; 9:41.
48. John 2:19–21; 4:20–24; 5:39–47; 6:27–30, 51–58; 8:12; etc.

that came through Jesus Christ, render the energizing power to fulfill them."[49] The Jewish opponents of Jesus, with their unyielding focus on the Mosaic law, thus miss the truth to which it pointed, Jesus Christ.

Abiding in the Gospel of John

The union of truth, knowledge, relationship, and obedience come together in the Gospel of John to formulate the notion of abiding. Those who reject the truth fail to abide in God because they believe the lies of Satan and carry out his will. Those who abide in God, even if imperfectly, accept the truth of the incarnation and seek to walk in obedience to Christ.

This concept of abiding is crucial to understanding the Gospel of John and especially chapter 14. In 14:2, Jesus says to his disciples, "In my Father's house there are many rooms," a phrase often understood to refer to living quarters in heaven. The broader concept of John's Gospel, however, indicates that Jesus is referring to the presence of God, not a heavenly dwelling place. Through Christ's work on the cross, his followers will be empowered to abide in the Father.

When chapter 14 is understood in the larger context of the Fourth Gospel, such an interpretation becomes apparent. Although the connection between "rooms" and "abiding" may not immediately be obvious, the Greek terms are closely related. We will thus proceed to analyze the concept of abiding in the Fourth Gospel before returning to chapter 14 and drawing further conclusions.

Abiding in Context

Compared with the Synoptics, John offers a more sophisticated and nuanced portrayal of the relationship between the Father, the Son, the Spirit, and the community of believers. As such, the author of the Fourth Gospel utilizes a range of terms to portray close interpersonal bonding. The most noteworthy is the term *menō*, which is typically translated as "to abide." Along with verbal cognates, *menō* is used forty times in the Gospel of John, in contrast to thirteen times in the other three Gospels combined.[50] The

---

49. Kanagaraj, "Implied Ethics," 59.

50. *Menō* has multiple nuanced definitions, including remaining in a state, condition, activity, or relationship: 3:36; 5:38; 6:27, 56; 8:31; 9:41; 12:24, 34, 46; 14:10, 17, 25; 15:4, 5, 6, 7, 9, 10, 16; remaining in a spatial area, but likely with a double meaning:

term is used most often in the sense of abiding or remaining in a certain state, condition, or activity (twenty-seven times out of the forty). Specifically in John, *menō* is "most often used to describe solidarity with Jesus and his faction."[51] The term can also be used in a spatial sense, as in staying put in a certain location (thirteen times). Yet even when the term is used spatially, it often has a double meaning, which will be discussed shortly.

Although John does not use this key term until 1:32, he establishes the concepts of abiding in the opening lines of his Gospel: "In the beginning... the Word was with God, and the Word was God" (John 1:1). The Word wasn't simply in close proximity to God. Rather, John's language implies a dynamic and intimate relationship. "It is not a static 'being with' which relates these two parties. There is a mutuality involved in the relationship that is difficult to render in succinct English.... The two parties of the relationship are so close that what one is, the other also is."[52]

Whereas 1:1 situates John's narrative within the entire scope of creation, in 1:14 the author hints that his narrative will take place in continuity with the people of Israel. By using *doxa*, "glory," and *skenoō*, "to dwell," key terms in the exodus narrative, John introduces a central theme—that of God tabernacling with his people.[53]

Yet by entering into creation in a physical body, God makes possible a deeper union, a more profound co-abiding than had previously been possible. In 1:18, John describes Christ's position as "in the bosom/by the side" of the Father, which reflects the "greatest possible intimacy with and knowledge of the Father." Such a relationship is also the basis for the mutual indwelling between Jesus and his followers, a relational orientation mirrored when the beloved disciple reclines upon the breast of Jesus in 13:25.[54] The position of Jesus upon the breast of the Father in 1:18 also serves to emphasize the concept of mutual indwelling throughout the prologue, as v. 18 forms an inclusio with v. 1 in affirming the oneness of

---

1:32, 33, 38–39; 4:40; 8:35; spatial only: 2:12; 7:9; 10:40; 11:6, 54; 19:31; and remaining alive: 21:22, 23.

51. Malina and Rohrbaugh, *John*, 174.

52. In addition, "The use of the preposition *pros* followed by the accusative case indicates the dynamism of the relationship." Moloney, *Belief in the Word*, 28.

53. Coloe, *God Dwells with Us*, 3; Coloe, "Temple Imagery," 370; Allen, *Grounded in Heaven*, 80.

54. Jobes, *John*, 39. Cf. Bauckham and Hart, *Hope against Hope*, 34; Carter, "Prologue," 38; Keener, *John*, 1:425; Neyrey, *John*, 77. Other scriptural examples of the idiom include Gen 16:5; Num 11:12; Deut 13:6; 1 Kgs 3:20; 17:19; Luke 16:22–23.

the Father and Son. Moloney explains that in v. 18 "there is certainly a return to the idea of a dynamic relationship which exists between the Word and God (v. 1). The dynamism of the relationship is expressed by means of the preposition *eis*, which captures the same idea of a motion toward the Father as *pros* in v. 1."[55] In other words, the terminology John uses does not simply imply Jesus is "in" the Father, but rather, that he is constantly moving "into" or "toward" God. A similar principle is expressed in 1:12 (and throughout the Gospel): Those who believe *into* Christ are those who have true fellowship with him.[56]

The stress on abiding continues in 1:32 with the first use of *menō* to describe the Spirit descending to "rest upon" (*emeinen*) Jesus. Whether the verb is used in the spatial sense or the relational sense is difficult to determine. Yet, since John often utilizes double meaning as a literary strategy, he is likely establishing that the concept of abiding has a greater nuance in his gospel than simply spatial. And, indeed, the next usage of *menō* seems to confirm this hypothesis. In vv. 35 and following, John describes a scene in which two disciples of John the Baptist begin to follow Jesus. When Jesus notices them, they ask: "'Rabbi[,] . . . where are you staying (*meneis*)?' He said to them, 'Come, and you will see.' So they came and saw where he was staying (*menei*); and they stayed (*emeinan*) with him that day" (1:38–39). While, in one sense, the uses of *menō* here seem to denote lodging, the usages clearly have theological overtones.[57] Along such lines, Malina and Rohrbaugh assert that John uses the word to convey the new loyalty and deep attachment the two disciples form with Jesus.[58] This new relationship then serves to foreshadow the deep abiding to which Jesus will call his subsequent followers.

The narrative of the Samaritan woman and her community also appears to reflect the double meaning of *menō*. After many of the Samaritans place their faith in Jesus, they request that he remain (*meinai*) with them. Indeed, Jesus remains in their midst for two days, but the narrative makes clear that the Samaritans have acknowledged the truth of his messiahship and, thus, the abiding will not cease once Jesus leaves their village (John 4:39–42).

55. Moloney, *Belief in the Word*, 49.

56. Scholars debate whether the pronouns *eis* and *pros* had lost their nuance of motion by the time of Koine Greek. However, John's use of the terms, especially *eis*, seems distinct in comparison to the Synoptics.

57. Brown, *John I–XII*, 75.

58. Malina and Rohrbaugh, *John*, 55.

The first overtly relational uses of *menō* can be found in John 6, which is also the context of the first of Jesus' well-known "I am" statements. These repeated assertions[59] again evoke the exodus theme and remind readers that Jesus, in himself, represents the very presence and activity of God among his people.[60] The setting of chapter 6 is a discussion between Jesus and the crowds regarding eating and drinking. In 6:27, Jesus advises his hearers not to work for food that perishes, but to seek food which remains (*menousan*), sustenance provided by Christ himself. As the passage continues, Jesus expands upon his admonition by explaining that the food is his own flesh, such that "he who eats My flesh and drinks My blood abides in Me, and I in him" (6:56). Thus, the abiding isn't simply an action undertaken by those who would seek to follow Jesus, or by Jesus himself, but a reciprocal action in which Jesus and his followers jointly participate.[61]

It is worth noting that Jesus describes "eternal life" as one facet of this mutual indwelling, but nowhere does the passage indicate that this life will occur in a place called "heaven."[62] In fact, eternal life is specifically associated with the resurrection in John 6:40 and 6:54; and in 17:2–3, Jesus directly equates eternal life to *knowing* God. Thus, the goal of co-abiding with Christ isn't getting to heaven but, rather, an increasing obedience to and deepening relationship with both Son and Father.[63]

This principle is succinctly illustrated in John 10. The parable of the sheep, John 10:1–18, contains two more "I am" statements as Jesus is described as both the gate for the sheep and the good shepherd who cares for them. Although viewing Jesus as "the gate" is at times understood to indicate that he provides the way into heaven, most scholars recognize that this parable isn't about going somewhere. Jesus is not a means of departure but a way into the Father's presence.

Although Jesus' works have already revealed his deity, the Messiah begins to assert his divine identity here as he takes the OT shepherding role of God upon himself. Likely drawing upon Jer 23 and Ezek 34, Jesus refers to the people as his sheep, connecting his own identity and purpose

---

59. John 6:35; 8:12; 10:7, 11; 11:25; 14:6; 15:1.
60. Exod 3:14; Kanagaraj, "Implied Ethics," 40.
61. Bauckham, *Gospel of Glory*, 12–13.
62. Eternal life: John 3:15, 16; 3:36; 4:14, 36; 5:24, 39; 6:27, 40, 47, 54, 68; 10:28; 12:25, 50; 17:2, 3.
63. Bauckham, *Gospel of Glory*, 10.

with that of the Father.⁶⁴ And just in case any reader misses the significance of the imagery, Jesus clearly asserts in v. 30, "I and the Father are one" (cf. 10:38). So, as the earthly incarnation of God, Jesus obediently carries out the Father's will, while Jesus' own followers listen to his voice and follow in his footsteps (10:25–27). Thus, in context, John 10 supports the theology of abiding and mutual indwelling, having virtually nothing to say about getting to "heaven."

This theology of mutual indwelling prepares readers to understand Jesus' words in chapter 14, but for now we must skip over our focal passage to examine the concept of abiding in the remainder of John's Gospel.

Jumping to the final "I am" statement, John 15 contains the highest concentration of *menō* usages in the entire Gospel, with a total of ten instances in the first ten verses of chapter 15. In this teaching, Jesus presents himself as the true vine, and once again the Gospel's author draws upon familiar OT imagery in which Israel was portrayed as a vine or vineyard and God as the vinedresser.⁶⁵ Thus, as the *true* vine, Jesus succeeds where Israel failed. He perfectly abides in the person and will of the Father. And as the mediator of truth, Jesus makes this relationship of mutual indwelling available to his followers.⁶⁶ Jobes explains, "Jesus pleads with his disciples whom he is about to leave behind in this world to continue his mission by remaining in him. But the remaining is not simply for the purpose of enjoying his fellowship; here they are told they must do something as a result of remaining."⁶⁷ In a more explicit manner than has been stated thus far, Jesus connects abiding with obedience (15:10). In other words, bearing fruit, i.e., living in obedience, indicates that one is truly abiding in Christ; lack of fruit implies the opposite. Peterson clarifies: "Fruit-bearing is proof of discipleship, and lack of fruit betrays that one never really was connected to the vine in a life-giving way."⁶⁸

Although John 15:16 is that last instance in which John uses *menō* in a relational sense, chapter 17 contains one further teaching on mutual indwelling that must be addressed. Often termed Jesus' "High Priestly Prayer," in John 17 Jesus prays for his followers just before he is

---

64. Bauckham suggests that the oneness of Father and Son also echoes the Shema. See Deut 6:4–5; John 8:41; 10:16, 30; 11:50, 52; 17:11, 21–23; 18:14. Bauckham, *Gospel of Glory*, 21–36.

65. Ps 80:8–16; Isa 5:1–7; 27:2–6; Jer 2:21; Ezek 15:2–6; 17:5–10; 19:10–14.

66. Malina and Rohrbaugh, *John*, 233.

67. Jobes, *John*, 37.

68. Peterson, "Union with Christ," 23.

betrayed and arrested. The portions relevant to our current discussion include the following:

- In 17:3, Jesus connects eternal life with knowing God in Christ. Such knowledge, as already discussed, is a key component of abiding.
- In 17:7–8, Jesus proclaims that his followers have received and believed in him, which are also key components of abiding.
- In 17:11 and again in 17:21, the theme of mutual indwelling becomes more overt as Jesus prays that his followers will be one as he and the Father are one.

As he has on multiple occasions throughout the Gospel, Jesus here mentions the connection between eternal life and abiding in himself (17:2–3). However, nowhere does Jesus mention that eternal life is oriented toward "heaven." Rather, eternal life is personal and missional. The disciples are to be sanctified in the truth so that they can abide in the presence of God and, as a result, carry on the mission of Jesus.[69]

Abiding in John 14

With context established, we may finally return to John 14. As the chapter begins, Jesus encourages his disciples, "Do not let your heart be troubled; believe in God, believe also in me. In my Father's house are many rooms (*monē*)" (John 14:1–2a). We should immediately note that our familiar term "believe," which is closely associated with abiding, is followed by a cognate of *menō*. Although this specific form, *monē*, is uncommon, the overwhelming context of relational, mutual indwelling in John should steer us away from a spatial interpretation. In other words, it is unlikely that *monē* represents a literal living space such as a "room." Nonetheless, the term is typically translated as "rooms," "mansions," or "dwelling places."

The translation difficulty arises because the term is rare in Greek literature, and appears only twice in the NT (John 14:2 and 14:23). Due to the scarcity of attestations, determining a precise meaning has presented interpreters with a particular challenge. As a result, *monē* has undergone a storied history of interpretation. Used twice in Josephus's *Antiquities*, both instances seem to refer to a spatial dwelling place.[70] However, in 1

---

69. Brown, *John XIII–XXI*, 765.

70. "And finding there a certain hollow cave, [Elijah] entered into it, and continued to make his *abode* in it" (Josephus, *Ant.* 8.13.7); "And thus did Jonathan make his

Macc 7:38, the single attestation in the Septuagint (the Greek translation of the OT), *monē* is associated with "continued existence," which accords well with our non-spatial understanding of the *monē* in John 14.[71]

The translation of *monē* in the Latin Vulgate—the Bible of the Catholic Church—made a deep, lasting, and regrettable impact on the church's interpretation of John 14. Translated from Greek to Latin as *mansiones*, the term was intended to convey stations or resting places along the soul's journey to heaven, once again a more Hellenistic than biblical understanding.[72] Yet, despite the inaccuracy of the translation, interpreters departed even further from the original meaning of *monē* by rendering the Latin term *mansiones* literally into English, which is reflected in the ASV and the KJV as "mansions." Along such lines, many people interpret the *monē* of 14:2 as heavenly dwellings into which believers go after the earthly state.[73] However, we have already seen that such interpretations are based more in Hellenistic thought than biblical theology.

Andreas Köstenberger, although he interprets *monē* more spatially than relationally, comes closer to an accurate interpretation by associating the term with the homes in which first-century people typically lived. During the time of Christ, a household was comprised of multiple dwellings; sons built onto their fathers' homes upon marriage, and family dwellings grew into a compound surrounding a central courtyard.[74] Yet, the context of John is clear that *menō* and its cognate *monē* describe relationships between the people more so than the structures in which they dwell.

Brown explains that interpreting *monē* in the light of its root, *menō*, is more in line with Johannine thought, as *menō* is "frequently used in John in reference to staying, remaining, or abiding with Jesus and with the Father."[75] The theological relationship between the verb *menō* and the noun *monē* is also noted by Keener, who points out that repeated uses of

---

abode at Jerusalem" (13.2.1).

71. *Monē* is used in this sense in John 21:22–23.

72. Jewish tradition does not provide any firm basis for interpreting *monē* as way stations or resting places on a journey; Beasley-Murray, *John*, 249; Brown, *John XIII–XXI*, 619; Carson, *John*, 489; Gundry, "In My Father's House," 69; Köstenberger, *Encountering John*, 426; McCaffrey, *House*, 73; Michaels, *John*, 767; Whitacre, *John*, 348.

73. Friedrich Hauck, "*Menō*," *TDNT*, 4:574–76; Lightfoot, *John*, 275.

74. Köstenberger, *Encountering John*, 426.

75. Brown, *John XIII–XXI*, 619. Cf. Moloney, *Glory Not Dishonor*, 33; Osiek, "Dwellings," 36.

the verb throughout John indicate that the present experience of believers "dwelling" in God's presence defines the use of the noun *monē* in John 14:2.[76] Similarly, Coloe describes the dwelling as "a series of interpersonal relationships made possible because of the indwellings of the Father, Jesus, and the Paraclete with and in the believer."[77] Although Hauck argues that a *monē* is a heavenly abode, he makes an apt point by describing the term as a permanent and indestructible dwelling wherein the believer is unified with God.[78] Stagg also makes a crucial point when he notes that *monē* designates a reciprocal indwelling that begins in life and remains unbroken by death.[79]

Along similar lines, the phrase "I will come again and receive you to myself, that where I am also you will be" (John 14:3b) is often understood as Jesus' promise to return to earth, gather his followers, and transport them to their heavenly dwellings. However, a close examination of the text reveals that Jesus does not promise to take his followers anywhere at all, other than "to himself."

The Greek term describing the action of "receiving" in 14:3 is *paralambanō*, which is often defined as "to take along with," designating a spatial movement. Yet when directed towards a person the term can be translated as "to take into a fellowship."[80] Gundry explains that Jesus' words, "receive you to myself" bear great depth of meaning as believers are guaranteed the immediate, personal presence of Jesus upon his resurrection, not a roomy, ethereal dwelling place.[81] Even McCaffrey, who sees primarily a spatial aspect to the phrase, concedes that the intimacy implied in *paralambanō* also has a spiritual sense in that it indicates "a deep spiritual union between the believers and Jesus."[82]

Along slightly different lines, Schnackenburg asserts that *paralambanō* can be interpreted as "receiving into a house," which has obvious connections with the phrase "my Father's house" (14:2).[83] If "the Father's house" is, as will be argued, the presence of God, such an

---

76. Keener, *John*, 2:935. Cf. Coloe, "Temple Imagery," 374–76; McCaffrey, *House*, 33; Gundry, "In My Father's House," 70.

77. Coloe, "Temple Imagery," 376.

78. Hauck, "*Menō*," *TDNT*, 4:574–76.

79. Stagg, "Farewell Discourses," 465.

80. Gerhard Delling, "*Paralambanō*," *TDNT*, 4:11–15.

81. Gundry, "In My Father's House," 70.

82. McCaffrey, *House*, 195.

83. Schnackenburg, *John*, 63.

interpretation accords well with reading *paralambanō* as being received into the presence of God/Christ and with the focus upon abiding in John.

Other Greek usages also prove informative. Hellenistic Jewish culture regarded *paralambanein* (receiving) as descriptive of the type of relationship in which a student is continually sustained by his teacher's impartation of religious tradition, most notably observed in the *talmidim* tradition. *Talmidim* were close pupils of a rabbi, as the disciples were of Jesus. The Mishnah indicates that the relationship between the *talmidim* and rabbi was more important than family ties: "If his father and his teacher were each taken captive, he must first ransom his teacher and afterward ransom his father."[84] Jesus, likewise, uttered statements along similar lines[85] and Plato describes the relationship between a student and a teacher as *paralambanōn* (one who receives) to *paradidous* (one who gives).[86]

An examination of NT references is helpful as well. While most usages of the term in the Gospels are spatial,[87] the Pauline epistles use *paralambanō* exclusively in the sense of receiving Christ or his teachings in line with the *talmidim* tradition.[88] For example, in 1 Cor 15:1 Paul declares, "I make known to you, brethren, the gospel which I preached to you, which also you received (*paralabete*), in which also you stand." The same type of usage is also attested in John 1:11-12: "He came to his own, but they did not receive (*parelabon*) him; but as many as received him (*elabon*), he gave the right to become children of God." Therefore, based on Jewish and Hellenistic traditions, as well as the precedent in John 1, we conclude that the usage of *paralambanō* in chapter 14 should be interpreted as a relational rather than spatial "receiving."

One problem does remain with such an interpretation. In John 14:3 Jesus is the subject of the verb, i.e., the one "receiving." If the "receiving" were in line with the Pauline/*talmidim* usages, one would expect the

---

84. M. B. Meṣ. 2.11. The term *talmidim* is only attested once in the OT (1 Chr 25:8) and is likely a late evolution of the verb *lamad*. See Walter Kaiser, "Lamad," *TWOT*, 480.

85. Luke 9:60-62; 14:26; Matt 8:22-23; 10:37.

86. Plato, *Theaetetus* 198b; Delling, "Paralambanō," *TDNT*, 4:11-15.

87. Matt 1:20, 24; 2:13-14, 20-21; 4:5, 8; 12:45; 17:1; 18:16; 20:17; 24:40-41; 26:37; 27:27; Mark 4:36; 5:40; 7:4; 9:2; 10:32; 14:33; Luke 9:10, 28; 11:26; 17:34-35; 18:31; John 1:11; 14:3; 19:16.

88. 1 Cor 11:23; 15:1, 3; Gal 1:9, 12; Phil 4:9; Col 2:6; 4:17; 1 Thess 2:13; 4:1; 2 Thess 3:6; Heb 12:28.

disciples to be the ones receiving. However, in the light of the reciprocal action described in the chapter (and the Gospel as a whole), the idea of Jesus receiving the disciples into his own presence is not incongruent at all.[89] John 15:1–17 describes Christ's followers as the branches that abide in the vine. Presumably, Jesus' followers could not abide in him if he had not taken the initiative to first receive them into his presence. Even more telling, in John 12:32 Jesus explicitly states that "if I am lifted up from the earth, I will draw all people to myself." While the verse does not use *paralambanō*, the message is clearly parallel—Jesus draws and receives his followers into his presence.

Jesus' assertion in 14:3, "I will come again and receive you to myself in order that where I am you will also be," also supports such an interpretation. Exactly where is Jesus? Jesus is already in "the Father's house." In other words, Christ is in a relationship of familial communion with God. The phrase, therefore, implies that Jesus will soon receive his disciples into their "dwelling place," not a room or mansion, but a relationship akin to that which Jesus already enjoys with the Father. For modern Christ followers, thus, the "room" or "dwelling place" of John 14:2 is a "present spiritual experience" that believers enjoy today, not at some point in the future.[90]

John 14:4–6 also shines additional light on the "receiving" that takes place. In v. 4, Jesus affirms, "And you know the way where I go." But in 14:5, Thomas responds, "Lord, we do not know where you go. How can we know the way?" Although Thomas seems to have interpreted the teaching spatially, Jesus offers gentle correction: "I am the way and the truth and the life; no one comes to the Father except through me" (14:6). In short, Jesus doesn't point the way, he *is* the way.[91] Christ never claims that the disciples know *where* he is going, only the *way*. In other words, if the disciples know the *way* (i.e., Jesus himself) their arrival at the correct destination is guaranteed.[92] Indeed, the "way" is not an indicator of direction, but a commitment to follow Christ, in line with the stress on abiding throughout the Gospel. Thus, being received (*paralambanō*) into a room (*monē*) in the Father's house does not suggest a room in a heavenly

---

89. John 12:26, 32; 15:1–17; 17:24.
90. Neyrey, *John*, 75.
91. Burns, "John 14," 299–315.
92. Michaels, *John*, 773.

mansion, but an intimacy of relationship and fullness of purpose.[93] Such a deep and abiding relationship is rooted in a knowledge of Christ and a faith in his divine identity.

---

93. Jobes, *John*, 226; Peterson, "Union with Christ," 22; Carson, *John*, 504.

3.

A Very, Very, Very Fine House
The Temple and Household of the Father

When my family moved into our current home, my youngest son Abel mourned the loss of our old house. It was the home in which he had lived his entire life, and in his five-year-old imagination, everything about the old house had been better than our new one. In reality, our new home was newer, nicer, and larger than our previous abode. Abel occupied a bigger bedroom and bathroom and acquired an entire playroom that he shared with his brother. Our new neighborhood even had a park and a pool, neither of which were available in our previous community. Clearly, Abel was seeing our old house through the lens of fond memories rather than reality. Nonetheless, our old home had felt safe and familiar, so he would periodically ask, "Why did we have to move?" and "Why can't we go back to our old house?" He couldn't enjoy the good things about our new house because he was so fixated on the old one.

Similarly, for individuals who have always held to the hope of a paradisal otherworldly heaven, shifting to belief in an embodied, earthly afterlife can evoke feelings of disorientation or even disappointment. Understanding the Father's house in John 14 not as a promise of heaven available upon death but as the immediate presence of God can feel jarring. But just as Abel's new house was superior to his old home in every way, the present and future hope of eternity in God's presence is simply better than our finite human minds can comprehend.

The Path Ahead

In this chapter, we will examine "the Father's house." As we've already seen, many of the terms in John 14 are spatial terms used relationally and none more so than the imagery of a "house." Just as the "rooms" in the Father's house represent the intimate relationship between God and his children, the "house" represents the presence of God and the temple of Jesus' body, *through* which believers enter the family of God.

In fact, the governing imagery for John 14, especially the opening verses, is that of "the Father's house" (*tē oikia tou patros*). This *oikia*, or "house," has been variously interpreted as heaven, the presence of God, the heavenly temple, the Jerusalem temple, the family of God, and Jesus himself. Examining the imagery in the context of John, however, brings clarity to the discussion and leads us to understand the Father's house on two levels. First, the Father's house is a clear reference to the Jerusalem temple, and second, it is an important symbol that Jesus appropriates and applies to himself. Jesus, the incarnate presence of God, is the reality to which the temple always pointed.

Grasping the temple implications of the passage is essential for a correct interpretation of the Father's house and John 14 as a whole. Dennis Olson writes, "I would guess that only a few would realize how central the theology of the temple was for ancient Israelites, how often it lies behind both the Old and New Testament texts, and how it continues to inform Christian theology."[1] To understand how temple imagery deepens our understanding of John 14, we will first examine the concept of sacred space and the manner in which biblical and extra-biblical literature portrays the temple as God's house. We will then, of course, survey the concepts in the context of John's Gospel and conclude by scrutinizing the Father's house in John 14.

Supporting Concept: Sacred Space

Sacred space, a foundational biblical concept that is closely related to temple theology, is exactly what it sounds like: a space holier than the surrounding area. More specifically, "Sacred space is the result of divine presence and serves as the center of order in the cosmos."[2] Biblically,

---

1. Olson, "Sacred Time," 126.
2. Walton, *Lost World*, 49.

sacred space is any hot spot of God's presence—the area surrounding the burning bush (Exod 3:2–10), Israel's wilderness tabernacle (Exod 40:34), the Jerusalem temple (2 Chr 7:16), or any other place God deigns to interact with his people.[3]

To fully elucidate sacred space, we must once more go all the way back to the beginning. God, as he created the cosmos and the earth then rested within it, generated a sacred space in which he could be with his people. In fact, the finale of the entire creation narrative is God dwelling with his people in his creation.[4] As such, most scholars agree that the creation account of Gen 1–3 is a "temple story."[5] Along such lines, many elements of the creation narrative reflect ancient temple-building accounts, and many characteristics of the garden of Eden reflect ancient temples.[6] That the garden was perceived as a temple is confirmed by the garden iconography in Israel's temple and tabernacle.[7] Walton explains that the inauguration of the Mosaic tabernacle reflects Gen 1–2 by telling "the story of sacred space established, sacred space lost and sacred space about to be regained."[8] The tabernacle would serve as a space in which God could, once again, dwell in the midst of his people as he had in Eden. And like the garden, the tabernacle and temple would be the central point from which God's blessings would flow to the rest of creation.[9]

The idea of temple is so closely intertwined with creation that the actual Jerusalem temple was later considered to be the "cosmic navel," or the source from which the rest of creation grew. In rabbinic literature, the temple was regarded as "a visible, tangible token of the act of creation, the point of origin of the world."[10] Along slightly different lines, the temple was also considered a microcosm of the entire universe, as each feature of the precincts typified some element of the cosmos. According

---

3. Gen 18:1–2; 28:12; 32:24–30; Num 22:22–35; Josh 5:13–15; etc.
4. Allen, *Grounded in Heaven*, 34.
5. Beale, *Temple*, 60–80; Levenson, "Temple," 287–89; Walton, *Lost World*, 49.
6. For example, the garden as the locus of God's presence, the garden as the dwelling of the high priest (Adam), the garden as a source of water, the garden as a place of precious stones, the garden being guarded by cherubim, and the eastern orientation of the garden; see Beale, *Temple*, 60–80.
7. Exod 25:31–40; 1 Kgs 6:31–36; Ps 92:12; etc.
8. Walton, *Lost World*, 51.
9. Hoskins, *Jesus as Fulfillment*, 65–66.
10. Levenson, "Temple," 283.

to Josephus, even the threads within the tapestries and the garments of the priests held cosmological significance:

> The veils, too, which were composed of four things, they declared the four elements; for the fine linen was proper to signify the earth, because the flax grows out of the earth; the purple signified the sea, because that color is dyed by the blood of a sea shell fish; the blue is fit to signify the air; and the scarlet will naturally be an indication of fire. Now the vestment of the high priest being made of linen, signified the earth; the blue denoted the sky, being like lightning in its pomegranates, and in the noise of the bells resembling thunder. And for the ephod, it showed that God had made the universe of four [elements]; and as for the gold interwoven, I suppose it related to the splendor by which all things are enlightened.[11]

Of course, the temple and tabernacle were only necessary because humanity, through their failure, had rendered themselves unable to approach the holy presence of God. Thus, the sacred spaces of Israel were localized, temporary accommodations. As a holy people called to reflect God to creation, the people of Israel needed a holy place in which they could encounter the God they were called to represent. Yet, even in the Mosaic period, which is often associated with legalism, the focus was not so much on the space as the relationship. The holy structures facilitated the communion of God with his people.[12] And living in proximity to God's presence would, in turn, empower the people to uphold his ethical requirements, thereby reflecting his character to the world.[13]

The sacred spaces of Israel recalled creation as it was meant to be.[14] The temple and tabernacle were places where heaven met the earth, where God dwelt among his people, and where God's people could worship him. Yet, because the holy presence of God was dangerous for sinful humans, certain procedures were required to approach him. The closer an individual came to God's presence, the greater the danger, and the more complex the ritual procedures. For example, Leviticus 16 prescribes priestly procedures for washing and bathing, as well as specific sacrificial rituals involving multiple animals before the priest could enter the most holy place, and that only once a year on Yom Kippur. Thiessen explains

---

11. Josephus, *Ant.* 3.7.7. Cf. Beale, *Temple*, 39–46.
12. Hoskins, *Jesus as Fulfillment*, 39; Mouton, "Torah Reimag(in)ed," 98–99.
13. Hoskins, *Jesus as Fulfillment*, 45.
14. Levenson, "Temple," 297.

that the ritual procedures and spatial boundaries "were meant not only to safeguard God's presence but also to protect God's people from the consequences of wrongly approaching God."[15] Although such procedures might seem archaic and confusing to modern readers, for Israel the rituals represented the process of restoring order and holiness to a creation that had descended into chaos.[16]

Upon the advent of Christ, however, God rendered such procedures obsolete (Heb 8). Humans would no longer require complex rituals to come near God's holy presence because God had come near to humanity. Sacred space was no longer a dangerous place entered only through ritual because the presence of God was located in Jesus. Further, no longer was sacred space a "space" at all, but a place of relational communion. And as already discussed, Jesus as "last Adam" was the "first fruits" of the new creation, a decisive step toward a return to the Edenic state in which God would dwell fully with his people.

But before that could take place, the locus of sacred space had to shift once more—into the believer. When Christ died and sent the Holy Spirit to his followers, the body of the believer became a temple of God, a new sacred space.[17] Thus, the presence of God was no longer restricted to one temple or even one person, but to an entire people, able to spread God's presence throughout the earth.

Supporting Concept: The Temple as God's House

Despite the importance of temple theology in the OT, no word for "temple" exists in the Hebrew language. When referring to the temple, biblical authors most often use the word *bayit*, "house," or *hekal*, "palace." As the terms imply, an ancient temple was the residence of a god. Whereas modern churches serve the needs of the faith community, temples existed to serve the divine resident.[18] Olson explains that the idea of the temple as a house was primary: "God in the temple was like a royal resident in a palace."[19]

---

15. Thiessen, *Jesus and Death*, 11. Cf. Hoskins, *Jesus as Fulfillment*, 41.
16. Mouton, "Torah Reimag(in)ed," 101.
17. 1 Cor 3:16–17; 6:19–20.
18. Olson, "Sacred Time," 127–30.
19. Olson, "Sacred Time," 127.

Though the temple was the locus of God's presence on earth, his primary dwelling place remained in the heavenly temple.[20] The earthly temple functioned as both a parallel residence and a gate through which God's presence could move throughout the earth.[21] Thus, even prior to Christ, the presence of God wasn't *restricted* to a certain place; he was simply more fully in one place—the temple—than others.[22] The concept is easy to grasp when one views the temple as the *house* of God, which is the most common name for the temple in the OT and other Jewish literature.[23]

Also like a house or palace, the temple was a complex of rooms and chambers. Although the focal point of the space was the sanctuary, the precincts also held quarters for lodging, cooking, and storage, in addition to the spaces for priestly ritual and the courtyards for worship.[24] Along such lines, the Temple Scroll from Qumran anticipates that a future temple will be built with chambers for every tribe of Israel.[25] Bryan explains that in this perfected eschatological temple "the people of God enjoy unprecedented access to the presence of God, in rooms that have been prepared for them."[26]

As God dwelt in both the heavenly and earthly temples simultaneously, the characteristics of both dwellings overlap and mirror one another in biblical and Jewish literature. As we've already seen in our "History of Heaven," many extra-biblical texts portrayed heaven as a place with rooms or chambers.[27] In the Psalms, the heavenly temple and earthly temple are often conflated such that distinguishing between the two is impossible.[28] Some texts even go so far as to indicate that the earthly temple was modeled after the heavenly one.[29]

---

20. 1 Kgs 8:32-34; 2 Chr 6:21; Ps 123:1; Ecc 5:2; Isa 6:1-6; 63:15; 66:1; Jer 25:30; Mic 1:2-3; Hab 2:20; Bar 2:16; etc.

21. Greene, "Jesus as Heavenly Temple," 427.

22. Hoskins, *Jesus as Fulfillment*, 103.

23. Pss 23:6; 27:4; 122:1; 1 Sam 1:7; 2 Chr 15:18; Bar 2:26; 1 En. 14:10-15; etc.

24. M. Mid. 5.3-4; Gibbs, "Already Dwelling," 25; McCaffrey, *House*, 67; Olson, "Sacred Time," 127.

25. 11QT^a XLIV.

26. Bryan, "Eschatological Temple," 192.

27. 1 En. 14:8-23; 21-22; 41:2; 91:13; 4 Ezra 4:35; 7:88-99; 8:20.

28. Pss 11:4; 20:2-6; 76:2, 8; 80:1, 14.

29. 2 Bar. 4:3-7; Wis 9:8; Heb 8:5. Cf. Bryan, "Eschatological Temple," 190-97.

Though the heavenly temple is one theological extension of God's "house," the imagery also bears an additional nuance. The "house of God" can also refer to the kingdom of God, or more specifically, the *people* of God.[30] Along such lines, "house" is often used in a familial or communal sense to refer to the household of a patriarch, such as Abraham, Israel, or Judah.[31] Thus, the notion that the "house of God" could refer to the people of God began to develop in the early stages of Judaism.

Aalen suggests that the shift from house-as-*temple* to house-as-*people* is reflected in 1 Chr 17:7–14. In this passage, the prophet Nathan relays God's promise that a descendant of David "will build for me a house, and I will establish his throne forever. I will be his father and he will be my son; and I will not take my covenant love away from him, as I took it from him who was before you. But I will enable him to stand firm in My house and in My kingdom forever, and his throne will be established forever" (1 Chr 17:12–14). Almost certainly the first reference to "house" describes the temple that is soon to be built. As the passage continues, however, the house of God is closely linked with the kingdom of God, as a descendant of David will be established in God's house/family/kingdom forever. Thus, the notion of house begins to shift away from a physical temple or a specific royal line to a community of God's people.[32]

Passages in extra-biblical literature also reflect a familial understanding of "house." The Qumran sectarians, who rejected the Jerusalem temple as corrupt, adopted such associations of house and community in calling themselves "a sure house" and a "house of holiness."[33] Although the author of the intertestamental book of Baruch doesn't necessarily identify God's house with people, he does describe it as a vast territory, in keeping with the idea of God's expansive kingdom.[34]

The associations of kingdom and community are carried forward into the NT as spatial and genealogical bonds are increasingly replaced by relational and spiritual ones.[35] In Eph 2:19, Paul tells the Ephesian church that they are members of "God's household . . . growing into a

---

30. Aalen, "'Reign' and 'House,'" 235–40.

31. Gen 12:1; 18:23–27; 34:19, 30; 50:4, 8, 22; Num 1:2–45; Isa 46:3; Bar 2:26; 2 Esd 1:33–35; etc.

32. Aalen, "'Reign' and 'House,'" 240.

33. For a sure house: CD I, 19; III, 19; a house of holiness: 1QS VIII, 5–10; IX:5–8.

34. Bar 3:24.

35. Aalen, "'Reign' and 'House,'" 235–36.

holy temple."[36] Aalen goes so far as to argue that John 8:35 exhibits a clear reference to 1 Chr 17, which relays the prophecy of a Davidic descendant who would establish God's kingdom forever. In John 8:35, Jesus affirms, "But the slave [of sin] does not remain in the house forever; the son remains forever." As such, Aalen argues, the references to God's house in John 2 and 14 should also be understood as referring to God's kingdom.[37]

The movement away from conceiving of the temple as the locus of God's presence was *not* a shocking development in the scope of Jewish history. As far back as the exilic period, centuries before Christ, the Jewish people had learned to define their relationship with God outside of land and sanctuary.[38] After the first temple was destroyed and the people were exiled, both Jeremiah and Ezekiel encouraged a movement toward personal holiness in the absence of cultic institutions.[39] Indeed, a humble spirit and obedient heart had long been essential aspects of experiencing God's presence whether in the temple or away from it.[40]

Nonetheless, the Jewish people never abandoned their hope of a restored future temple.[41] And a second temple was, indeed, rebuilt during the time of Ezra/Nehemiah (ca. 515 BCE) and refurbished during the reign of Herod (ca. 20 BCE). At the same time, many Jewish people continued to anticipate a perfected eschatological temple that would usher in the messianic age. Yet, even as they worshiped in the Jerusalem temple and hoped for the eschatological one, Jewish sages continued to affirm that intimacy with God was available to his people through the medium of torah and wisdom.[42]

When Herod's Temple was destroyed by Rome in 70 CE, just prior to the composition of John's Gospel, the Jewish people were in dire straits as they sought to articulate how they would relate to God without the focal point of their faith. Just as the Jewish people were beginning the process of redefining themselves, so were Christians defining and refining their own identity. Both groups sought to understand the actions of God in recent history. With the destruction of the temple, the Jewish people

---

36. Eph 2:19, 21; cf. 1 Tim 3:15; 1 Pet 4:17.

37. Aalen, "'Reign' and 'House,'" 237–38.

38. Coloe, *God Dwells with Us*, 51.

39. Ezek 36:24–28; Jer 31:31–34; cf. Coloe, *God Dwells with Us*, 49–51.

40. Isa 57:14–15; Mic 6:6–8; Hoskins, *Jesus as Fulfillment*, 104.

41. For an in-depth analysis of Ezekiel's temple vision in Ezek 40–48, see my published dissertation *Temple of Presence*.

42. Wis 7:21–30; 8:21; Sir 24; cf. Coloe, *God Dwells with Us*, 54–55.

turned to torah to replace what they had lost, while John reveals Jesus to be the new temple and the truth to which it had always pointed.[43]

Sacred Space in the Gospel of John

Understanding Jesus as a new locus of sacred space is fundamental for understanding the entirety of the Fourth Gospel.[44] Sacred spaces throughout the history of Israel, most notably the temple and tabernacle, had all pointed toward the role and identity of Christ. The author of the Fourth Gospel, thus, offers an overt and sustained presentation of Jesus as the replacement of such holy places.[45] At a number of points, Jesus himself uses spatial terms to define spiritual and relational concepts.[46] Coloe succinctly explains, "The intimate union of Father and Son, in the person of Jesus, creates a new sacred place that does away with regional sanctuaries, and provides a new mode of worship of the Father in spirit and truth."[47]

Sacred Space in Context

The opening words of John's Gospel, "In the beginning," are an obvious allusion to Gen 1:1 and the creation account. The reference evokes the time during which humanity enjoyed unbroken fellowship with God as well as the disastrous events of the fall. Through his incarnation, Jesus is both the remedy for the rift as well as the incarnate presence of the Creator, come again to dwell among his people. Although John does not, as yet, utilize explicit temple imagery, the very reference to creation evokes images of the garden-temple in which Adam and Eve dwelt.[48]

The first overt temple imagery emerges in John 1:14, in which the Word comes to "dwell" among humanity, a phrase "pregnant with

---

43. Coloe, "Temple Imagery," 369; Coloe, *God Dwells with Us*, 1; Schaefer, "Sinn der Rede Jesu," 210–17.

44. Mouton, "Torah Reimag(in)ed," 103.

45. Davies, *Gospel and the Land*, 334.

46. Neyrey, *John*, 408.

47. Coloe, *God Dwells with Us*, 86.

48. Siliezar argues that John utilizes creation imagery to highlight the close relationship between the Father and Son. He also demonstrates that creation imagery underscores the universal scope of the gospel; Siliezar, *Creation Imagery*.

theological significance."⁴⁹ To describe the act of "dwelling," John uses *skenoō*, a verbal cognate of the noun *skēnē*, used over 100 times in the OT to refer to the tabernacle.⁵⁰ As such, John almost certainly evokes the exodus narrative "in which the tent (or tabernacle) symbolizes the presence of God in the midst of Israel."⁵¹ Had John *not* intended to evoke images of the tabernacle, he would likely have used his favored term *menō*, "to abide," already discussed in the previous chapter.⁵²

Along similar lines, that Jesus reflects God's glory, *doxa*, is another overt link to Israel's holy sanctuaries. When the wilderness tabernacle and temple were completed, God's radiant, visible presence—his *doxa*—descends upon them.⁵³ Alternately, when the second temple is defiled by the corruption and idolatry of its priests, God's *doxa* departs (Ezek 10:18).

Thus, God has come in visible form to tabernacle among his people just as he dwelt in the temple and tabernacle. In Christ, God takes upon himself a more perfect medium for contact with humanity than the architectural structures of the past. The Messiah embodies the perfection of God and makes available the true essence of worship.⁵⁴

An eschatological aspect also underlies John 1:14 when viewed in the light of OT expectations. Included in the new covenant promised by the prophets was a new temple in which God would permanently dwell among his people.⁵⁵ The inception of this future temple would usher in an age of peace and prosperity during which all nations would gather to the temple, from which blessings would flow.⁵⁶ In John, thus, the bringing together of God's children in Christ, the promised temple, is the inauguration of the blessed eschatological age.⁵⁷

We will return to such expectations later, but for now, our next overt mention of sacred space occurs in John 1:51. As Jesus addresses

---

49. Collins, *Studies on the Fourth Gospel*, 198.

50. Exod 25:9; 26:30; 27:9; 35:11; 40:2; Lev 8:10; Num 1:50; Josh 22:29; etc.

51. Malina and Rohrbaugh, *John*, 33. Cf. Mouton, "Torah Reimag(in)ed," 96; Jobes, *John*, 36, 72.

52. Greene, "Jesus as Heavenly Temple," 430.

53. For tabernacle: Exod 40:34; temple: 2 Chr 5:11–14; cf. Hoskins, *Jesus as Fulfillment*, 58–60, 117–20.

54. Tenney, "Old Testament," 306.

55. Ezek 43:4–5; Collins, *Studies on the Fourth Gospel*, 200.

56. McCaffrey, *House*, 60.

57. Jonge, *Jesus*, 174.

Nathaniel, whom he had just dubbed "a true Israelite," he says, "You will see the heavens opening and the angels of God ascending and descending upon the son of man" (John 1:51). Two OT references are in view here, a subtle echo of Gen 32:23–32 and an explicit allusion to Gen 28:12–17.[58]

We will deal first with the clear allusion: John's reference to "Jacob's ladder." In Gen 28:12–19, Jacob has a dream in which he sees a ladder reaching into heaven. God stands at the pinnacle of this ladder while angels ascend and descend upon it. When Jacob awakens, he refers to his location as "the gate of heaven" and names it "the house of God," or *Beth-El*.

In John's allusion to the passage, the ladder is replaced by Jesus himself. By describing Jesus as such, John likely intends to convey that the Messiah is currently enthroned in heaven with the Father, even as he stands upon the earth.[59] Thus, the focus is not on "heaven" or on the angelic beings, but upon Jesus as the locus of God's presence.[60] Because Jesus is both in heaven and on earth, no ladder is needed. Jesus functions as a mediator between the two such that when the disciples look at Jesus, they are, in fact, gazing into heaven.[61]

The positioning of the Father and Son reinforces concepts discussed in our previous chapter. That both are simultaneously on earth and in heaven is a subtle reminder of the reciprocal relationship between them. As the Father dwells with the Son on the earth, so also the Son dwells with the Father in heaven. Thus, once again, heaven does not equate to a geographical space, but rather a relational co-abiding—a mode of existence or inter-dimensional communion perhaps beyond our present frame of comprehension.

The second echo of Genesis in John 1:47–51 also involves Jacob. In Gen 32:23–32, the patriarch wrestles with God, *sees* the face of God, and is renamed *Israel*. In like manner, Nathaniel, to whom Jesus is speaking in John 1:47–51, is called *Israel* as he *sees* God in Christ. According to Neusner, "[Nathaniel] is like Jacob, not the devious character who grabbed his brother's heel at birth and stole his birthright and blessing,

---

58. Mouton, "Torah Reimag(in)ed," 94; Neusner, "Jacob Allusions," 589–91; Neyrey, *John*, 101.

59. John 1:2 and 1:18 likewise indicate that Jesus is in the presence of the Father even while he is on earth. Cf. Neusner, "Jacob Allusions," 598–600; Neyrey, *John*, 101.

60. Brown, *John I–XII*, 91; Hoskins, *Jesus as the Fulfillment*, 132–35; Jobes, *John*, 53; Mouton, "Torah Reimag(in)ed," 108.

61. Hoskins, *Jesus as the Fulfillment*, 126; Neusner, "Jacob Allusions," 589.

but the perfect Jacob, the man of wisdom."[62] Nathaniel along with true Israel, i.e., all who believe in Jesus, are the ones who see God in truth. Hoskins explains further, "Jesus therefore fulfills a purpose associated with Bethel, the Tabernacle, and the Temple. By implication, he is a suitable replacement for these holy places."[63]

These initial allusions to the sacred spaces of the past foreshadow John 2:19–21 and 4:20–24, in which Jesus unequivocally announces that he will replace the temple.[64] Initially, when Jesus identifies his body as the temple in 2:19–21, his words make no literal sense. Readers are, thus, "required to puzzle out how the notion of 'Templeness' could relate to the body of Jesus, and conversely, what is it of Jesus that can be called 'Temple.'"[65] Yet, readers have already learned from John chapter 1 that Jesus' relationship with the Father is key to understanding his purpose and identity.[66] Just as the defining characteristic of the temple was the presence of God, Jesus, as the embodiment of God, likewise embodies the temple.

Further, with the words "destroy this temple, and in three days I will raise it up" (2:19), Jesus anticipates his work on the cross. Thus, the "templeness" of Jesus is also closely related to his crucifixion and resurrection. Jobes explains that "all of the promise and hope of [the temple's] sacrifices and rituals have been fulfilled, according to John, in the one, final sacrifice of Jesus on the cross. The people's relationship with God is no longer mediated through the priests of the Jerusalem temple, but through Jesus Christ God's Son."[67] In referring to the temple as Jesus' body, the author of the Gospel has begun to move away from the "temple-as-building to something more personal and relational."[68] The new temple of Jesus' body becomes the place where humanity can approach God's presence, a new community of faith embodying a new way of life with God.[69]

The particular episode in which Jesus identifies his body as the temple is often called the "temple cleansing." Though Jesus drives out

62. Neusner, "Jacob Allusions," 588.
63. Hoskins, *Jesus as the Fulfillment*, 135. Cf. Greene, "Jesus as Heavenly Temple," 436.
64. Hoskins, *Jesus as the Fulfillment*, 135; Gibbs, "Already Dwelling," 17.
65. Coloe, *God Dwells with Us*, 5.
66. Moloney, *Belief in the Word*, 97.
67. Jobes, *John*, 211. Cf. Neyrey, *John*, 71.
68. Coloe, "Temple Imagery," 365. Cf. Coloe, *God Dwells with Us*, 161.
69. McCaffrey, *House*, 252; Dodd, *Founder*, 90; Davies, *Gospel and the Land*, 350.

the money changers and merchants, such figures actually provided an essential function within the temple by selling animals to those who traveled from afar and were unable to bring livestock with them. The functionaries also changed Roman currency, which bore idolatrous images, into coinage that could be used to pay the temple tax.[70] Such services made it possible for any Jewish person to take part in the daily *tamid*, or whole-offering. "And to the accomplishment of that holy purpose, the money-changers, as a matter of fact, were simply essential. They formed an integral part in the system of atonement and expiation for sin."[71] Thus, Jesus' rejection of the merchants and money changers represented a rejection of the most important Israelite ritual and the entire system it represented.[72] In addition, Jesus' actions function as an indicator that a different means of atonement would soon be available.

Perceptive readers may notice that John places the temple cleansing at the start of Jesus ministry whereas the Synoptic Gospels place the event during the final week of Jesus' life. Such an apparent discrepancy is easily resolved. The literary and theological purpose of John's Gospel does not revolve around a strict chronology of Jesus' life. John arranges his material in such a way as to help his readers understand the spiritual significance of events in Jesus' life and in God's salvific work throughout history. By situating the temple cleansing so early, John emphasizes the importance of the temple in the narrative.[73] In addition, the temple cleansing provides an interpretive key for the manner in which John utilizes temple imagery throughout his Gospel.[74]

Moving on to the next passage in which sacred space is prominent, John has already prepared readers for the encounter between Jesus and the Samaritan woman with his prior references to Jacob. Once again, in John 4, Jesus is portrayed as one who would inaugurate a better mode of worship than was practiced by Jacob and his descendants, a new experience of God that would surpass all spatial and ethnic boundaries.[75]

---

70. Moloney, *John*, 76.

71. Neusner, "Money-Changers," 288–89.

72. Coloe, *God Dwells with Us*, 81; Gibbs, "Already Dwelling," 17; Neusner, "Money-Changers," 290.

73. Davies, *Gospel and the Land*, 289–90; Jobes, *John*, 70–75; Porter, *Sacred Tradition*, 138; Porter, "Traditional Exegesis," 411.

74. Coloe, *God Dwells with Us*, 84.

75. Coloe, *God Dwells with Us*, 86.

The primary theme of John 4 is that of true worship, which John highlights by referencing additional traditions associated with Jacob. In the well-known narrative, Jesus approaches a Samaritan woman at the site of Jacob's Well. Over the course of a theological discussion, Jesus offers the woman "living water" and informs her that "a time is coming and now is, when the true worshipers will worship the Father in Spirit and truth" (4:24). No longer will people need to travel to Mt. Gerizim, Jerusalem, or any other sacred site. God's presence can now be experienced through Christ himself (4:23–26). As the one who abides in the presence of the Father, Jesus is the first true worshiper and the channel through which others may experience God. Along such lines, Jesus inaugurates *true* worship, a worship toward which the incomplete modalities of the past pointed. Because Jesus is the embodiment of the Father, true worship is now available through knowledge of Christ himself.[76] "Thus the narrative of 4.1–42 develops the point, begun in the Cleansing of the Temple and continued throughout the Gospel, that the locus of worship lies . . . no longer in a specific sacred place, but rather through the believing community in whom the Spirit of Jesus abides."[77]

Although we will address the Spirit in a later chapter, we should note that worship in "Spirit and truth" does not simply refer to an internal, spiritualized walk with God. In John's Gospel, the Spirit is a powerful agent of real-world transformation and action. Worship in "Spirit and truth," thus, refers to "the total orientation of one's life and action toward the Father."[78]

Returning to the matter of Jacob's Well, no specific biblical account of such a place exists. Instead, John appears to combine several streams of tradition from Jewish targumic[79] and rabbinic literature. The extrabiblical material is based upon Gen 29, in which Jacob travels to Haran in search of a wife and meets Rachel at a well. Certain targums expand upon the narrative by proclaiming that Jacob's presence draws forth a

---

76. Coloe, *God Dwells with Us*, 103–4.

77. Lee, *Symbolic Narratives*, 83. Cf. John 14:16–17; 15:26; 16:7, 14–15.

78. Moloney, *Belief in the Word*, 152–53. Cf. Hoskins, *Jesus as the Fulfillment*, 143–44.

79. A targum is a translation of the Hebrew Bible into Aramaic. The translations often take the form of paraphrases that reveal how the translators interpreted the original text. Most targums arose around the time of Christ in the first century CE.

miraculous overflow of water that lasts for the entire twenty years Jacob resides at Haran.[80]

Separate lines of tradition associate Jacob's Well with Shechem/Sychar, a plot of land Jacob gave to his son Joseph (Gen 33:19; 48:22) and the site of Jesus' encounter with the Samaritan woman (John 4:5). The tradition is significant because the well in question is likely the same well associated with Abraham, Isaac, Jacob, Miriam, and the children of Israel. This well, according to tradition, was created before the founding of the world and would spring up as needed for God's people.[81] Thus, the miraculous drawing of water by Jacob and the children of Israel seems to underlie the discussion between Jesus and the Samaritan woman. In such a light, John continues to reveal the superiority of Jesus over past traditions, as even the miraculous waters from the very well of creation cannot quench thirst as absolutely as Christ.[82]

Yet other traditions associate Jacob with special knowledge of a future temple and messiah who would arise upon the advent of the eschatological age.[83] This messiah would hold even greater knowledge than Jacob as he inaugurates the new temple. The Samaritan woman seems familiar with such traditions as she remarks: "I know that messiah is coming.... When that one comes, he will reveal everything to us" (4:24). Thus, as the woman dialogues with Christ, she begins to realize that Jesus is speaking to her of an eschatological reality: a future hope that was becoming a present reality through the one even greater than Jacob (4:12).[84] Yet, John does not present Jesus as a new Jacob who would decide generational disputes over the proper location of the temple, i.e., Mt. Gerizim or Jerusalem. He circumvents the discussion entirely. Neyrey explains, "Jesus *declassifies* . . . all temples and mountains as sacred, even as he presents his body as the new temple, the new sacred space. Hence his body becomes the dwelling of God."[85]

The themes of living water, eschatological hope, and sacred space again converge in John 7. The chapter is set within the Jewish Feast of Tabernacles, or *Sukkot*. This sacred holiday commemorated the period

---

80. Tg. Neof. Gen 28:10; Tg. Yer. I Gen 29:1. Cf. Coloe, *God Dwells with Us*, 91.

81. Tg. Yer. I Num 23:17–31. Cf. Neyrey, "Jacob Traditions," 421–22.

82. Neyrey, "Jacob Traditions," 422–24.

83. Gen. Rab. 65.23; Pesiq. Rab. 30.3; 17.2; Midr. Ps. 78.6; Sifre Num. 119; Neyrey, "Jacob Traditions," 431.

84. Greene, "Jesus as Heavenly Temple," 435.

85. Neyrey, *John*, 80–81 (emphasis original). Cf. Neyrey, "Jacob Traditions," 432.

in which the Israelites lived in temporary shelters following their escape from Egypt. Key elements of the festival included light, which recalled God's guiding pillar of fire (Exod 13:21–22) and water, which recalled God's miraculous provision (Exod 17:1–2).[86] As a whole, *Sukkot* was a memorial of God's protective care for and presence with his people.[87] It was also one of three holy holidays for which all Jewish people were instructed to make a pilgrimage to the temple. According to Reubenstein, "When worshippers came to the temple [for *Sukkot*]—the divine house, domain, throne, and footstool—they rededicated themselves to their God and renewed their devotion to his sovereignty. The community expressed its subservience to its God and king at his terrestrial abode where his presence was most keenly experienced."[88]

By the time of Christ, *Sukkot* had developed a strong eschatological element. As the feast memorialized the past, it also anticipated a future time of prosperity in which all nations would be gathered toward Jerusalem and experience Edenic blessings.[89] Here in chapter 7, John draws upon prophecies articulated in passages such as Ezek 47 to expand upon the water imagery of the feast.[90] Ezek 47:1–12, which typifies many biblical and extra-biblical expectations, describes the eschatological river that flows *from the temple* and revivifies the barren land and the people that live upon it. Similarly, in John 7:37–38, "Jesus stood and shouted, saying 'If anyone should thirst, let him come to me and drink. The one who believes in me, as the Scripture says, from his inward being will flow rivers of living water.'" Thus, once again the "living water" that Christ provides is associated with the messianic future. In this case however, Christ replaces the *temple* as the source of the living water.[91] And further, the living water that Christ offers not only flows from himself but through those who place faith in him. In other words, through Christ, the locus of sacred space shifts into believers, who are charged with bringing God's presence throughout the earth.

In chapter 8, the *Sukkot* narrative continues as John's focus shifts from water to light. During the feast, God's presence was signified by

---

86. Coloe, "Temple Imagery," 373; Jobes, *John*, 140.
87. Coloe, *God Dwells with Us*, 120.
88. Reubenstein, "*Sukkot*," 190.
89. Zech 14:16–19; Isa 2:2–4; 56:6–8; Brown, *John I–XII*, 326; Coloe, *God Dwells with Us*, 121; Hoskins, *Jesus as the Fulfillment*, 163–64; Reubenstein, "*Sukkot*," 185–86.
90. Cf. Isa 12:3–4; 44:3; 55:1; 58:11.
91. Brown, *John I–XII*, 327; Coloe, *God Dwells with Us*, 126–27.

large bonfires throughout the temple courtyards and the golden candelabrum within the sanctuary. The flames both memorialized God's guidance in the wilderness and represented his presence currently within the temple.[92] Into this setting Jesus declares, "I am the light of the world" (8:12), thus affirming that he is the same God who guided Israel in a pillar of fire and who presently embodies YHWH's sacred presence in the temple. As such, Jesus claims not only that he replaces the temple and tabernacle with his body but that he is the truth to which the associated symbols of water and light point.

The theme of sacred space carries forward subtly into chapter 10 with the parable of the sheep. As the narrative begins, Jesus teaches, "Truly, truly, I say to you, anyone who does not enter by the door into the fold (*aulē*) of the sheep, but climbs up another way, is a thief and a robber" (John 10:1).[93]

The "fold," or *aulē*, is best understood as an open-air enclosure, such as a sheep pen or courtyard.[94] In addition to sheepfolds, the term is frequently used to refer to the temple courtyard as, for example, when Peter follows Jesus into the court, *aulē*, of the high priest in John 18:15.[95] Although it was an outer courtyard, the *aulē* was an essential part of the temple complex and as such, was included in the sacred space of God's presence. Thus John, as he does in numerous other instances, cleverly takes advantage of an available double meaning. Metaphorically, Jesus offers "sheep" a way into the "sheep-pen," but in a more literal sense he is the means by which believers enter the sacred space of God.

In the latter half of chapter 10, John returns to the Jewish festivals with a narrative that takes place during the feast of Dedication, or *Hanukkah*, which is closely associated with *Sukkot*. The author of 2 Maccabees explains that *Hanukkah* was inaugurated because the Jewish people were unable to celebrate *Sukkot* when their temple was occupied by "foreigners" (Seleucids).[96] Therefore, two months after *Sukkot*, a new feast, *Hannukah*, was instituted when the people victoriously reclaimed and reconsecrated their temple.

92. M. Sukkah 5:2; Brown, *John I–XII*, 344; Jobes, *John*, 139; Malina and Rohrbaugh, *John*, 156.

93. Cf. John 10:16.

94. "*Aulē*," BDAG, 150.

95. See also Matt 26:58, 69; Mark 14:54, 66; Luke 22:55; Rev 11:2; LXX: Lev 6:16; Isa 1:12; Ezek 10:4; 40:20; 46:1; Ps 28:2; Neh 13:7; etc.

96. 2 Macc 10:5–8; cf. Reubenstein, "*Sukkot*," 189.

The lighting of the *Hannukah* lampstands played an important role in the festival by commemorating the fire that God miraculously sustained during the rededication of the temple, but light is not a focus in this portion of the Johannine narrative. Rather, in the context of a feast that celebrated the *reconsecration* of the temple, Jesus describes himself as the one who is consecrated. As such, the Messiah implies he is a new temple by applying to himself the terminology used for the consecration of the tabernacle, Solomon's temple, and the Second Temple,[97] as "one who the Father *consecrated* (*hagiazō*) and sent into the world" (10:36).[98] In short, Jesus claims that "God is no longer present in the consecrated stone altar, but in the flesh and blood of the consecrated and sent Son of God."[99] The use of *hagiazō* may also foreshadow the means of Jesus' death, as the same term was used of sacrificial animals.[100]

Returning to the imagery of family and household, one final scene should be mentioned before moving to John 14. As Jesus perishes upon the cross, he speaks to the individuals dearest to him: "When Jesus saw his mother and the disciple whom he loved standing nearby, he said to his mother, 'Behold, your son.' Then he said to the disciple, 'Behold, your mother'" (John 19:26–27a). Though often interpreted as Jesus' affectionate concern for his mother, the verses likely bear a greater depth of meaning. In fact, Coloe regards the interchange as the climax of the entire Gospel.[101] At the hour of Jesus' death, a new family is born. "Jesus' flesh and blood relationships are completely transcended as he fulfills the work the Father has given him to do."[102] Indeed, after his resurrection, Jesus exhorts Mary Magdalene to go tell his "brothers" the good news (20:17). The promise of John 1:12 has been fulfilled: all who believe in Christ will now become "children" of God and members of the Father's household.

To conclude our survey of sacred spaces in John, Jesus fulfills every symbol and institution in his own person. He is the God who established the tabernacle in the wilderness and the divine Son who brings heaven to earth. He is the source of creation, the fiery light in the desert, and the water that brings life to the world. He is the temple incarnate and the

---

97. For tabernacle: Num 7:1; Exod 29:36, 43; Lev 8:11; For Solomon's Temple: 1 Kgs 8:64; 9:3; 2 Chr 7:7, 16, 20; For Second Temple: 1 Macc 4:48.

98. Coloe, *God Dwells with Us*, 145; Moloney, *Signs and Shadows*, 147.

99. Moloney, *Signs and Shadows*, 150.

100. Cf. John 10:15.

101. Coloe, *Dwelling*, 55; Coloe, *God Dwells with Us*, 185–90.

102. Culpepper, "Johannine Passion," 29. Cf. Moloney, "Johannine Passion," 42.

God who now comes bodily so that such subpar modalities are no longer needed. As God in human form, Jesus removes every limitation upon access to the Father. Through his death and resurrection, he opens the door to the Father's household and institutes a new family of faith. With such foundations established, we may now turn our attention to John 14.

Sacred Space in John 14

John's use of familial language and sacred space throughout the Gospel prepares readers to understand the Father's house in John 14:2–3. For convenience, we will reproduce the verses under consideration:

> In my Father's house are many rooms; unless it were so, would I say to you that I go to prepare a place for you? And if I should go and prepare a place for you, I will come again and receive you to myself, that where I am also you will be. (John 14:2–3)

Some scholars have argued against a reference to the temple here, but several factors indicate that temple imagery must be considered.[103] First of all, the phrase "my Father's house" (*tē oikia tou patros mou*) exhibits a clear link to the nearly identical phrase in 2:16 (*ton oikon tou patros mou*). Almost certainly, the usage in John 14 should bring to mind the narrative of John 2, in which "the Father's house" refers to the temple.[104] Second, as discussed earlier in the chapter, "house" was the most common term used to refer to the Jerusalem temple in biblical and extra-biblical literature.[105] Third, in accordance with the temple-as-house imagery, John draws upon the traditional Jewish imagery of the temple as a house with rooms for God's people. Fourth, John repeatedly uses spatial metaphors to describe relational and spiritual concepts.

So, assuming that the temple imagery of John 2 can be carried forward into John 14, we will continue to use 2:19–21 as an interpretive guide to 14:2–3. And, as discussed, in 2:19–21, Jesus' body is identified as the temple. In referring to the temple as Jesus' body, the author of the

---

103. Scholars who see no reference to the Jerusalem temple include: Fischer, *Die himmlischen Wohnungen*; Holwerda, *Holy Spirit and Eschatology*; Köstenberger, *Encountering John*, 426; McKelvey, *New Temple*; Michaels, *John*, 767.

104. McCaffrey, *House*, 30; Wright, *Resurrection*, 446.

105. Pss 23:6; 27:4; 122:1; 1 Sam 1:7; Isa 56:7; 60:7; 2 Chr 15:18; Bar 2:26; Luke 2:49; 11:51; Mark 2:26; et al; Michel Otto, "*Oikos*," *TDNT*, 5:119–20; Coloe, *God Dwells with Us*, 73; Keener, *John*, 2:932; McCaffrey, *House*, 30.

Gospel has already begun to transition away from a spatial temple to a relational one.[106] Further, a minor shift in terminology from chapter 2 to chapter 14 emphasizes the transition to a more relational form of dwelling. John 2:16–17 makes use of the term *oikos*, which is used exclusively of physical dwellings, whereas *oikia*, used in 14:2, bears a broader range of meaning. *Oikia* can be used for a building[107] or a *household*.[108] Accordingly, John leads his readers to understand the "Father's house" relationally rather than spatially.

More specifically, temple shifts to a single person, that is, Christ.[109] The new temple of Jesus' body becomes the place where humanity can approach God's presence, as Jesus bridges the chasm between heaven and earth.[110] In the past, the temple (and tabernacle) had been the primary means by which God fulfilled the covenant promise to dwell among his people.[111] But in Christ, sacred space was unmoored from a geographical location. As Neyrey quips, "There is no 'there' there."[112] Thus, when Jesus invites the disciples into the Father's House, he doesn't invite them to a heavenly home that they will enter upon death, but into a new relational reality through which they themselves will encounter God's presence and become mediators of it.

As chapter 14 continues, Jesus' meaning becomes increasingly clear. Starting in 14:6 Jesus shortens "the Father's house" to "the Father" as he says "I am the way and the truth and the life; no one comes to the Father except through me. If you have known me, you will also know my Father. And from now on you know him and have seen him" (14:6–7). Then, later in the chapter, Jesus says, "If anyone should love me, he will keep my word, and my Father will love him, and we will come to him and we will make our home with him" (14:23). Neyrey explains, "Once more, the key to this 'geography' is relationship: 1) a disciple *loving* Jesus and *keeping*

---

106. Coloe, "Temple Imagery," 365; Coloe, *God Dwells with Us*, 161. Other familial language in John also reinforces the relational nature of "the Father's house": "children," *teknia* (1:12; 13:33); "I will not leave you as orphans," *ouk aphēsō humas orphanous* (14:18).

107. John 2:16–17; 11:31; 12:3

108. Aalen, "'Reign' and 'House,'" 238; Coloe, *God Dwells with Us*, 161–62; Gundry, "In My Father's House," 71; Neyrey, *John*, 75.

109. Aune, *Cultic Setting*, 130; Coloe, *God Dwells with Us*, 3.

110. McCaffrey, *House*, 252.

111. Exod 25:8; 29:45; Lev 26:11–12; Ezek 37:26–28; et al.

112. Neyrey, *John*, 82.

his word, 2) the Father *loving* the disciple, and 3) the Father and Son *coming to him* and making a '*home*' with him."[113]

Although Jesus is "going" to the Father, John's Gospel has already made it clear that Jesus' dwelling in the presence of God does not preclude his presence on earth.[114] Just as Jesus mediates between heaven and earth in 1:51, Jesus will remain with his followers *and* go to his father in chapter 14. Bryan explains succinctly, "Jesus' words . . . are not so much concerned with the removal of his followers from the earth as they are about the dissolution of the divide between heaven and earth; God's earthly house is no longer separate from his heavenly house."[115] As such, Jesus can promise, "I will not leave you as orphans" (14:18).

As members of the Father's household, Christ's followers constitute a new sacred space.[116] Unbound from the institutions of the past, they are now called to meet the high holy standards of abiding in God's immediate presence. For the followers of Jesus in the Gospel of John, "every aspect of life—time, place, people—is oriented and connected to God, Jesus and the Spirit, and therefore regarded as holy."[117] As Christ's people would seek to live in the light of such an intimate relationship—in the Father's house—they would become mobile incarnations of the temple, spreading God's sacred presence throughout the earth, not seeking an escape to heaven, but a return to "the world of creation . . . as it was meant to be."[118] The means by which believers enter the presence of God and accomplish this calling is the subject of our remaining chapters.

---

113. Neyrey, *John*, 408.

114. Coloe, *God Dwells with Us*, 159; Neyrey, *John*, 407.

115. Bryan, "Eschatological Temple," 198.

116. Coloe, *Dwelling*, 1, 193; Coloe, *God Dwells with Us*, 3; Mouton, "Torah Reimag(in)ed," 94–104; Neyrey, *John*, 64.

117. Mouton, "Torah Reimag(in)ed," 96.

118. Levenson, "Temple," 297. Cf. Mouton, "Torah Reimag(in)ed," 108.

4.

Walk This Way

The Halakah *of Jesus*

MANY YEARS AGO, MY aunt had begun visiting a new church. On the Sunday in question, she decided to mow her lawn before heading to the worship service. Being a nature-loving gal, she neglected to wear shoes while mowing and enjoyed the soft, fresh-cut grass under her feet. Upon finishing the yard, she threw on a pair of shoes and headed to church. As the service commenced, she learned that this was a special Sunday—a foot washing Sunday. All the congregants would remove their shoes and wash one another's feet. So, with great mortification, my aunt proceeded to remove her shoes and reveal her green, grass-stained feet. And her foot washer got to work. The devout saint went above and beyond, not simply going through the ceremonial motions. She scrubbed and scrubbed, washing away every speck of green until my aunt's feet were clean and shiny.

I've always loved this story, not just because it makes me laugh but because I believe it reveals a truth behind the foot-washing narratives in Scripture. The faith to which Christ calls us isn't a shallow spirituality of token ritual; it is an elbow-grease kind of belief that doesn't balk in the face—or feet—of hard work and selfless service.

The Path Ahead

In this chapter we will examine the sacrificial model that Christ provides through his life, ministry, and death. Faithful service and obedience are inextricable from true belief and authentic relationship in John's Gospel.[1] Faith and works are not opposite poles, but complementary aspects of abiding in Christ. The Mosaic laws, central to the Jewish faith, are not set aside but reinterpreted in Christ. The Messiah himself would become the focal point of faith and as such, a perfect model of obeying God's law. With the words "Come, follow me," which frame John's entire Gospel (1:43; 21:19–22), Jesus sets the expectation for all who would believe *into* him.[2] Just as Christ walked in obedience to the Father, those who have true faith will follow in the footsteps of Christ.

Specifically in John 14, Jesus is about to go where he has been going throughout the whole Gospel: to the cross. In doing so, he both opens the door to God's presence and provides the perfect model of obedience. In other words, those who place faith in Christ aren't going to a heavenly dwelling, but following Jesus' model of carrying out God's mission in the world.

Such a mode of faithful obedience is defined by the Jewish concept of *halakah*. Though obscured somewhat by the transition from Hebrew to Greek terminology and again by translation into English, *halakah* describes both God's law and the manner in which one walks in obedience. In this chapter, we will first elucidate the concept itself and then examine its expression in the Gospel of John.

Supporting Concept: *Halakah*

While *halakah* might be an unfamiliar concept for Christians, it is well-known in Jewish circles. The literal sense of the verb *halak* is "walking" or "journeying," but the moral sense is well-attested and well-known. Such a multifaceted understanding is reflected in passages such as Deut 5:33, which instructs, "You shall walk (*halak*) in every way which the Lord your God commands." In other words, the way in which a person "walks" reflects his or her degree of faithfulness and obedience to the Lord.[3]

---

1. Lund, "Joys and Dangers," 283.
2. Collins, "Follow Me," 47.
3. Collins, "Follow Me," 52; Culpepper, "Creation Ethics," 84.

Because Jewish adherents desired to keep the statutes of the written torah—the laws and commandments outlined in Scripture—an additional body of teaching emerged to facilitate obedience. This supplementary material is known as the "Oral Torah." Much like Bible commentaries throughout history have equipped Christians to apply God's word in changing times and cultures, the Oral Torah was often refined and updated in order to help God's people navigate changing circumstances. However, unlike Christian Bible commentaries, the Oral Torah was regarded nearly as sacred as Scripture, as the Jewish people believed it was given to Moses along with the written Torah at Sinai. Thus, the term *halakah* came to describe the written commandments of God in addition to the oral traditions that developed around it.[4]

By extension, *halakah* can also refer to "the way" an individual lives out God's law. Davies explains, "Judaism is essentially *halakic* and not theological: it is not orthodoxy but orthopraxy that marks Judaism."[5] In other words, Judaism is defined more by obedience to the law than by belief in a set of theological propositions.

Freedom from the law is often regarded as an aspect of Christianity that is superior to Judaism. However, the emphasis upon obedience should serve as a corrective to the sentimentality, mysticism, and overspiritualizing of which the Christian faith is sometimes guilty.[6] Many Christian scholars and pastors would certainly agree that the Western church desperately needs an infusion of holy living that would set the saints apart from the culture at large.

In the earliest centuries of the Christian faith, *halakah* was a ubiquitous concept. In fact, the first converts were called people of "the Way," a definite echo of the Jewish concept.[7] Numerous OT passages equate the *ways* of God with adherence to his will, as reflected in Psalm 1:1, "Blessed is the man who does not walk (*halak*) in the counsel of the wicked, nor stand in *the way* of sinners" (emphasis mine).[8] The more specific usage

---

4. *Halakic* traditions were often attributed to particular teachers (e.g., *halakha le-Moshe mi-Sinai*), and older *halakha* were afforded more authority. Today, the term refers to any matter of Jewish law. Patte, *Early Jewish Hermeneutic*, 14–15; Telushkin, *Jewish Literacy*, 153–57.

5. Davies, "Torah and Dogma," 91.

6. Davies, "Torah and Dogma," 93.

7. Matt 22:16; Mark 12:14; Luke 20:21; John 14:4–6; Acts 18:25–26; 1 Cor 4:17; 12:31; 2 Pet 2:21.

8. Cf. Ps 118:30; Prov 21:16; Job 24:13; Isa 26:7; 35:8; etc.

as applied to Christianity is attested in Acts 9:1, in which Saul/Paul seeks permission from the high priest that "if he should find anyone belonging to the Way, both men and women, he might deliver them, being bound, to Jerusalem." Paul continues to refer to Christianity as "the Way" even after his conversion, and in Acts 24:14 asserts that adhering to the Way entails believing everything in the Law and prophets.[9]

Yet, over the centuries, focus upon theological *belief* eventually overrode the early focus on *praxis* in the Christian faith. Davies again explains, "It is well to recognize that a complete separation of Judaism as a religion of *Torah* from Christianity as a religion of *Dogma* [a set of beliefs] cannot be justified. Christianity too is a halakah."[10] Though the Christian faith should never become legalistic, the commandments of God are a primary means by which Christ followers abide in him. In other words, one's *halakah*, or way of living, reveals what one truly believes. Only through proper *halakah* can followers of Christ "worship in spirit and truth" and bring the presence of God to the world.

Halakah in the Gospel of John

The concept of *halakah* permeates the Gospel of John. Though Jesus is often at odds with "the Judeans," the Messiah never denigrates the traditions of his people. In fact, Jesus seems genuinely committed to the observance of Jewish law.[11] "Jesus' presence at the great feasts of Israel—Sabbath, Passover, Tabernacles, and Dedication—affirm that the former order has been perfected, not destroyed."[12] Along similar lines, discussions of the Jewish law form "a central pillar" of Jesus' dialogues in the Gospel, and neither Jesus nor his opponents regard the law negatively.[13] The law is not the problem, but rather the Pharisaic interpretation of it. In an overt and sustained manner, thus John portrays Christ as a newer and truer version of God's revelation to Israel and Christianity as a transformation of Judaism, not a replacement.

---

9. Cf. Acts 19:9, 23; 22:4; 24:22.

10. Davies, "Torah and Dogma," 94.

11. Though Thiessen makes this point in regard to the Synoptics, I believe the same applies to the Gospel of John. Thiessen, *Jesus and Death*, xii.

12. Moloney, *Signs and Shadows*, 152.

13. Van der Watt, "Ethics of/and the Opponents of Jesus," 189. Cf. Van der Watt, "Ethics and Ethos," 156.

While Christ doesn't call his followers to follow Jewish *halakah*, his teaching reveals a new way of walking with God that grows out of his heritage. In fact, the teachings of the Decalogue seem to undergird the ethical framework of John's entire Gospel as each of the Ten Commandments is redemptively reinterpreted in the person and work of Christ.[14] As a result, those who follow Christ are empowered to fulfill the law by walking according his perfect example.

Halakah in Context

As with the concepts of abiding and sacred space, John establishes his interpretive foundations in his prologue. Since the first words of the Gospel, "In the beginning," open the Hebrew Scriptures, it is fitting that the same words be used for this new era of history.[15] And this new beginning, as presented by John, carries not-so-subtle echoes of torah.

The wisdom sages of Israel connected creation with torah, ethics, and law.[16] Culpepper explains, "By the first century, wisdom speculation had merged with the rising importance of the Torah, so we begin to hear that the Decalogue, the revelation at Sinai, or the Torah preexisted the creation."[17] As an inherent aspect of creation, thus, torah establishes sacred times and sacred spaces, as well as the sanctity of human life. For example, the command to love one another (Lev 19:17) flows from the recognition that all humans bear the sacred image of God. In fact, the very incarnation "implies an encounter between Creation and Creator. As human beings are made in God's image (Gen 1.26–27), so in the Johannine view salvation involves centrally the human capacity to image the divine being."[18] In sum, creation establishes the foundational patterns of life desired by the Creator. Along such lines, the commands of Jesus

---

14. Further validating that the Fourth Gospel reinterprets the Decalogue in the light of Christ is the heavy use of Passover and exodus imagery throughout the Gospel, which is the setting in which the Ten Commandments are given to Israel. See Kanagaraj, "Implied Ethics," 33–60.

15. Bernard, *John*, cxlv; Brown, *John I–XII*, 23; Moloney, *Belief in the Word*, 27; Thompson, *Humanity of Jesus*, 50–51.

16. Prov 8; Job 28:15–28; Sir 24:23; Bar 4:1; LAB 32:7; Gen. Rab. 1:1, 4; b. Šabb. 88a.

17. Culpepper, "Creation Ethics," 78. Cf. Carter, "Prologue," 47; Longenecker, *Christology*, 146.

18. Lee, *Symbolic Narratives*, 23–24.

aren't simply moral guidelines, "they involved a whole way of life in loving union with him."[19] This way of life entails an increasing movement toward and return to God's original created intent.

The themes of light and darkness (1:4–9), which will reemerge later in the Fourth Gospel, reinforce the connection between creation, torah, and Christ.[20] Torah was commonly regarded as a source of light, yet John asserts that Jesus himself is the source of light.[21] Collins explains, "It is difficult to escape the conclusion that Jesus's self-designation as the light of the world points to—among other things as well—his role as a teacher, as one who conveyed divine wisdom for the benefit of the disciples. He was one who taught them how to *walk* in the light rather than in the darkness."[22]

Alternately those who do not walk in the light of God do not abide in God's Word—the *Logos*, Jesus Christ.[23] As such, John almost certainly alludes to the OT concept of "the word of the Lord," or *dabar YHWH*, which describes God's activity in his creation and among his people.[24] Richard Morgan explains, "When God spoke, he did something. So Jesus is God's final Word to man, a word not merely spoken through the lips of prophets, or written in the Torah, but a Word which became flesh and dwelt among us."[25] As the very embodiment of torah, Jesus could teach his people how to live it out in truth. Individuals or groups (i.e., "the Judeans") who scorned Jesus' interpretation of the law didn't simply reject his teaching but his "origin, identity, and authority."[26] Accordingly, the author of the Fourth Gospel teaches that walking according to the light of Christ is the proper response, nay, the only response of those who desire to abide in God the Father.

As the prologue draws to a close, John makes explicit the relationship between living Word and legal code. Though Moses gave Israel the law, the reality to which it points—the grace and truth of God—is

---

19. Brown, *John XIII–XXI*, 638. Cf. Kanagaraj, "Implied Ethics," 36; Beasley-Murray, *John*, 256.

20. Brown, *John I–XII*, 4.

21. Pss 19:8; 119:105; Bar 4:1–2; Sir 24:23; 2 Bar. 54:13–14; T. Levi 14:4.

22. Collins, "Follow Me," 54 (emphasis mine).

23. John 5:38; 8:37, 43; cf. 4:41; 5:24; 7:40; 8:31, 51–52, 55; 14:23–24.

24. Pss 33:6; 107:20; 119:105; Prov 30:5–6; Amos 1:3; Isa 55:11; Jer 23:29; Ezek 12:1; Zech 4:6.

25. Morgan, "Fulfillment," 159–60.

26. Carter, "Prologue," 48.

realized in Jesus (1:17–18).[27] Moloney clarifies, "The Prologue (1:1–18) affirms that God's former gift through the Law of Moses is perfected by the fullness of the gift of the truth in Jesus Christ (1:16–17). There is no conflict between the two gifts; one leads to the other, but the latter gift of the truth through Jesus Christ surpasses the gift of the Law through Moses. It is the fullness of God's gracious gifts."[28] Whereas Moses had only glimpsed God (Exod 33:17–23; 34:5–7), Jesus reveals the full glory of the Father, embodies his will, and restores his presence to creation. This true and enlightened manner of abiding and walking, modeled by Jesus for his followers, will continue even after Jesus departs bodily from the earth.

John hints at the new reality in 1:19 when "the Judeans" from Jerusalem send priests and Levites to question John the Baptist. Though these temple functionaries are as yet unaware, the narrative implies that their role is becoming obsolete as John the Baptist prepares "the way" for the Messiah and his kingdom (1:23).

As chapter 1 draws to a close, the theme of *walking* with Christ continues to advance as a narrative undercurrent. In 1:38–43 Jesus extends the call to follow himself, terminology echoed later in the Gospel (cf. 10:27; 12:26; 21:19–22), and terminology related to the nuance of active abiding previously discussed. Jobes asserts, "Jesus' command to 'follow me' is clearly a command to start walking. From the Old Testament we know that walking was a metaphor for living [and] for how one conducted one's life. . . . The call to follow him entails a growing awareness of the God Jesus came to reveal and a growing willingness to conform our lives to that revelation."[29]

The theme of doing the will of the Lord is maintained subtly in John 2. Mary, after inducing Jesus to aid the wineless wedding party, articulates the proper response to her son: "Do whatever he tells you."[30] The compliance of the servants then leads to a powerful miracle in which water is transformed into wine. That the water in the six jars was previously used for ritual washing is significant (2:6): "The newness of the Gospel is such that the old order of the waterpots has given place to the new wine

---

27. John 1:17 seems to exhibit Semitic parallelism, in which two or three lines of text closely relate to emphasize a point. As such, I believe that "grace and truth" (1:17b) synonymously corresponds to "the Law" (1:17a).

28. Moloney, *Signs and Shadows*, 1. Cf. Hoskins, *Jesus as the Fulfillment*, 121–23.

29. Jobes, *John*, 50.

30. Jobes, *John*, 67–68; Moloney, *Belief in the Word*, 103; Moloney, *Love in the Gospel*, 82.

of the Gospel."[31] The obedience of the servants thus leads to a powerful transformation that foreshadows even greater miracles to come.[32]

Moving on to chapter 3, we would be remiss not to mention the most prominent ethical command found in John: love. As discussed in the section "Faith, Truth, and Knowledge" in chapter 2, an internal disposition was inextricable from its external expression in the first-century Mediterranean world. Therefore, love doesn't simply describe a feeling of warm affection; it means taking action that fosters wholeness in others.[33] God himself demonstrates his love, as articulated in John 3:16, by sending his son; the Son then embodies love by laying down his life (15:13). As love is enacted between Father and Son, it is likewise extended to humanity.[34]

John explicitly links love and obedience in 3:19–21 as he contrasts those who believe God and perform good works with those who don't love God and act wickedly. Consequently, in the Gospel of John, love is implicitly and explicitly connected with believing, abiding, and walking in obedience to Jesus.[35]

Starting in John 3, a number of "unless" (*ean mē*) statements throughout the Gospel clarify that following Jesus requires belief *and* action:

- unless one is born again (3:3)
- unless one drinks Jesus' blood and eats his flesh (6:53)
- unless one is willing to surrender his or her life (12:24)
- unless one is washed by Christ (13:8)
- unless one abides in Christ (15:4)

In other words, unless one believes the truth of the incarnation and lives accordingly, one will not experience God's kingdom.[36]

Possibly the most shocking of the new mandates, especially to a Jewish audience, is the command to consume the flesh and blood of Christ. The exhortation is given in the context of the feeding of the five thousand and the Feast of Passover in John 6. Maloney explains, "The reader senses from the beginning of the narrative (vv. 5–6) that the feeding is linked to

---

31. Davies, "Torah and Dogma," 101.
32. See especially John 5:8–9; 9:6–7; 11:43–44; 20:11–18.
33. Malina and Rohrbaugh, *John*, 228.
34. Moloney, "God," 201–2.
35. Cf. John 14:15; 15:10, 12, 14, 17; Neyrey, *John*, 345.
36. Malina and Rohrbaugh, *John*, 212.

a food that only Jesus can give. But the disciples are unable to transcend the purely physical impossibility of feeding such a crowd (vv. 5, 7). Paralleling and yet surpassing the gift of the manna in the desert (see Exodus 16; Leviticus 11), Jesus feeds the multitude, and begins a feeding that endures, as the fragments are gathered into twelve baskets."[37] Even greater than the baskets of bread in John 6 or the miraculous manna, however, the "self-rising" bread of Christ yields eternal life and satisfies the needs of the entire world.[38]

Yet, God's provision in the wilderness wasn't solely associated with manna. As the law was given during Israel's wilderness wandering, manna came to represent the gift of the law.[39] Though manna and law had sustained Israel in the past, Jesus reminds the crowd that their forefathers all died (John 6:49). Even the supernatural manna wasn't preserved as it grew rancid and produced maggots (Exod 16:19–20). Yet Christ offers enduring bread from heaven such that all who rely upon him for sustenance will live forever (6:47–48). According to Moloney, "Jesus promises eternal life to those who would perfect their adherence to the Law by believing in the Son sent by the Father. . . . This 'living presence,' the visible assurance that God cares for and guides his people, is no longer found in a written law. It is to be seen and believed in the presence of the Son."[40]

The backdrop of the exodus persists in John 7 and 8 with the Feast of Booths, or *Sukkot*, which followed on the heels of Passover and commemorated God's provision for Israel in the wilderness. As noted previously, the lighting of the bonfires and candelabra during the feast reminded the Jewish people of the pillar of fire God provided in the wilderness (Exod 13:21). Such imagery is a reminder of God's presence and protection, but it also bears a moral connotation. The dualism of light and darkness, both then and now, carries well-known ethical significance. The Community Rule from Qumran provides a helpful description of those who walk in the darkness. Such people are characterized by greed, sluggishness, wickedness, falsehood, pride, haughtiness, dishonesty, cruelty, insincerity,

---

37. Moloney, *Signs and Shadows*, 38–39.

38. Neyrey, *John*, 185. Cf. Peterson, "Union with Christ," 10; Koester, "Hearing, Seeing, and Believing," 339; Hoskins, "Deliverance from Death," 296.

39. Jobes, *John*, 129–31; Köstenberger, *Encountering John*, 210; Thompson, *Humanity of Jesus*, 151; Harstine, *Moses as a Character*, 61.

40. Moloney, *Signs and Shadows*, 50. Cf. Jobes, *John*, 129; Keener, *John*, 1:677; Van der Watt, "Ethics and Ethos," 158.

impatience, foolishness, lust, blasphemy, and the list goes on.[41] In short, "to walk the paths of darkness is to live a vile life of sin, and it will not go unpunished."[42] By contrast, Jesus is the light of the world (1:4–9), and those who follow him will not *walk* in darkness (8:12); indeed, they will not stumble because they *walk* in the light (11:9).[43] In short, the metaphor of light and dark for good and evil is directly tied to walking according to the way of Christ—the new *halakah*.[44]

To conclude the *halakic* implications of John 7–8, John presents Jesus as a teacher who is greater than those who promulgate the Mosaic law. In 7:14, Jesus goes to the temple and begins to teach. The Jewish crowd is amazed at his knowledge of Scripture, but Jesus asserts that he simply speaks the truth of God, which *should* align with the law around which they base their identity. In 7:19, Jesus asks, "Has not Moses given the law to you? Yet not one of you keeps the law. Why do you seek to kill me?" The Jewish leaders, priests, and Pharisees of Jerusalem fail to recognize the true form of the living torah and walk accordingly. Even worse, they seek to destroy Christ, who is a threat to their entrenched traditions and power structures. Yet, Jesus is not simply a rival prophet or rabbi, he is the embodiment of God's word and a truer version of the torah, an incarnate truth that catalyzes both internal and external transformation.[45]

The next topic in our *halakic* investigation of John's Gospel is the practice of foot washing. In the ancient Mediterranean culture, even more so than now, feet were associated with purposeful action. Neyrey notes that, "As part of their cultic behavior, priests wash before offering sacrifice (Exod 30:17–21; 40:30–32); likewise warriors in a Holy War washed their feet to symbolize that they were assuming duties requiring ritual purity."[46] The anointing of Jesus' feet, thus, indicates that Jesus is about to undertake "something of singular significance."[47]

As Mary washes Jesus' feet with costly oil, her actions subtly contrast with the behavior and motives of Jesus' opponents (12:3–8). Though Judas

41. 1QS IV, 9–11; cf. LAB 11:1.

42. Collins, "Follow Me," 51–52.

43. Cf. John 12:35–36.

44. In contrast, Bultmann divorces the Fourth Gospel from its Jewish context and argues that metaphors such as "walking in the light" and "eating the bread of life" refer "only to faith." Bultmann, *John*, 344. See Culpepper, "Creation Ethics," 84.

45. Jobes, *John*, 92, 140–41.

46. Neyrey, *John*, 365.

47. See John 12:3; Malina and Rohrbaugh, *John*, 205; cf. 223.

was actually greedy for the wealth that the oil represented, he criticized Mary for wasting it rather than donating to the poor. Despite the criticism she receives, Mary makes a personal sacrifice on behalf of her Lord. Sherri Brown notes, "Believing in the word of Jesus means taking action, even in small ways that counter the status quo . . . sometimes in the face of skepticism from one's allies."[48] Whereas Mary loved Jesus and honored him with her actions, Judas loved money and betrayed the Savior.

In the following narrative, yet again, the duplicitous actions of Judas contrast with those of the true disciples of Christ. In 13:1–16, Judas leaves the final meal with his fellow disciples to betray Jesus to the authorities. Conversely, through being washed by Christ, the disciples are prepared to take action, or walk, in Jesus' footsteps.

In washing the feet of his disciples, Jesus provides an example of sacrificial love that he calls his followers to imitate.[49] When Peter objects in 13:8, Jesus says, "Unless I wash you, you have no part in me." Thus, as Jesus prepares his followers for action, he reminds them that co-abiding is an essential element of following. But more than simply fellowship, Jesus indicates that Peter must be washed by Christ to obtain his *meros*. *Meros* was a term used to describe the portion of the promised land that each tribe of Israel would receive. In other words, the term "describes the God-given heritage of Israel."[50] In the context of the Fourth Gospel, however, John redefines the term not as an inheritance of land, or even heaven, but as a place in the household of God.

Although the act of foot washing was an act of humility on Jesus' behalf, it signified much more. By mentioning Jesus' pending death in 13:1–2, John connects the sacrificial death of Jesus with the symbolic act of foot washing. In vv. 3–4 John makes the connection even more explicit as he informs readers that Jesus girded himself for the foot washing *because* he knew that he was about to return to the Father. Brown clarifies, "The simplest explanation of the foot washing, then, remains that Jesus performed this servile task to prophecy symbolically that he was about to be humiliated in death."[51]

---

48. Brown, "Believing," 20.

49. Brown, *John XIII–XXI*, 569; Gibbs, "Already Dwelling," 20; Moloney, *Glory Not Dishonor*, 12–16; Skinner, "Love One Another," 29; Van der Watt, "Ethics and Ethos," 173.

50. Brown, *John XIII–XXI*, 565.

51. Brown, *John XIII–XXI*, 568; cf. 563–65.

The following chapters speak more directly about following the commands of Jesus than any others in the book. Of thirteen uses of the term "command" (*entolē*) in John, eight are found in chapters 14–15 alone. In 14:15, 21; 15:10, 12, 14, and 17, Jesus explicitly equates keeping his commandments with mutual indwelling and love: "If you keep my commands, you will abide in my love; just as I have kept my Father's commandments and abide in his love" (15:10).[52] Yet these commands aren't simply moral guidelines, as evidenced by the stark absence of explicit moral instruction in the Fourth Gospel. The commands of God in Christ involve a whole new way of walking in truth and sacrificial love made possible through union with God.[53] Further, "the basis of this love is not emotion but relationships that are expressed in actions. Love exists in activity. When God loves, he *gives* his Son. . . . When Jesus loves intensely he *washes* feet and *gives* his life for his friends (13,1ff.; 15,9ff.), when believers love they follow the example of Jesus of serving and caring, even if it means shifting their own interests aside in order to serve God and one another (13,12–20; 12,24–26)."[54]

Although love is defined by the value system of torah, it is birthed anew in Christ. The command to love one another hearkens back to Lev 19:18, but Jesus alters the original language from "love your neighbor as yourself" to "love as I have loved you" (15:12).[55] In doing so, Jesus calls his disciples to love others with the type of self-sacrificing service that he demonstrates on the cross.[56]

Such depth of love flows from a relationship of mutual indwelling with God in Christ, which makes sacrificial obedience possible. DeSilva writes, "For almost every facet of the Christian walk that John holds up for us, Jesus is presented as our example, particularly with regard to the values of servanthood, Christian love and Christian unity, but also notably in the encouragement of ongoing witness and obedience in the face of the world's hostility and rejection."[57] While modern readers of John readily reach such conclusions when studying John 15, somehow, a totally different, often otherworldly, interpretation is attached to John

52. John 10:18; 11:57; 12:49, 50; 13:34; 14:15, 21, 31; 15:10 (2x), 12, 14, 17.

53. Brown, *John XIII–XXI*, 638; Kanagaraj, "Implied Ethics," 36; Beasley-Murray, *John*, 256.

54. Van der Watt, "Ethics and Ethos," 161 (emphasis original).

55. Van der Watt, "Ethics and Ethos," 166; Jobes, *John*, 239.

56. Skinner, "Love One Another," 35.

57. DeSilva, *New Testament*, 433.

14:1–3. Yet, perhaps if we view Jesus' words in the light of that which comes before and after, we might arrive at a more cohesive interpretation of John 14.

To summarize our conclusions thus far, in John 1 and 6, Jesus is portrayed as the very embodiment of torah. Christ is the living incarnation of God's will who walks in perfect obedience. In doing so, he shines God's light and shows humanity how to live according to God's perfect plan (1:4–9; 8:12; 11:9). Through his incarnation, Christ both models obedience and, with the words "follow me," invites true believers to emulate his example (1:43; cf. 21:19–22). This theme is borne out throughout the Gospel as genuine relationship with God is closely connected to obedience. Conversely, the behavior of those who walk wickedly—in darkness—reveals that they do not know God (3:16–21; 8:12; 15:10–17).

The anointing and foot washing scenes (John 12–13) narratively establish that just as Jesus walks in sacrificial obedience—all the way to the cross—he expects his followers to walk likewise, even after he departs bodily. This mode of sacrificial living is the basis of the intimate love between the Father, the Son, and those who would follow Christ. Such a relationship doesn't take the form of an insubstantial *belief*, but a whole new way of walking in sacrificial service, a death to self that brings new life. Conversely, those who don't know God, exemplified by Judas, live for self, perform evil deeds, and breed eternal death.

Thus, when Christ *goes* in John 14, nothing in the immediate or larger context implies that he is going to heaven. Rather, Christ walks in perfect obedience as he willingly submits to his horrible death on the cross. And instead of transporting his disciples to heaven, he is preparing them to walk in his footsteps.

Halakah in John 14

The references to departure and return in 14:2–3 underlie the entire Farewell Discourse (John 14–17) as fundamental themes. The "going" and "coming" of Jesus is developed especially within the center section (ch. 14) in order to emphasize the importance of the Messiah's actions.[58] Almost certainly, Jesus sought to comfort his disciples, as "knowing that he

---

58. Segovia, "Structure," 477; Dodd, *Interpretation*, 403; Becker, "Die Abschiedsreden Jesu."

knew he would depart, and that it was not an unplanned disaster, should reassure them."[59]

The term used to describe Jesus' "going" is the Greek verb *poreuomai*, which is frequently used to translate the Hebrew *halak*. Both the Greek and Hebrew verbs can indicate spatial movement from one place to another, as in "walking," "journeying," or "going."[60] Yet, the moral connotation is also reflected in NT verses such as Luke 1:6: "And they [Zacharias and Elizabeth] were both righteous in the presence of God, walking blamelessly in all the commands and requirements of the Lord."[61]

Specifically in regard to John 14, Jesus does make a spatial movement, but the Fourth Gospel emphasizes Jesus is going to the cross, not heaven. In chapter 13, Judas departs from Jesus and the disciples in order to betray the Messiah, an action that leads directly to arrest and crucifixion (13:21–30). In response, Peter affirms his commitment to follow Christ, but the Messiah asks "Will you lay down your life for me?" (13:36–38). Then, in 15:13, Jesus says, "Greater love no one has than this, that one should lay down his life on behalf of his friends." In short, Jesus' death, anticipated throughout the gospel and now close at hand, dominates the narrative, especially the Farewell Discourse. According to Gibbs, "Jesus is going where only he can go—to his glory on the cross."[62] Therefore, in the light of the ethical overtones inherent in the idea of *halakah/poreuomai*, as well as the pending threat of crucifixion, Jesus' words in 14:2b might better be interpreted as, "For I walk [to the cross in obedience to the Father] in order to prepare a place for you." Along such lines Jesus' "going" not only reconciles believers with the Father but provides the perfect model of obedience.

The ethical interpretation of *poreuomai* accords well with McCaffrey's classification of the usage in 14:2 as a "futuristic present," which describes a journey in progress, yet still in the future. Through dying on the cross and rising to new life in the present, Jesus opens the way into the Father's house and teaches believers how to continue following him in the future.[63] The unique aspect of Jesus' departure is that in the OT

---

59. Malina and Rohrbaugh, *John*, 232.
60. "*Poreuomai*," *L&N* 15:10.
61. Cf. Acts 9:31; 1 Pet 4:3; 2 Pet 2:10; 3:3; Jude 11:16, 18.
62. Gibbs, "Already Dwelling," 21.
63. Jobes, *John*, 224–25; McCaffrey, *House*, 86–88.

death is synonymous with separation from God, but in John 14 Jesus' death provides ongoing access to God.

The use of *poreuomai* may also evoke the context of the exodus, especially considering the recurring references to Moses and the Passover in John. Whereas the unbelief of the Israelites prevented them from entering the promised land, the faith of Jesus' followers will usher them into a "prepared place." The potential for danger in Jesus' role also accords well with Israel's journey to the promised land. Deut 1:30 reads, "The Lord your God who goes (*halak/poreuomai*) before you, he himself will fight for you, just as he did for you in Egypt before your eyes." Along such lines, the author of the Fourth Gospel likely is presenting Jesus as a new leader who goes before his people for the purpose of liberation.

In his "going away" Jesus provides the perfect model of obedience, fulfills the law, and cleanses believers through his sacrifice. McCaffrey suggests that, in line with temple imagery, Jesus' movement might be interpreted in the light of the Day of Atonement. As the high priest, Jesus enters into the holy of holies, i.e., the presence of God, upon death. His return could then be interpreted in line with the priest's reemergence after making atonement for the nation. Not surprisingly, Lev 16, the principal Yom Kipper passage, utilizes same terms as John 14 (*erchomai* and *poreuomai*; 16:17–18) to describe the going and coming of the high priest.

Yet, as noted, the "going" of Christ does not imply that his work will cease. Indeed, his disciples will carry on his mission, as the continuing context of John 14 makes clear. In 14:12, Jesus affirms that his disciples will do even greater works than himself. Though a seemingly impossible goal, the works of those who follow Christ will be greater because they are accomplished according to the new paradigm of Spirit-led grace brought about by the life, death, and resurrection of Christ.[64] As John has already made clear, the commandments of Christ bring about the truth to which the Mosaic law pointed—a loving relationship with God that leads to his will being done upon the earth.[65] "Just as the Ten Commandments of the Old Testament defined the moral quality of ancient Israel's relationship with God, Jesus' commands transpose them into a higher key that involves inner spiritual transformation. Love for Jesus will result

---

64. Jobes, *John*, 228.
65. John 14:14–15; cf. 1:16–18; 6:4–14, 26–58; 7:14–19.

in, both by one's will and by the promise of one's spiritual transformation, obedience to the whole truth that Jesus reveals."[66]

Another echo of *halakah* can be identified in the dialogue between Jesus and Thomas in 14:4–6. Jesus declares that the disciples know the *way* where he is going, but Thomas misunderstands: "Thomas said to him, 'Lord, we do not know where you go. How can we know the *way*?' Jesus said to him, '*I am the way* and the truth and the life; no one comes to the Father except through me'" (John 14:5–6, emphasis mine). As noted earlier in the chapter, the way (*hodos*) is closely connected to *halakah*. The appearance of *hodos* here supports our assertion that Jesus is exhorting his disciples to follow in his footsteps by walking in obedience and abiding in the presence (and household) of the Father.

As such, Jesus never promises to take his followers out of the world. The only movement the disciples make is toward, or into, Christ.[67] As such, Jesus' teaching does not entail an escape from the world, but greater engagement within it. Jesus demonstrates what he expects of his followers by going to the cross, and thus, walking according to the way, or *halakah*, of Christ should consist of obedience to the Father that results in sacrificial love.[68] But before Christ-followers can transform the world, they must *be* transformed by abiding in God's loving presence. Rensberger incisively explains that we must first save "the world as it has been structured by human will and rationality, but also and especially by human self-absorption and selfishness in opposition to God and to the good of other people."[69]

The laws of the OT, which would have created an ideal society, were impossible to fulfill because access to the transformative presence of God was limited. But in Christ, the sacred space of God has moved into the hearts of his people, sanctifying them from the inside out.[70] As God's presence transforms the inner reality of his people, they, in turn, bear his presence to the world and create outward transformation. In doing so, God's salvific work through Christ should recall the world "from its self-absorption to its stance as creature before its Creator, yielding an obedience to God that could undo the structures that maintained it apart

---

66. Jobes, *John*, 229. Cf. Moloney, "God," 214.
67. Gibbs, "Already Dwelling."
68. Brown, "Believing," 22; Malina and Rohrbaugh, *John*, 232.
69. Rensberger, *Johannine Faith*, 146.
70. Olson, "Sacred Time," 150.

from God in the darkness of its hatred."[71] In fact, the entire ministry of Jesus was oriented toward healing God's broken people and corrupted world. From healing the sick to dying on a cross and rising again, Jesus demonstrated the radically transformative power of God's love.

Matthew 28:19–20, often called the Great Commission, reflects God's intent to restore his creation through his people. Yet, the passage is actually a "renewal of the first commission to humanity in Gen 1:26–28."[72] In like manner, the entirety of John 14, including vv. 1–3, serves as a call to those who would follow Jesus. Will God's people walk in the way, the truth, and the life so that others can experience his love (14:6)—or, like Israel at the entrance to the promised land, balk in fear? Will disciples of Christ die to self so others may live—or like the opponents of Jesus, live for self and perpetuate the corrupt structures of a diseased and distressed world?

---

71. Rensberger, *Johannine Faith*, 142.
72. Beale, *Union*, 116.

5.

Paradise Lost and Found

Prepared Place and Promised Land

MY POPS WAS OF the "greatest generation." In addition to facing the death of his father at a young age and helping his family survive the Great Depression, he fought in World War II. More specifically, Pops fought in the Ardennes Offensive, otherwise known as the Battle of the Bulge—one of the most significant conflicts of the entire war. Also one of the bloodiest, the battle incurred nearly ninety thousand casualties.

Ardennes was the last major offensive of the Axis powers. The surprise attack by Germany and her allies devastated the largely American forces holding the Belgian front, where Pops was stationed. Yet, the valiant Allied soldiers held the line in sub-freezing temperatures and heavy snowstorms. Their crucial victory marked the beginning of the German retreat and, ultimately, the end of the war.

My Pops was among the ninety thousand casualties, but thankfully not among the deaths. He was shot twice, once in the chest, a scant inch from his heart, and once in the hip, an injury from which he never fully recovered. He lay on the battlefield, among the other injured and dead, for an entire day before being rescued. Although he was awarded two Purple Hearts for his bravery, the experience caused such severe emotional (and physical) scarring that he would never talk about his days in the war. He simply had no desire to revisit the horrors he'd experienced.

The portrait of a man who survived unimaginable trauma during the first twenty years of his life seems inconsistent with the Pops I knew and loved—the compassionate grandfather who took me fishing, the gentle gardener who grew roses, the wise mentor who taught me the value of hard work. Yet, I think such a combination of suffering and love reflects the heart of Christ. Although Pops wasn't especially "religious," I'm confident he knew and loved the Lord. In fact, he explicitly told me so. But more than that, his life proved it. His sacrificial service goes beyond that which most humans, at least most contemporary Westerners, will ever be called to give. He literally laid down his life so that others could have freedom.

The Path Ahead

In this chapter, we will examine the sacrificial death of Christ. John doesn't simply describe Jesus as a new law, or *halakah*, for his disciples to follow; he portrays Jesus as the atoning sacrifice that provides deliverance from death and entry into the Father's household.

The structure of our analysis will depart somewhat from the previous chapters due to the number of themes that converge around Christ's cruciform work. First, though we've touched on John's use of Passover imagery, we have yet to give the theme the attention it deserves. As most readers are already familiar with the exodus and Passover narratives, we will forgo a "supporting concept" section and proceed directly into our examination of the Passover theme in the Fourth Gospel. Throughout the analysis, we will discuss the atoning work of Christ, which is closely related to the function of the Passover lamb. By dying as the perfect Passover sacrifice, Jesus leads his people out of slavery to sin and into the household of God. In doing so, he defeats death and cleanses people of the sin that causes it.

Second, we will revisit the concept of sacred space. In particular, we will focus on the gradations of holiness around the sacred spaces of Israel. Prior to Jesus, access to God was highly regulated. The atoning work of Christ, however, renders the presence of God available to everyone everywhere. Indeed, there are "many rooms" in the Father's house—plenty of space for whosoever would believe, whether Jew or gentile, male or female.

Third, we will examine the place prepared by Jesus, a concept closely associated with the promised land and the Jerusalem temple. As Jesus leads his people out of slavery, he simultaneously leads them into the place he prepares, a new promised land in the presence of the Father.

Passover and Atonement in the Gospel of John

Symbolism of the exodus and Passover narratives permeates John.[1] In fact, "most of the dramatic imagery of the first Exodus is found in this Gospel."[2] John either explicitly or implicitly refers to the themes of redemption from slavery (8:33–34; 15:15, 20), light in the wilderness (8:12), God's provision of water and manna (6:31–59; 7:37–39), the brazen serpent (3:14–15), the tabernacling presence of God (1:14), and Moses himself.[3] Even the death of Christ takes place in the context of the Passover Feast, which is mentioned more in John than in any other NT book.[4]

The celebration of Passover was of great memorial value, bringing to mind God's deliverance from slavery and commemorating the start of a journey toward the promised land. Along such lines, Jesus asserts that "salvation is from the Judeans" (4:22). And salvation in the Fourth Gospel takes the form of a new exodus—the deliverance of God's people by means of Christ, the true paschal lamb.[5]

More than simply a Passover lamb, however, Jesus is portrayed as the *perfect* Passover sacrifice. Through the sacrificial lamb, the concept of vicarious sacrifice had already been established in Israel. Just as the Jewish people sprinkled the blood of the paschal lamb on their doorposts to avert the Lord's judgment and redeem their own sons, the blood of the Lamb of God, Jesus Christ, was spilled.[6] The redemption that had previously been accomplished through sacrificial animals would now be accomplished by the death of Jesus. But the blood of Christ achieved a far greater good than the redemption of one nation. Jesus "achieved the opening of eternal life after death for the entire human race."[7]

Christ is first introduced as the Lamb of God in 1:29–36, wherein John describes Christ as the *amnos* who takes away the sin of the world.

---

1. Hoskins, "Deliverance from Death," 285–99; Howard, "Passover and Eucharist," 329–37; Lee, "Paschal Imagery," 13–28; Morgan, "Fulfillment," 155–65; Porter, "Traditional Exegesis," 396–428; Porter, *John*, 206.

2. Morgan, "Fulfillment," 158.

3. Moses is referenced thirteen times in John: 1:17, 45; 3:14; 5:45–46; 6:32; 7:19, 22–23; 8:5; 9:28–29.

4. The term "Passover" (*pascha*) is used ten times in John: 2:13, 23; 6:4; 11:55; 12:1; 13:1; 18:28, 39; 19:14; and referenced with the term "feast" (*heortē*) nine times: 2:23; 4:45; 5:1; 6:4; 11:56; 12:12, 20; 13:1, 29.

5. Morgan, "Fulfillment," 158–61.

6. Jobes, *John*, 222; Morgan, "Fulfillment," 158.

7. Jobes, *John*, 293.

The Greek term *amnos* is found only four times in the NT, twice of which are found in this passage.[8] Although *amnos* is not used of the lamb in the plague of the firstborn (Exod 12), other passages in the Greek OT do use the term in a Passover context.[9] In addition to being used of the Passover lamb and other sacrificial lambs, *amnos* is the term used in Isa 53:7 to describe the afflicted servant of the Lord who pours himself out for many and bears the iniquity of all.[10] Thus, John appears to combine the concept of the Passover sacrifice with the figure of the suffering servant, who functions as a guilt and/or sin offering.

Though the work of the suffering servant is expiatory, whether the original Passover sacrifice had any atoning value is debated.[11] On the surface, the blood of lamb only protected God's people from the plague of the firstborn; it did not cover over or bear away *sin*.[12] Nonetheless, the sacrifice seems to have become associated with atonement at some point in the history of Israel.[13] Josephus, whose writings are roughly contemporaneous with the Gospel of John, indicates that the Passover sacrifice had expiatory value even during the original plague (Exod 12), as the blood of the lamb purified the homes of the Hebrews when applied.[14] Some scholars, likewise, argue that the Passover sacrifice always bore atoning value. Carey explains that "a vicarious, expiatory explanation is clearly at the heart of the Exodus."[15]

Either way, John surely intends to link the Passover lamb with the work of Christ. The blood of the original Passover sacrifice saves God's people from a plague that would have resulted in death. Similarly, "as the fulfillment of the Passover lamb, Jesus delivers believers from death due to God's wrath and judgment by removing their sin and guilt."[16] In addition, John merges the function of the Passover sacrifice with the sin

---

8. John 1:29, 36; Acts 8:32; 1 Pet 1:19.

9. See especially Num 28:19.

10. Carey, "Lamb of God," 111; Longenecker, *Christology*, 50.

11. Though expiation and atonement are roughly equivalent, expiation refers more to taking away sins, while atonement bears the nuance of covering over them.

12. Carey, "Lamb of God," 101–2; Hoskins, "Deliverance from Death," 285.

13. See Num 28:22; Ezek 45:21–25; Porter, "Traditional Exegesis," 411; Porter, *Sacred Tradition*, 136; Hoskins, "Deliverance from Death," 386–87. For more on the possible sources of John 1:29, see Christopher W. Skinner, "Another Look," 89–104.

14. Josephus, *Ant.* 2.14.6.

15. Carey, "Lamb of God," 118–19. Cf. Hoskins, "Deliverance from Death," 287.

16. Hoskins, "Deliverance from Death," 293.

offering because the atoning work of Christ not only saves people from death but restores them to fellowship with God.[17]

Yet, the Lamb of God in John 1:29 represents not only a fusion of OT concepts but an escalation. Whereas the threat of death in Exod 12 applies only to the firstborn sons of Israel, all humanity is now faced with death—and not just mortal death but eternal death. In response, Jesus both saves people from death and eliminates the disease that causes it—sin.[18] As such, Christ is a more perfect sacrifice who brings a greater degree of deliverance, restoration, and purification.[19] The sacrificial lamb of John 1:29 not only bears the sin of Israel, but has the capacity to cleanse the whole world.[20] Further, in addition to salvation from death, "the Johannine model of salvation is, in the light of the Exodus, an act of liberation from the dominion of slavery to the freedom of children within the household/Temple of God."[21]

The next clear Passover scene takes place in 2:13–25, the temple cleansing. The narrative is framed by references to the Passover in both 2:13 and 2:25. That John has already introduced Jesus as the Lamb of God in chapter 1 implies that he intends to carry the imagery forward into the Gospel's first Passover.[22] During this visit, Jesus drives the merchants from the temple, signifying that animals will no longer be needed for sacrifice. In doing so, he reveals that the temple and its institutions have become obsolete because the true lamb has arrived. Just as Jesus bodily replaces Bethel, the house of God (1:51), and the temple itself (2:19–21), he likewise replaces the sacrifices that took place at such holy sites.[23]

As we've already discussed, the placement of the temple cleansing early in John's narrative, as opposed to the Synoptics' placement near the end of Jesus' ministry, almost certainly has a narrative and theological purpose. Porter explains that the "equation of Jesus with the Passover lamb is not simply a plot marker but potentially a major motivating factor for Jesus's actions throughout the entire Gospel, including his actions

---

17. DeSilva, *New Testament*, 430.

18. Jobes, *John*, 45.

19. Hoskins, "Deliverance from Death," 291; Tenney, "Old Testament," 305.

20. Porter, "Traditional Exegesis," 411; Porter, *Sacred Tradition*, 135; Westcott, *John*, 20.

21. Coloe, *God Dwells with Us*, 194.

22. Jobes, *John*, 68; Moloney, *Belief in the Word*, 95.

23. Gibbs, "Already Dwelling," 17; Jobes, *John*, 283; Porter, "Traditional Exegesis," 413; Porter, *Sacred Tradition*, 138.

in the temple."²⁴ As Jesus ejects the money changers and turns over tables, he doesn't simply replace the institution of the temple and the lamb of the Passover; the Messiah inaugurates a new way of living, one that is borne out over the course of the Gospel and which culminates in a prepared place even better than the promised land toward which Israel trekked after the exodus.²⁵

The original journey toward the promised land was fraught with difficulty because Israel repeatedly sinned against the Lord. In 3:14–15, John refers to a specific incident during which the people complain against God and curse the food he has provided. As a result, God sends venomous snakes, which infect and kill many within the camp. As Moses prays for his ungrateful compatriots, God instructs him to mount a serpent upon a pole. Those who have been bitten are then able to gaze upon the uplifted snake and recover (Num 21:4–9).

In 3:14–15, John draws an analogy between the crucifixion of Jesus and the lifted serpent. Tenney explains, "Just as looking upon the serpent in response to the divine command brought healing, so trust in the uplifted Christ will result in eternal life. . . . The bronze serpent was an antidote to the poisonous death that rebellion had caused; Jesus became the antidote to the sin of a world."²⁶ Once again, John portrays Jesus as the truth behind events of the OT, especially those of the exodus narrative. The Israelites were saved from death in the wilderness not because of a serpent on a stick, but because they trusted in the God who would take away their sin and disease.

The next prominent concentration of Passover imagery can be found in John 6, specifically vv. 1–14 and 26–58. We've already discussed the feeding of the five thousand, which is set during the Feast of Passover and saturated with exodus imagery. Although God's provision of water and manna sustain the children of Israel in the wilderness, the physical sustenance is a gift that offers only temporary relief.

In 6:51, Jesus' conversation with the crowd takes an offensive turn as Jesus begins to speak of consuming his flesh and blood.²⁷ While such language would have been shocking to both a Jewish and Hellenistic

---

24. Porter, *Sacred Tradition*, 137.

25. Davies, *Gospel and the Land*, 289–90; Jobes, *John*, 70; Porter, *Sacred Tradition*, 138; Porter, "Traditional Exegesis," 411.

26. Tenney, "Old Testament," 306.

27. Although the passage may also reflect eucharistic themes, the Passover motif dominates. See Peterson, "Union with Christ," 13; Keener, *John*, 1:687–91.

audience, just as it is today, precedent exists for metaphorical usage. Seneca relates eating and drinking to violence in battle, 1 Enoch equates the suffering of Israel to being consumed by wild animals, and even Paul portrays interpersonal conflict as "biting and devouring."[28] In addition, the clear Passover context implies that Jesus alludes to the Passover meal. According to Hoskins, "Giving his flesh sounds like he is talking about his death in sacrificial terms, especially in combination with the mention of blood in 6:53. Flesh/meat and blood are the two main components of a sacrifice (Exod 12:7–8). In 6:51–56, one can readily see a possible relationship between eating the flesh of Jesus and the Passover, since the Passover Lamb was eaten (Exod 12:8)."[29]

The imagery of drinking Jesus' blood is more complex and difficult to parse. Celebrants drank the blood of grapes, i.e., wine, during the Passover Feast, but the blood of the Passover lamb was not to be ingested.[30] Hoskins suggests that the key to interpreting the imagery can be identified in John 6:63, as Jesus teaches "the spirit is the one who gives life; the flesh accomplishes nothing. The words I have spoken to you are spirit and life." In John, spirit, water, and blood are closely associated such that the Spirit gives life *by means of* Jesus' sacrificial blood.[31] Thus, "drinking" Jesus' blood is closely associated with partaking of the life-giving Spirit of God. Further support for the association can be found in John 19:30–34, as both blood and water gush from the side of Christ after he releases the Spirit.

The subsequent context of John 8, especially vv. 21–51, reinforces the concept that the sacrificial death of Christ brings life. True disciples, those who abide in Christ and keep the commands of God, will never see death (8:51). Conversely, those who reject Christ align themselves with the devil, are enslaved in his kingdom (8:32–34, 44), and will die in sin (8:21–24). Accordingly, "the transfer from the kingdom of the world/devil to the kingdom of God requires redemption from that kingdom. The Passover lamb is the preeminent sacrifice associated with the redemption of the people of God in the OT."[32] In the Fourth Gospel, the Lamb of God is the sacrifice that redeems people from sin so that they

28. Seneca, *Controversiae* 1.8.16; 1 En. 90:2–4; Gal 5:15; Keener, *John*, 1:688.

29. Hoskins, "Deliverance from Death," 297.

30. Exod 12:7; Lev 17:10–14.

31. Hoskins, "Deliverance from Death," 297. Cf. John 7:37–39.

32. Hoskins, "Deliverance from Death," 293. Cf. Hoskins, "Freedom from Slavery," 47–63; John 3:36; 12:47–50.

will not die in sin. At the same time, the individual is granted freedom, being transferred from the realm of slavery to the devil to the household of God.

Though Christ offers deliverance—as the Passover lamb delivered the Israelites from slavery and death in Egypt—Jesus' opponents refuse to accept his sacrifice. Just as many within the camp of Israel begged to return to Egypt, "the Judeans" of the Fourth Gospel refuse to understand and appropriate the freedom Christ offers.[33]

Though only tangentially related to Passover, the language of consecration in 10:36 and 17:19 is closely associated with atonement. In 10:36, Jesus describes himself as "one who the Father *consecrated* (*hagiazō*) and sent into the world." While the imagery of Christ as a new temple is prominent in John's Gospel, considering that the term *hagiazō* was often used of sacrificial animals, Jesus' function as sacrificial lamb is also implicit.[34]

Comparing 10:36 with 17:17–19 yields additional insight. Speaking of his disciples, Jesus prays, "Sanctify them in the truth. . . . On their behalf I sanctify myself, so that they themselves also might be sanctified in truth" (17:17a, 19). Through his sacrificial death as Passover lamb, Jesus sanctifies his followers; just as the Passover lamb redeems the firstborn sons of Israel, Jesus' death atones for and redeems each son and daughter of true Israel, enabling them to receive a place in the household of God.[35] Further, true believers who are sanctified by Christ are called, in turn, to sacrifice their own lives on behalf of others (15:13).

The next section with prevalent exodus imagery is comprised by 11:47—12:8, which takes place in the context of the third Passover mentioned in John. In these chapters, the raising of Lazarus has just precipitated the final plot to kill Jesus. As chapter 11 ends, the council of the chief priests, led by the high priest Caiaphas, is planning to take action against Christ (11:47–57), a scene which leads into chapter 12 with the anointing of Jesus for his burial (12:1–8). With the two explicit references to the Passover in 11:55 and 12:1, John is careful to ensure his readers understand Jesus' anointing in the light of Caiaphas's words, and that both scenes anticipate the events which will soon take place in Jerusalem.[36]

---

33. Exod 14:11–12; 15:24; 16:2–8; Moloney, *Signs and Shadows*, 51.
34. Moloney, *Signs and Shadows*, 147–50; Coloe, *God Dwells with Us*, 145.
35. Hoskins, "Deliverance from Death," 294.
36. Porter, "Traditional Exegesis," 416; Porter, *Sacred Tradition*, 142.

The dialogue concerning the death of Christ between Caiaphas and his fellow priests is loaded with irony (11:47–53). When Caiaphas contends that it is better for one man to die so that the people not perish, he refers to saving the Jewish people from the wrath of Rome (11:50).[37] Yet, he has unknowingly made a statement about the substitutionary efficacy of the Passover lamb, who prevents the destruction not just of the Jewish people but of all people.[38] Brown insightfully articulates, "[Caiaphas] was anxious to get rid of Jesus lest, as one more in a series of revolutionaries, this troublemaker provoke the Romans to action against the [Judeans]. . . . [And] Caiaphas was right; the death of Jesus would save the nation from destruction. Yet Caiaphas could not suspect that Jesus would die not in place of Israel but on behalf of the true Israel."[39]

The chapter that follows, John 12, serves as a transition into the Farewell Discourse and passion narrative. After the Jewish leaders plot to take Jesus' life, Mary anoints the feet of Christ. As is often noted, the volume and quality of Mary's oil represented a lavish sacrifice, one befitting a king. Though the scene evokes undercurrents of Jesus' kingship and priesthood, the Passover setting remains primary.[40] Keener points out that Jesus' enthronement takes place upon a cross, and "so a royal anointing is inseparable from an anointing for burial."[41] Further, Jesus' sacrificial role is intimated by the site of the anointing—the feet. Kings and honored guests were typically anointed on the head, while anointing the feet bears more similarity to the ministrations performed upon a corpse.[42]

Mary's anointing of Christ anticipates the foot washing and final meal between Jesus and his disciples in John 13. In 13:1, John reveals that the intimate gathering took place just prior to the Passover festival. Thus, though John does not explicitly say so, the meal is portrayed as a Passover-like meal.[43]

---

37. The fear that Rome would take away the place and nation of the Jewish people (11:48) was valid. Most likely, Rome had already razed Jerusalem and her temple by the time John's Gospel was written.

38. Bauckham, *Gospel of Glory*, 31; Keener, *John*, 2:855–56; Porter, *Sacred Tradition*, 142; Porter, "Traditional Exegesis," 415.

39. Brown, *John I–XII*, 442.

40. Jobes, *John*, 198.

41. Keener, *John*, 2:865.

42. Brown, *John I–XII*, 454; Keener, *John*, 2:863.

43. Culpepper, "Johannine *Hypodeigma*," 135; Porter, *Sacred Tradition*, 143.

In addition to the themes of preparation, fellowship, and faithful obedience discussed in our previous chapter on *halakah*, the foot washing of John 13 is an act of cleansing in which the physical points toward the inner work of Christ.[44] In 13:10, Jesus seems to indicate that the disciples have already been washed, likely a reference to the ritual cleansing required before the Passover meal. Although hand washing was typically required before all meals, taking part in Passover required a greater degree of ritual purity.[45] Nonetheless, Jesus declares that the disciples require yet another layer of cleansing; they must have their feet washed by himself in order to be wholly clean.[46] Yet, even the foot washing Christ provides is not enough to cleanse all of the disciples, as Judas has already turned his heart against the Messiah. In other words, more than outward rituals are required to abide in Christ and enter the household of the Father. At the same time, no longer would those who place faith in the true Word of God require the purification rituals of the Mosaic law to approach God.[47]

Jesus' act of foot washing is efficacious because it points to the act that brings about true purification—his passion. The Messiah has already been anointed for burial, and he now goes to his sacrificial death.[48] Although no explicit references to the Passover *lamb* are made in chapter 13, the Passover themes remain overt. According to 13:1: "Before the Feast of the Passover, Jesus knowing his hour had come that he would transition out of this world to the Father. . ." Thus, the identification of a Passover timeline in addition to the mention of Jesus' impending death, especially following the ominous narrative of 11:47—12:8, implies that John intends to keep the substitutionary and expiatory work of the Lamb of God in the minds of his readers.

Such themes continue into John 15, although they are obscured in most English translations. As 15:1–10 elucidates, the disciples are purified by abiding in Christ and his word. On the surface, the passage seems to be a straightforward metaphor about God (the vinedresser), Jesus (the true vine), and the disciples (the branches). According to the symbolic teaching, those who love Christ abide in him and obey the commands of

---

44. Culpepper, "Johannine *Hypodeigma*," 133–52.

45. Keener, *John*, 2:909.

46. Though Jesus is speaking to Peter in 13:10, he uses the plural "you" indicating that, as a group, the disciples have been purified.

47. Keener, *John*, 2:910.

48. Culpepper, "Johannine *Hypodeigma*," 137; Hoskins, "Deliverance from Death," 295; Keener, *John*, 2:902; Neyrey, *John*, 363–64.

the Father. Yet, an additional layer of meaning is conveyed by purity language, which is obvious in the original Greek. According to 15:2, "Every branch in me [Jesus] not bearing fruit, [the Father] takes away (*airō*), and each that bears fruit, he prunes (*kathairō*) so that it may bear more fruit." John, always fond of double meaning, uses *kathairō* cleverly. Though the verb can refer to pruning a plant, as in cleaning away dead foliage, it can also refer to cleansing in the sense of purification. Immediately following, John 15:3 confirms that John's word play is intentional: "Already you are clean (*katharos*) because of the word that I have spoken to you." Thus, John recalls and reinforces Jesus' teaching about cleansing from the foot washing narrative (13:10–11).[49]

Conversely, those who reject Christ, like Judas, remain separated from the Father (15:2, 6). Such non-fruit-bearing branches are not pruned/cleansed but "taken away." This action, described by the verb *airō*, is the same term used in 1:29: "the Lamb who *takes away* the sin of the world." Thus, those who do not abide in Christ are "taken away" from the presence of God along with the sin that causes the separation. Instead of following Christ into the family of God, they remain enslaved to sin and the devil (15:15–16).

The final passage in our examination of the Passover theme is John 18:28—19:42. In the light of the prevalent Passover imagery throughout the Gospel, readers should not be surprised to see the theme carry forward into Jesus' crucifixion. Events of the last night of Jesus' life are framed by references to Passover in 13:1; 18:28, 39; and 19:14. Just as John has correlated the events of Jesus' ministry with Passover themes, he now continues to do so as Jesus goes to his death. More specifically, situating Jesus' passion in the context of the Passover accomplishes a similar symbolic purpose as the temple cleansing in 2:13–25, which was also framed by explicit Passover references. In chapters 18–19, Christ is again revealing the truth of the old rituals by embodying their true form.[50]

The chronology of the passion narrative closely links the final hours of Christ to the Passover festival. In fact, the three references to the "day of preparation" (19:14, 31, 42) correspond roughly to the beginning, middle, and end of the passion account. Unlike the Synoptics, John is careful to articulate that Jesus was sentenced to death around the same

---

49. Neyrey, *John*, 365.

50. Beasley-Murray, *John*, 341; Bultmann, *John*, 677; Porter, *Sacred Tradition*, 145; Porter, "Traditional Exegesis," 418.

time the slaughter of Passover lambs would begin in the temple (19:14).[51] Beasley-Murray explains, "The place, the day, and the hour are all mentioned, for the Evangelist is conscious of the momentous nature of the event now taking place. . . . In *this* celebration the [Jewish people] gathered before Pilate are about to play a decisive part in the fulfillment of the Passover, a second Exodus, wherein God would achieve an emancipation for all nations, not for Israel alone, giving them life in the promised land of his eternal kingdom."[52]

Specific elements of the passion account also evoke the Passover theme. The reference to a hyssop branch, with which a vinegary sponge is lifted to Christ (19:29), is likely significant since none of the Synoptics mention it. In the OT, hyssop regularly appears in blood rituals that effect cleansing from impurity or sin.[53] In the context of the Passover, hyssop bundles were used to apply the blood of the lamb to the lintels of Israelite homes, thus averting death (Exod 12:22).[54] Yet, hyssop was typically a weak plant—too weak to lift a sponge saturated with liquid. Keener suggests that "the very implausibility of the literal portrait reinforces the probability that John intended his audience to envision the symbolic allusion to Passover."[55]

Other elements also evoke the Passover context. In Exod 12:46, God commands, "You shall not break any of [the lamb's] bones."[56] Similarly, in 19:33, John informs readers that the soldiers did not break Jesus' legs.[57] In addition, John indicates that Jesus' body was not permitted to remain on the cross overnight, just as food from the Passover meal was not to be left until the next morning (Exod 12:10).

The flow of blood and water from Jesus' side is more complex, yet no less a vehicle for Passover symbolism. Just as the lamb's blood covered

51. Bultmann, *John*, 677; Jobes, *John*, 283; Keener, *John*, 2:1130–31; Malina and Rohrbaugh, *John*, 273; Mouton, "Torah Reimag(in)ed," 102; Porter, *Sacred Tradition*, 145. Cf. John 19:14, 31, 42.

52. Beasley-Murray, *John*, 341 (emphasis original).

53. Exod 12:22; Lev 14:4–7; Num 19:6, 18; Ps 51:7; Heb 9:19–22; cf. Hoskins, "Deliverance from Death," 288.

54. Jobes, *John*, 278; Malina and Rohrbaugh, *John*, 274.

55. Keener, *John*, 2:1147. Cf. Culpepper, "Johannine Passion," 33; Hoskins, "Deliverance from Death," 296; Jobes, *John*, 278; Malina and Rohrbaugh, *John*, 274; Porter, *Sacred Tradition*, 146.

56. Cf. Num 9:12.

57. Hoskins, *Jesus as the Fulfillment*, 178; Jobes, *John*, 280; Keener, *John*, 2:1156; Porter, "Traditional Exegesis," 405.

the homes of the Israelites, Christ's blood covers the sins of his people. For Israel, the blood of the lamb affected deliverance from slavery and death, and for the true Israel, it affects deliverance from slavery to sin and eternal death. Yet, such theology only explains the function of the blood, not the water.

Several factors converge to offer a promising avenue of interpretation. First, a passage in the Mishnah indicates that the southwestern corner of the temple's altar had two small holes for sacrificial blood. Blood would run through the holes and down into the Kidron brook, where it would mingle with the flow of water (m. Mid. 3:3). Second, the term used for Jesus' side, *pleura*, is commonly used to refer to side walls or chambers of the temple.[58] Third, Jewish tradition held that water would flow from the foundation stones of the temple in the eschatological age, a tradition that John connects with Jesus in chapters 4 and 7. As such, in John 19:34, Jesus is the sacrifice whose blood is poured out in addition to the temple from which water and blood flow. Both fluids mingle as they pour from Christ, simultaneously bringing atonement and life to the world. With the flow of water and blood from Jesus' body, John thus culminates the passion of Christ by merging paschal and eschatological imagery.

In summary, from the very start, John has established a foundation without which it is impossible to understand his Gospel—Jesus is the "Lamb of God." Throughout, Christ is portrayed as the paschal lamb, yet as he recapitulates the story of Israel, his work also represents an escalation of the ancient events. Whereas Israel lived by eating manna in the wilderness, those who "eat" the flesh of Christ, the Passover lamb, receive eternal life. Further, the sacrificial lamb of John 1:29 and 36 not only bears the sin of Israel but has the capacity to cleanse the whole world. Jesus not only saves his people from slavery to the realm of death but eliminates the disease that causes it—sin.

Though the atoning value of the original paschal sacrifice is debatable, John blends various themes to confirm that Christ's sacrifice cleanses his people by atoning for their sin. In the wilderness, Moses raised up a snake, upon which the Israelites could gaze and be healed. On the cross, Christ is lifted up—along with the sin he bears for humanity—so that those who believe into him may receive new life (3:14–15). In 11:47–53, Caiaphas unknowingly speaks prophetically when he indicates that Christ will die on behalf of his people. Soon after, as Jesus washes

---

58. 1 Kgs 6:5, 6, 8, 16; Ezek 41:5, 6, 7, 8, 9, 26; etc. Cf. Coloe, *God Dwells with Us*, 206–7.

his disciples' feet (ch. 13), he indicates that his work begins the process through which they will receive a cleansing more efficacious than mere ritual could ever provide. In chapter 15, the cleansing work of Christ is reaffirmed as Jesus indicates that the Father prunes/cleanses branches who abide in Christ.

By the time readers of the Fourth Gospel reach the passion narrative, they should be well prepared to see clear references to the paschal lamb in Christ's body. As the true Passover sacrifice, Christ would make a way for the true people of God to be permanently cleansed from sin, liberated from the kingdom of the devil, and led into the kingdom and household of God.

Supporting Concept: The Accessibility of Sacred Space

We learn from the Hebrew Bible that, prior to Christ, access to the presence of God was restricted almost exclusively to the Jewish people. And even within Israel, only certain members of the community—priests and Levites—were permitted to access God's presence more directly in the tabernacle and temple. Yet, the work of Christ made the presence of God available to all of humanity, i.e., he prepared a place in the household of the Father.

In the Fourth Gospel, although not explicitly stated, Jesus' work as Passover lamb is the activity that renders the sacred space of God's household available to the world. In the following sections we will, therefore, examine the manner in which Jesus makes the presence of God available to those who were formerly excluded from it. Before discussing the theme of accessibility in John's Gospel, however, we must first revisit a supporting concept: sacred space.

The holiness of the Jewish land and people was highly stratified. Restrictions upon sacred space served both to preserve the presence of God among his people as well as protect humans from the dangerous presence of God. According to Coloe, "The Temple's cult was a means of continual purification, thus enabling God to be present in Israel's midst."[59]

Entering any sacred space, especially the temple or tabernacle, without proper procedures could result in dire consequences, as when Nadab and Abihu were incinerated for offering "strange fire" upon the altar (Lev

---

59. Coloe, *God Dwells with Us*, 180.

10:1–3). Shortly after, the Lord gives Moses instructions to relay to Aaron: "Do not enter, at any time, into the holy place inside the veil before the mercy seat, which is upon the ark, so that [you] will not die" (Lev 16:2). The Lord then goes on to outline detailed procedures for entering the holy place on Yom Kippur, the only day Aaron and future high priests would be allowed to approach the innermost sanctuary.

The temple and tabernacle weren't the only holy spaces in Israel, however. From the Mishnah, we learn that ten degrees of holiness exist in geographical space. In increasing levels of holiness: "the Land of Israel is holier than any other land. . . . The walled cities are still more holy" (m. Kelim 1.6–7). The city of Jerusalem is holier still, then the Temple Mount within it. The rampart (or outer court) surrounding the inner courts of the temple, the Court of the Women, the Court of the Israelites, and the Court of the Priests are next. Finally, the area between the porch and altar, the inner sanctuary, and the holy of holies comprise the most sacred spaces (m. Kelim 1.8–9).

Each holy space carried restrictions as to who was allowed to enter. For example, lepers weren't allowed in walled cities, and no man with a "flux" or a menstruating woman could approach the Temple Mount. Sources disagree whether gentiles were allowed to enter the outer court of the temple, but non-Jewish people certainly weren't allowed to go beyond it. Women weren't permitted beyond the Court of the Women, and only ritually pure Jewish men were allowed into the Court of the Israelites. Only priests were allowed into the court of the priests and only the high priest on the Day of Atonement could enter the holy of holies.[60]

An inscription unearthed from the balustrade around the court of the Israelites proves enlightening. The message prohibits access to gentiles and warns those who would trespass. The prohibition reads, "No foreigner is to enter within the forecourt and the balustrade around the sanctuary. Whoever is caught will have himself to blame for his subsequent death."[61] In sum, access to the presence of God was highly restricted, and violating the prescribed spaces could result in severe consequences, whether from God or from the Jewish leaders.

The restrictions upon sacred space also reflected sociocultural concerns. The concept of limited good was a staple of first-century Mediterranean thought. If one family or individual gained resources, fewer

---

60. M. Kelim 1.6–9; Nylund, "Court of the Gentiles."

61. Segal, "Penalty of the Warning Inscription," 79–84. Cf. Josephus, *Ant.* 15.11.5; *J.W.* 5.5.2; Neyrey, *John*, 64.

resources were available for others. Intangible concepts, by extension, were also perceived to be finite. For example "a prophet has no honor in his own country" (John 4:44) because the only way to increase one's status was to take status away from others in the community. Neyrey explains, "Jesus' increase in respect throughout Galilee lifts him high above his village peers, a situation which his neighbors perceive as an intolerable and unbalancing force that means their corresponding loss of honor in proportion to Jesus' gain."[62] Thus, in order to be considered an honorable person, one was expected to maintain the status quo and remain within the social standing ascribed at birth.[63]

Along similar lines, to encroach upon a sacred space disproportionate to one's status and heritage was to act dishonorably, even sinfully. Such behavior threatened the well-being of the entire society by disrupting boundary lines that maintained cosmic order and ensured the well-being of the group.[64] As such, stepping into a prohibited sacred space would classify as a dangerous action, not just for the offender but for the entire community.

By bodily tabernacling among humanity, however, Jesus erases the religious and cultural boundary lines that limit access to God. Olson explains, "The Incarnation changes the dynamic of God's real presence to the people. The Incarnation expresses God's 'descent' into human reality, cutting against the need to elevate humanity to find God's presence. . . . This presence does not map, nor does it form areas of separation."[65] Jesus can remove the boundaries around sacred space because he himself is the embodiment of the temple and associated rituals. By becoming the atoning sacrifice—the Passover lamb—that is offered upon the altar of God—his own body—he fulfills every ritual necessary to approach the Father.

The Accessibility of Sacred Space in the Gospel of John

We will now examine specific passages in the Gospel of John that reveal the accessibility of sacred space accomplished through the work of Christ. As with virtually every other significant Johannine theme, John

62. Neyrey, *John*, 133.
63. Malina, *New Testament World*, 90.
64. Malina, *New Testament World*, 105; Olson, "Sacred Time," 142.
65. Olson, "Sacred Time," 140.

establishes his foundations in the prologue. By anchoring the Gospel in creation (1:1), John reveals that God's love is universal in nature. In 1:9, the concept is made explicit as John affirms that the true light of the world, Christ, "enlightens every person."

The availability of God's presence is illuminated further in the dialogue between Jesus and Nicodemus (3:1–10). Prior to Christ, access to God was mediated through the Jewish people. One's heritage and birth, for the most part, determined whether one could enter God's kingdom. Yet, Christ makes the startling claim that a person can be born again, in fact *must* be born again, to enter God's kingdom. No longer would Jewish descent be required for access to the Father. As John says explicitly in 3:16–17: "For God so loved the *world* . . . that *anyone* who believes" will receive access to his presence (emphasis mine).

Jesus' encounter with the woman at the well further develops the theme (John 4). Multiple factors barred the Samaritan female from the sacred space of the temple: she was a woman, a Samaritan, and a person of questionable character with five previous husbands. According to Neyrey, "The narrator has concentrated in this one figure many of the characteristics of the marginal persons with whom Jesus regularly deals in the Synoptic Gospels. She is an amalgam of cultural deviance . . . [and] embodies most of the social liabilities which would marginalize her in her society."[66] More specifically, Samaritan women were perpetually and irrevocably defiled. According to the Mishnah, "The daughters of the Samaritans are [deemed unclean as] menstruants from the cradle."[67] So, not only were Samaritan women permanently impure, but they were highly contagious. Similar to a menstruating woman, everything they lie or sit upon becomes unclean, impurity that is transmitted to anyone who comes into contact with such items.[68] Nevertheless, Jesus welcomes her and her people into his presence. He is even willing to drink from the same water jug, a scandalous and defiling action, at least according to socioreligious conventions.[69]

The topic of conversation between Christ and the Samaritan woman further emphasizes the accessibility of sacred space as readers learn that worship will no longer be restricted to a specific geographical location.

66. Neyrey, *John*, 169.

67. M. Nid. 4.1.

68. Lev 15:19–33; cf. Malina and Rohrbaugh, *John*, 99.

69. Jobes, *John*, 99; Malina and Rohrbaugh, *John*, 164; Daube, "Jesus and the Samaritan Woman," 137–47.

John reveals that Jesus is opening a new way into the presence of the Father entirely apart from the temple or sacrificial system. Incomplete and imperfect institutions of the past are being replaced as "true worshippers will worship the Father in Spirit and truth" (4:23).[70] Any person, regardless of gender or racial heritage—even a Samaritan woman—will be able to enter God's presence. As a result, the first people to proclaim Jesus as Savior in the Fourth Gospel aren't the Jewish people, the learned Pharisee Nicodemus, or even Jesus' own disciples, but the "half-breed" Samaritans (John 4:42).[71]

Jesus continues to create access for marginalized and disenfranchised people in the following chapters. In both John 5 and 9, Jesus heals individuals who have no hope for inclusion in the community of faith. Porter describes the invalid of chapter 5: "Here is a person who had virtually no status within the social structure of the times. He has been ill for thirty-eight years without anyone to put him in the pool when the waters were troubled, and he was destined to remain there until he died—perhaps the only surprising element is that he was still alive."[72] Though the man is made well by Jesus, it is only his flesh that seems to be healed. The beggar offers no praise, or even thanks, for his healing. He immediately reports to the temple leaders and aligns himself with those who oppose the Messiah and will eventually kill him.

Instead of receiving honor for the miracle of healing, Jesus is accused of being a sinner who has broken the Sabbath (5:16). Jesus, however, proclaims his innocence; he is acting on God's behalf and demonstrating a *halakah* that is better than the Pharisaic interpretation of the law (5:19–30).[73] Though Christ departs from the letter of the law, or at least the prevailing version of it, he accomplishes the redemptive purpose toward which it pointed: "By revealing God as deliverer and by freeing people from oppressive forces, Jesus fulfills the sabbath ethic of the Old Testament."[74]

The contrast between the Pharisaic law and Jesus' redemptive *halakah* continues into chapter 9. The ungrateful beggar of chapter 5 serves

---

70. Gibbs, "Already Dwelling," 17; Jobes, *John*, 95–103; Malina and Rohrbaugh, *John*, 100; Neyrey, *John*, 118.

71. Jobes, *John*, 103–4.

72. Porter, *John*, 54.

73. Neyrey, *John*, 175.

74. Kanagaraj, "Implied Ethics," 46–47. Cf. Barrett, *John*, 321; Olson, "Sacred Time," 7; Thiessen, *Jesus and Death*, 7.

as a foil for the gracious blind man in chapter 9; whereas the first beggar aligns himself with "the Judeans," the blind man confesses loyalty to Christ (9:24–34). After Jesus' healing, the Pharisees question the man intently, again condemning Christ for failing to keep Sabbath. The Pharisees base their authority on the word of God as given through Moses, rejecting the man's claim that Jesus healed him through the power of God. Brown elucidates:

> While the former blind man is gradually having his eyes opened to the truth about Jesus, the Pharisees or "the [Judeans]" are becoming more obdurate in their failure to see the truth.... The care with which the evangelist has drawn out his portraits of increasing insight and hardening blindness is masterful. Three times the former blind man, who is truly gaining knowledge, humbly confesses his ignorance (12, 25, 36). Three times the Pharisees, who are really plunging deeper into abysmal ignorance of Jesus, make confident statements about what they know of him (16, 24, 29).[75]

Despite opposition, the beggar continues to affirm Jesus' divine authority (9:31–33). Though he is swiftly expelled from the synagogue, the man again encounters Jesus, proclaims his faith, and begins to worship (9:34–38). Kanagaraj explains aptly, "For John the sabbath is meant for encountering God in Christ, [and] for being made whole."[76] Thus, in these two narratives, John reaffirms that no temple is required to approach God and that all people may choose to worship the Father in Spirit and truth, even though some will choose not to.

Shortly after the healing of the two beggars, Jesus performs an even more spectacular miracle. In chapter 11, Jesus raises Lazarus from the dead and reveals that not even death can separate true believers from the presence of God. Even more so than a Samaritan woman, "corpses were the most powerful sources of impurity in the priestly ritual purity system."[77] Dead bodies could transmit defilement not only through touch but through proximity. Further, such defilement was long-lasting (seven days) and contagious. But just as he sat with the Samaritan woman, Jesus approaches the tomb of Lazarus, risking uncleanness and contagion. Jesus, however, is not defiled; the sacrificial Lamb overcomes the very

---

75. Brown, *John I–XII*, 377. Cf. Keener, *John*, 1:639.
76. Kanagaraj, "Implied Ethics," 47.
77. Thiessen, *Jesus and Death*, 122. Cf. Num 19:12.

powers of death and defilement. The explanation of Thiessen is worth quoting at length:

> The tabernacle and temple were the divinely given tools to deal with impurities as they arose. But the functions that God gave to the Jerusalem temple and its priests were predominately *defensive*. They had a divinely ordained limitation: they could not and were never meant to wipe out death itself.... The temple could not eradicate the *sources* of ritual impurity, but it could eliminate the *aftereffects* once those sources of impurity left a person's body.... [Yet through Jesus] God has unleashed a force of holiness in the world that goes on the offense against impurity—Jesus is the holy one of God. A holy power emanates out of Jesus's body and can overcome all sources of impurity. He embodies God's holiness let loose on earth. Whereas the temple apparatus removes the effects of sources of impurity, Jesus addresses the sources of impurity themselves.[78]

While the Passover lamb of Exod 12 was able to rescue Israelites from death, Jesus defeats death itself. The atoning power of his sacrifice overcomes every source of defilement, leading to eternal life and union with God. Although Lazarus's resurrection becomes the catalyst for Jesus' crucifixion, it is also a foreshadowing of Christ's own resurrection.[79]

In sum, the Fourth Gospel reveals that Jesus renders the presence of God available to people of *every heritage and social standing*. No longer would individuals formerly excluded from sacred space be kept outside the perimeter of the Father's house. According to Porter, "Jesus' ministry includes revealing his nature and identity in clear and obvious ways to people in all walks of life, including Galileans (chs. 1 and 2), Judeans (chs. 3 and 11), Samaritans (ch. 4), the physically infirm (chs. 5 and 9), nobility (ch. 4), and Roman political leaders (chs. 18–19)—in other words, the height and breadth of society."[80] The ritual procedures of the past, so vital in their time, were never intended to cordon humans off from God but to facilitate access to his presence. Yet, the incomplete and faulty execution of the law by those in power had distorted its true purpose. Through Christ, finally all of God's people could be restored to the Father.

---

78. Thiessen, *Jesus and Death*, 180 (emphasis original).
79. Lee, *Symbolic Narratives*, 226; Thiessen, *Jesus and Death*, 122.
80. Porter, *John*, 43.

Supporting Concept: A Prepared Place

Though we would typically turn to John 14 at this point in our chapter, one further concept requires discussion before we can synthesize the various themes. In 14:2, Jesus promises that he will go to prepare a place for his followers: "In my Father's house are many rooms; unless it were so, would I tell you that I go to prepare a place for you?" As already discussed, the *going* entails Jesus' obedient journey to the cross, but what precisely is the "place" that Jesus prepares? If the *monai*, or rooms, in the Father's house represent the co-abiding of God and his family, we might suspect that the prepared place reflects a relational rather than a spatial geography.

An examination of Greek terminology once again proves enlightening. In the NT, the idea of preparing, *hetoimazō*, often indicates some type of spiritual action. For example, the messianic prophecy of Isa 40:3, which is referenced in John 1:23 and repeated verbatim in Matt 3:3, reads, "Prepare (*hetoimazō*) the way (*hodos*) of the Lord." The authors of Scripture aren't describing the construction of a highway but the spiritual process by which hearts are prepared to receive the love, grace, and truth of the Messiah.[81] In Luke 2, when the righteous man Simeon sees the infant Christ, he rejoices to see the salvation God has *prepared*—Christ himself (Luke 2:31). Similarly, Matt 25:34 describes the inheritance *prepared* for the righteous, a kingdom that consists primarily of a relationship with Christ and an execution of God's will rather than a tract of land or heavenly abode.

The language of a "prepared place" exhibits profound theological significance in the OT as it expresses God's faithful work among his people, especially in the preparation of the promised land.[82] According to Ezek 20:6, when God led the people out of Egypt, he led them into the land he had prepared (*hetoimazō*) for them, "a land flowing with milk and honey," i.e., the promised land.[83] Yet, even in the era of the OT, the prepared place, or promised land, wasn't as much about the land as it was about a place where Israel was free to live as a people of God in the presence of God without outside oppression or interference.[84]

---

81. Cf. Mark 1:3; Luke 1:17, 76.

82. McCaffrey, *House*, 88–89; Köstenberger, *Encountering John*, 427.

83. Exod 23:20; Num 20:5; 32:1; Deut 1:29–33; Josh 1:3; Judg 18:10; Ezek 20:6; 45:4; Jdt 3:3; Bar 3:24.

84. Gen 17:6–8; Exod 6:4–7.

Because the land belonged to God and because he dwelt within it, his presence imbued the land with holiness.[85] The presence of God was so closely associated with the land that the gift of prophecy, the gift of the Spirit, and the gift of resurrection were considered largely unavailable outside of it.[86] According to the Babylonian Talmud, "For whoever lives in the Land of Israel is as though he has the true God, but whoever lives abroad is as though he has no God."[87] Due to God's pervasive presence and the resulting holiness of the land, retaining the land was contingent upon obedience to God's law and maintaining a state of holiness within the community. If the people disobeyed, they could be expelled.[88] At the same time, God's promise was irrevocable. Covenant breaches could be forgiven on the basis of the Abrahamic covenant. "In this way, the promise to Abraham becomes a ground for ultimate hope."[89] Even when God's people were expelled from the land, they could have faith in eventual restoration.

Language of a prepared place is also used of the ark of the covenant,[90] rooms within the temple,[91] and the temple itself.[92] In particular, Jewish tradition presents the messiah as the one who will prepare the eschatological temple.[93] In Mic 4:1 and Isa 2:2, use of the term evolves to describe the eschatological temple as the place prepared for the ingathering of all nations.[94] Along similar lines, God prepares (true) Israel to be his people for eternity. David says in 2 Sam 7:24 (LXX): "You prepared (*hetoimazō*) for yourself your people Israel, as a people for eternity, and you, Lord, are their God." In the light of such usages, the evolution of the verb might be considered complete in regarding Jesus as the messiah who prepares the eschatological temple, i.e., his own body, while drawing all the peoples of the earth to the Father.[95]

---

85. Lev 25:23; Num 35:34.

86. Mek. Pisha I:III.3B; b. Ketub. 111.17A; Neusner, *Mekhilta*, 3; *Talmud of Babylonia*, 139. Cf. Davies, *Gospel and the Land*, 61.

87. B. Ketub. 111.5C–D

88. Lev 18:28–29; 19:2; Deut 4:40.

89. Davies, *Gospel and the Land*, 21; cf. 22–35.

90. 1 Chr 15:1–3; 2 Chr 1:4.

91. 2 Chr 3:1; 31:11.

92. Exod 15:17; Sir 47:13; 49:12; Wis 9:8; 2 Chr 8:16.

93. McCaffrey, *House*, 91–99.

94. Cf. Rev 21:22; 4 Ezra 13:32–36; 1 En. 90:28–36.

95. Aalen, "'Reign' and 'House,'" 227–28.

The "place," *topos*, likewise bears implications that surpass a simple geographical space. For a seemingly generic term, a surprising number of attestations are used in a precise manner. In Gen 28, a passage referenced in John 1:51, *topos* is used six times.[96] Jacob declares, "The Lord is in this *place*," and "How awesome is this *place*" (Gen 28:16). He then names the *place* Bethel, the House of God (Gen 28:19). Similarly, the "*place* where Yahweh has chosen to establish his name" is repeated twenty-one times in various forms throughout the Greek OT, apparently referring to the Jerusalem temple.[97]

Along such lines, "the place," *topos*, frequently refers to the presence of God.[98] Montgomery explains that in the ancient Near East, divinities were often considered to be attached to a particular territory. Thus, for the Israelites, the "dwelling place" of God became an appellation for God himself.[99] Along such lines, "the place" was roughly equivalent to the person and presence of God.

Over the course of Jewish history, *topos* continued to evolve and develop associations not just with the person and presence of God, but also with the fulfillment of his promises to his people—with "the eschatological consummation and salvation for the people of God after the trials of this age."[100] In sum, the prepared place isn't simply a space delineated by a geographical boundary (the land of Israel) or architectural structure (the tabernacle/temple) but the space in which God's people experience the culmination of the Father's love and consummation of his promises.

A Prepared Place in the Gospel of John

Though *hetoimazō*, the act of preparing, is used only twice in the Fourth Gospel—in John 14:2–3—*topos* is used seventeen times. The term is used in a straightforward spatial manner in eight verses,[101] but as McCaffrey points out, "the fourth gospel also provides us with a highly technical

---

96. Gen 28:11 (3x), 16 (2x), 19.

97. Deut 12:11, 21; 14:24; 1 Kgs 6:6–49; 11:36; 14:21; 2 Kgs 21:4, 7; Ps 75:3; Dan 8:11; Ezek 42:13; 46:19–20; Ezra 6:3; 2 Macc 5:20.

98. Gen 28:17; Exod 3:5; 33:21; Josh 5:15; Zech 13:1; Isa 4:5; 33:21; 66:1; et al.

99. Montgomery, "Place," 17–20.

100. Aalen, "'Reign' and 'House,'" 238. Cf. McCaffrey, *House*, 98–100.

101. John 5:13; 6:10, 23; 10:40; 11:6, 30; 18:2; 20:7.

use of the term *topos* to designate the Jerusalem temple."[102] In 4:20, the woman at the well describes the Jerusalem temple as a *place* of worship and in 11:48 the chief priests worry that Rome will take away their *place*, i.e., the temple. John may also allude to the sacred place Abraham is asked to sacrifice Isaac as he uses *topos* four times to describe the place Jesus was crucified (19:13–20), just as *topos* is used four times in Gen 22:3–14.[103] So, *topos* can be used spatially, but it can also be used to delineate a place of God's presence. In other words, a spatial interpretation is possible but not required, especially in conjunction with the idea of preparation.

In John 14:2–3, Christ himself makes the preparation required for his people to receive their place. Such action does not consist of getting heavenly rooms ready for occupants who will arrive upon death. Rather, Jesus makes preparation by going to the cross so that his followers can abide in the presence of God, the Father's house.[104] As Jobes explains, "He died to provide, not a mansion, but an eternal relationship with the triune God."[105] Not at odds with such a view is Augustine's suggestion that Jesus prepares believers as the vessels of God's presence.[106] Thus, in John 14, as Christ prepares the way by going to the cross, believers are simultaneously prepared, not only through Christ's atoning work but also by knowing the Father through knowing Christ (vv. 6–7, 9, 17, 20), abiding in the Father and Son (vv. 3, 6, 10–11, 20, 25), carrying out God's will (vv. 12, 15, 21, 23–24, 31), and loving Jesus (vv. 15, 21, 23–24, 28).

Though John does not reference the preparation, *hetoimazō*, or the place, *topos*, in 17:24–26, the verses describe the place Jesus prepares, a space that transcends traditional geography. Jesus prays,

> Father, I desire that they also, the ones you have given me, would be with me, where I am, so that they might see my glory, which you have given me, because you loved me before the foundation of the world. O righteous Father, even though the world has not known you, yet I have known you, and these have known that you sent me; and I made your name known to them, and will continue to make it known, so that the love with which you loved me may be in them, and I in them. (John 17:24–26)

102. McCaffrey, *House*, 98.

103. Coloe, *God Dwells with Us*, 165.

104. Barrett, *John*, 457; Brown, *John XIII–XXI*, 627; Coloe, *God Dwells with Us*, 167; Gundry, "In My Father's House," 71; Keener, *John*, 2:937; Whitacre, *John*, 349.

105. Jobes, *John*, 226.

106. Augustine, *John*, 68.2.1–2.

Jesus' words here echo the language of love and co-abiding between the Father, Son, and true believers from John 14. In addition Jesus speaks of a relational space that will appertain after he departs from the world, just as in John 14. Thus, associating the relational space of John 17 with the prepared place of John 14 bears merit. Maloney explains, "Swept up into the love that united the Father and the Son, those who believe in Jesus will no longer be 'in the world' (v. 25). They dwell in the glory generated by the loving unity between the Father and the Son that existed between them from all time, before the world was made."[107] Thus the place Jesus prepares could be viewed as even more than a relational space. It is a place prepared from the very beginning, lost, and made available again through Christ—a place where God's will is done upon the earth through a perfect obedience made possible by a perfect love.

Atonement, Sacred Space, and Prepared Place in John 14

Surveying the cruciform access to sacred space in John's Gospel equips us to better understand the geography of the Father's house in John 14. As Jesus prepares a place in God's house, his preparation takes the form of going to the cross, not to heaven. As he prepares the temple of his body for death and resurrection, he likewise prepares his followers to abide in the loving presence of God, both now and into eternity.[108]

Christ's cruciform preparation also effects cleansing for those who place faith in him. Just as purity was required for Israelites to maintain the promised land, and later, enter the temple, Jesus' followers must be cleansed of sin in order to enter the presence of God. So, by bearing away the sins of his people and becoming a sacrificial offering, Christ atones for the sin that separates people from God. No longer would complex rituals or rigid boundaries be needed for God's people to safely approach his holy presence.

Along similar lines, Jesus ushers the community of believers into the kingdom of God by delivering them from death. Through his sacrificial blood, the Lamb of God redeems God's people from slavery to sin in the kingdom of the devil. In doing so, Christ leads his people into a new promised land. And because sin has been definitively defeated, never

---

107. Moloney, "God," 210.
108. Coloe, *God Dwells with Us*, 377; McCaffrey, *House*, 119.

again will God's people be expelled from his presence. Yet, this "place" isn't a geographical tract of land, a disembodied paradise, or a mansion in the clouds, but the household of God.

Although John does mention "heaven" on several occasions throughout the Gospel, it is never presented as a place to which believers will go. Further, eschatological nuances throughout John, which are rooted in Jewish tradition, associate Christ with the eschatological temple. As such, John portrays Jesus as the temple to which all peoples will gather in the end-times. Not just Israel, but all the world will be redeemed from sin and death.

Accordingly, the household of God and the prepared place are available to anyone whosoever might believe in Christ. Jesus' promise that *many* rooms, i.e., abiding places, are available in the Father's house indicates that he has opened up space for every person, regardless of race, gender, or social status. Yet, all who accept a place in the Father's house also receive the mission that is inseparable from the place. Believers are called to follow in the footsteps of Christ and spread the sacred space of God's kingdom throughout the world.[109] The means by which this calling is accomplished is the subject of our next chapter.

---

109. Mouton, "Torah Reimag(in)ed," 108.

6.

Coming and Going
The Return of Christ as Spirit-Paraclete

About a decade ago, I traveled to Mexico with a group of ladies to help a midsize church put on a ladies' conference. Our group members took turns speaking and leading sessions in addition to assisting with prayer and altar ministry. On the first night of the conference, I was part of the altar ministry praying for various ladies who came forward. Being pre-COVID, it was natural to lay hands upon people as I prayed. So I quickly noticed that one particular lady for whom I was praying seemed a bit unsteady on her feet. Before long, she began to fall backwards, and not wanting her to get hurt, I wrapped my arms around her and lifted her back up. As I quickly concluded our prayer and looked around, I immediately realized my faux pas. Ladies were dropping across the room—being "slain in the Spirit." While I had known the church in which we were ministering was "Spirit-filled," I'd never been in a service quite so charismatic. I quickly learned to go with the flow and gently guide my prayer partners to the floor as they engaged in their own silent communion with the Lord.

Whether or not you believe such pneumatic expressions are theologically legitimate, our ladies clearly desired a greater intimacy with God and a greater measure of the Holy Spirit. In fact, individuals in less developed countries are often more open to the supernatural and, thus, more sensitive to God's Spirit. Unlike Westerners, their worldview isn't as dependent upon reason and science, which often crowd the Holy Spirit out of our modern church culture. Though each church tradition responds differently to the Holy Spirit, Western churches often treat the Spirit like a substandard replacement for Jesus. In fact, he is often regarded as little more than a "babysitter," as I heard him referred to in one recent church service.

The Path Ahead

In this chapter, we will examine language and themes surrounding the Spirit to help us understand his role in John 14. Water, in particular, is a symbol upon which John draws to convey the manifold work of the Spirit in the life of the believer. However, the theme of water fades into the background in the Farewell Discourse as John focuses, instead, upon the Paraclete. Jesus says, "And if I should go and prepare a place for you, *I will come again* and receive you to myself, that where I am also you will be" (14:3; emphasis mine). Similarly, in John 14:16–18, Jesus says, "And I will ask the Father, and he will give you another Helper [*paraklētos*], so that he should be with you forever.... You know him for he abides with you and is in you. I will not leave you as orphans. *I will come to you*" (emphasis mine). This coming again is not Christ's return to individual believers to transport them to heaven when they die. Rather, Jesus tells his followers exactly what form his return will take: the Paraclete. As such, Jesus' return in the form of the Spirit empowers believers to continue Jesus' own work in the world.

Though Christ's return as Spirit-Paraclete is dominant in John 14, the larger setting of the Gospel anticipates a broader work of the Spirit. Thus, the immediate return of Christ as Spirit-Paraclete anticipates an end-time return of Christ in which he will complete the process of redemption and restoration. As such, the return of Christ through the Spirit fulfills the cosmic scope and OT focus of John. The same Spirit who hovered over the waters in Genesis brings new life to creation as the incarnation, death, and resurrection of Christ inaugurates the final era of history. The Spirit, anticipated by the Jewish prophets, would now begin to pour out the living water that renews and restores all of Creation.

Supporting Concept: Spirit and Water

Water, the most vital necessity for life, is saturated with symbolic meaning in Jewish literature. Most notably, water has a strong association with

Jewish purification rituals. The expression "living water" (*hydōr zōn*) typically refers to fresh water that is running or flowing as opposed to water in a pond or cistern.[1] Immersion in such water was necessary for ritual purification, thus, living water "took away defilement and made acceptable worshippers out of unclean men."[2] Along with blood, water was one of the two strongest purifying agents available.[3]

Water also has numerous other symbolic connotations.[4] In OT prophetic literature, water often represents God's revelatory word,[5] and in proverbial teaching, water is often associated with wisdom.[6] As time passed and wisdom became associated with the law, the imagery of water took on additional associations with torah.[7] For example, Ezekiel speaks of a future in which God will cleanse his people with water so that they can walk according to his ways. In doing so, God doesn't indicate that the law will change but that human nature will be purified (Ezek 36:25–27).[8]

Along similar lines, many prophetic texts anticipate the restoration of God's people and land in conjunction with the fullness of the Spirit. In such passages, water often represents the Spirit, who imparts the blessings. Though many prophecies initially anticipated a Jewish nationalistic restoration, they also came to be associated with the eschatological age.[9] In Isa 44:3, which typifies such passages, God says,

> For I will pour out water on the thirsty *land*
> And streams on the dry ground;
> I will pour out My Spirit on your offspring,
> And My blessing on your descendants. (NASB, emphasis original)

---

1. See Gen 26:19; Lev 14:5–6, 50–52; Num 19:17; Zech 14:8.

2. Morris, *John*, 260. Cf. Beasley-Murray, *John*, 60; Bultmann, *John*, 181; Keener, *John*, 1:604.

3. M. Miqw. 1. 4–8; Lev 14:4–6, 50–52; 15:13; Num 19:17; Deut 21:4; Ezek 36:25; Zech 13:1; Matt 27:24; Heb 10:22.

4. For a detailed survey, see Allison, "Living Water." Cf. Coloe, *God Dwells with Us*, 93.

5. Isa 11:9; 55:1, 10, 11; Amos 8:11–12; Hab 2:14; Jer 51:15–16.

6. Prov 13:14; 16:22; 18:4; Sir 15:3; 24:25, 30.

7. Sir 24:23–29; m. 'Abot 1.4, 11–12; 2.8; cf. CD III, 16; VI, 3–5.

8. Thiessen, *Jesus and Death*, 180.

9. Isa 30:23–26; 41:17–20; 43:19–21; 44:3–4; 48:21; 49:10; Ezek 47:1–12; Joel 3:18; Zech 13:1; 14:8.

Thus, water, especially "living water," is a biblical symbol that came to represent the fulfillment of God's ultimate promise of restoration. Allison explains,

> It is not difficult to determine why Jewish pictures of the ideal future included flowing fountains and great streams of water. To begin with, water, without which there is no life, was not always in abundant supply in ancient Palestine. Not only was there rarely any rain between May and October, but surface water was scarce, desert areas were large, and complete droughts of a year or two were not unknown. So the Jewish people did not take water for granted, and it is hardly remarkable that when they thought of paradise they thought of water.[10]

In sum, water points to the eschatological cleansing of creation in which God's living water, i.e., Spirit, will pour out, returning creation to its original Edenic state and restoring God's people to his presence.[11] In the eschaton, there will be no lack of water or God's Spirit; both will be readily available for anyone who thirsts.

In passages that feature eschatological water, the temple often figures as the source of the flow. While representing the life-giving character of God's Spirit, the water from the temple also signifies the absence of evil in the new creation. The ancients believed that the temple was situated above the primeval deep and that the proper functioning of the temple "was necessary to ensure that sufficient [water] was released to ensure fertility, but not so much as to overwhelm the earth with a flood."[12] Thus, the temple was a bastion of order that prevented the eruption of chaotic, destructive waters.[13] A similar concept is expressed in Rev 21:1 where John describes a temple-city, i.e., the new heaven and earth, in which "the sea is no more."[14]

---

10. Allison, "Living Water," 146. Cf. Bultmann, *John*, 182; Coloe, *God Dwells with Us*, 143; Mounce, *The Book of Revelation*, 385.

11. Gen 2:10; Pss 36:8-9; 46:4; Isa 32:1-2, 15; 35:1-6; 44:3; Ezek 36:25-27; 47:1-12; Joel 2:28-29; 3:18; Zech 14:8; Rev 22:1-2; 4 Ezra 7:30; 8:52; 1 En. 90:33-36; T. Levi 18:5-8; cf. Jobes, *John*, 97.

12. Barker, *Gate of Heaven*, 18.

13. Barker, *Gate of Heaven*, 19; Lundquist, "Temple, Covenant, and Law," 299. Cf. Ps 29:10; Let. Aris. 89-91.

14. For the absence or destruction of the sea, see Sib. Or. 5:158-59, 447-48; T. Levi 4:1; Pss 18:15; 106:9; Isa 44:27; 50:2; 51:10; Jer 51:36; Nah 1:4; Zech 10:11.

The associations of water with the temple, the renewal of creation, and the presence of God's Spirit culminate in Ezek 47, in which "the establishment of the new Temple and the return of God's glory are a prelude to the advent of the miraculous river flowing from the new temple (Ezek 47:1–12)."[15] Such miraculous waters bring life to the Dead Sea, cause fruit trees to grow, and bring healing to the land. In addition, Ezekiel's vision conveys the restoration of people to the land, the reversal of sin, and a new ability to keep God's commands. The symbols communicate both an "outward physical restoration of the land as well as a spiritual transformation of the people."[16]

The author of the Fourth Gospel, always fond of a layered meaning, likely drew upon the rich symbolic domain of water to convey an equally rich theological point.[17] Understanding living water simply as a means of cleansing *or* torah *or* wisdom *or* the Holy Spirit is an oversimplification that cannot encompass all that the author of the Fourth Gospel intended to convey.[18] Equipped with such an understanding, we may now examine John's robust and multifaceted use of water and Spirit in his gospel.

Spirit and Water in the Gospel of John

The Gospel of John, unlike the Synoptics, conveys the teachings of Jesus in lengthy dialogues, a technique that the author utilizes to introduce and develop characteristic language and symbols.[19] Water and Spirit are two closely related symbols the author helps readers progressively understand. As the Fourth Gospel begins, the Spirit rests upon (or abides with) Christ, who offers a baptism of Spirit instead of water (1:32–33). As the narrative proceeds, readers learn that Christ himself is the source of living water and Holy Spirit. And finally, as the Gospel closes, water pours from Christ as he gives up the Spirit (19:30, 34) in order to bestow him upon the disciples (20:33).

Nearly every passage in which John utilizes the imagery of Spirit and/or water is linked by the common theme that Jesus fulfills Jewish

---

15. Hoskins, *Jesus as Fulfillment*, 78. Cf. Allison, "Living Water," 46; Beale, *Temple*, 196; Beale, *Revelation*, 1106.

16. Manning, *Echoes of a Prophet*, 182. Cf. McCaffrey, *House*, 232.

17. Allison, "Living Water," 145. Cf. Barrett, *John*, 196; Brown, *John I–XII*, cxxxv.

18. Barrett, *John*, 196; Beasley-Murray, *John*, 60; Morris, *John*, 260.

19. Bauckham, *Testimony*, 120.

traditions.[20] Because Christ is the new temple of God from which living water flows, he brings cleansing, healing, and not just restoration but complete transformation, as anticipated by the OT.

John establishes the Holy Spirit from the outset by presenting Jesus as the one who bears the Spirit and baptizes in him (1:32–34). Water is first mentioned in the same narrative as readers learn that John the Baptist baptizes in water, but another—Christ—will offer a baptism of a wholly different magnitude (1:26–30). In the following chapter, Jesus' miraculous transformation of water to wine reinforces the theme that the waters of the past are being transformed into something new and better (2:1–10).

In chapter 3, the water/Spirit imagery becomes more complex as Jesus tells Nicodemus that he must be born of water and Spirit to enter God's kingdom (3:3–5). Though water often symbolizes Spirit in the Gospel of John and in the wider canon of Scripture, the terms diverge in John 3. Indeed, if water is equated to Spirit in John 3:5, Jesus would be saying redundantly that one must be "born of Spirt and Spirit" to enter God's kingdom.[21] Instead, the context seems to indicate that Jesus is referring to physical birth (water) and spiritual birth (Spirit).

In the ancient Near East, water was a common euphemism for semen, amniotic fluid, and the process of birth itself.[22] Semitic literature roughly contemporaneous with the Gospel of John also reflects similar usages of the term.[23] Witherington explains, "Notice that in John 3, Nicodemus's reference to going back into a mother's womb immediately precedes reference to birth from or out of water. The logical sequence of this passage quite naturally suggests . . . that the 'water' the Evangelist has Jesus speak of must have something to do with birth or coming forth from the womb."[24] As such, John may be countering proto-gnostic thinking in which mortal bodies were considered corrupted vessels from which the soul desired to escape. Such lines of thinking were antithetical to the very incarnation of Christ, as according to gnostic thought, a

---

20. Barrett, *John*, 190.

21. Though in the minority, some scholars have chosen to interpret "spirit and water" as a singular means of birth from above and thus translate the phrase as something akin to "born of spiritual water." See Westcott, *John*, 108.

22. Witherington, "Waters of Birth," 156.

23. M. 'Abot 3.1; 4 Ezra 8:8; 1QH V, 13–16; Witherington, "Waters of Birth," 157–58.

24. Witherington, "Waters of Birth," 156.

divine soul would never deprecate itself by voluntarily taking on a corporeal body. To the contrary, the incarnation of Christ is the event that makes Spirit birth possible.[25] *Because of* Christ's embodied life, death, and resurrection, humans can become something more—something like Christ himself—as they partake of the new birth Jesus offers. This new birth delivers believers from the kingdom of the world to the kingdom of God, into an existence both corporeal and spiritual that begins at the moment of regeneration and extends into eternity. As Beale explains, "The idea of being 'born again' in John 3 is likely tied to the OT concept of resurrection and thus to new creation."[26] Along such lines, these new creation beings, those who believe into Christ, perceive the world differently and begin to transform it from within.

Before moving on, we should briefly address the mention of heaven in John 3. According to 3:12, Jesus is one who has ascended to and descended from heaven, and in 3:31, Jesus is one who has come from above/heaven. Hopefully we are by now aware that such references are not statements about the location of heaven; John isn't communicating that heaven is somewhere in or above the sky. Rather, Jesus' heavenly origin is a figurative way of explaining that Jesus is of a divine nature; he is different from every human who has come before him. All prophets, priests, and kings were merely human men and women; Jesus, however, is of a qualitatively different nature and origin. Indeed, the "location" of one's birth is an indicator of the manner in which one lives, speaks, and acts. Those born of the kingdom of God, the kingdom "above," practice the truth and manifest deeds wrought in God himself (3:20–21).[27]

Spirit and water again converge in John 4. Though Jesus' dialogue with the Samaritan woman seems to be, initially, about literal water, John soon reveals that the Messiah's offer goes far beyond bodily hydration. Building upon foundations established in chapter 3, Jesus communicates that eternal life in God's kingdom is available through the living water that he, himself, offers (4:14). Just as birth through water and Spirit result in eternal life in chapter 3, partaking of Jesus' living water likewise leads to eternal life in John 4.

Although water and Spirit are not explicitly equated in John 4, the themes are brought together by familiar traditions that associate living

---

25. Witherington, "Waters of Birth," 160.
26. Beale, *Union*, 70.
27. Moloney, *Belief in the Word*, 114; Jonge, *Jesus*, 161–62.

water with the eschatological age.[28] As previously discussed, the site of the narrative, Jacob's Well, may have alluded to traditions surrounding the primordial well of creation that nourished God's people.[29] Possibly upon the same well that the eschatological temple would sit and pour out living water, Jesus—the new temple—now sits. Coloe summarizes, "As Ezekiel prophesied a new Temple whose waters would overflow to bring life and healing, so Jesus, the dwelling place of God with us, is able to give waters welling up for eternal life."[30] The eschatological water that flows from the temple and the living water that flows from Christ are one and the same: the Holy Spirit—the true agent of transformation in God's creation.

Several features of John 4 hint that the eschatological age has arrived. First, Jesus' statement that "an hour is coming and now is" (4:23) indicates that the time anticipated by God's people and predicted by the prophets was at hand. According to Coloe, "In his [Jesus'] own person the dwelling place of God is being established in the midst of the people (cf. 1:14). The children of Jacob who had once been given land (Ezek 37:25) have now been given a far greater gift in the true sanctuary present in their midst."[31] Indeed, the hour has come when God's people can "worship in spirit and truth" without the intermediaries of priests, rituals, or even the Jerusalem temple (4:24).

Second, the imagery of the harvest (John 4:35) and ingathering of the nations (John 4:39–45) is a prevalent eschatological theme throughout Scripture. Numerous passages indicate that the day of the Lord's return will be a time of harvest in which God will punish the wicked, vindicate his people, regather the scattered tribes, and draw all nations to himself. Joel 3 is worth quoting at length:

> Hurry and come, all you surrounding nations,
> And gather yourselves there [to Judah].
> Bring down, Lord, Your warriors.
> Let the nations be awakened
> And come up to the Valley of Jehoshaphat [Yahweh Judges],
> For there I will sit to judge
> All the surrounding nations.
> Put in the sickle, for the harvest is ripe.

---

28. Coloe, *God Dwells with Us*, 96.
29. For previous discussion, see "Sacred Space in the Gospel of John" in ch. 3.
30. Coloe, *God Dwells with Us*, 95.
31. Coloe, *God Dwells with Us*, 112.

> Come, tread *the grapes*, for the wine press is full;
> The vats overflow, for their wickedness is great. . . .
> The Lord roars from Zion
> And utters His voice from Jerusalem,
> And the heavens and the earth quake.
> But the Lord is a refuge for His people,
> And a stronghold for the sons of Israel.
> Then you will know that I am the Lord your God,
> Dwelling on Zion, My holy mountain.
> So Jerusalem will be holy,
> And strangers will no longer pass through it.
> And on that day
> The mountains will drip with sweet wine,
> And the hills will flow with milk,
> And all the brooks of Judah will flow with water;
> And a spring will go out from the house of the Lord
> And water the Valley of Shittim. (3:11–13, 16–18 NASB, emphasis original)

The eschatological themes of nations, harvest, and God's nourishing water are all reflected in Joel 3 and many more OT and NT prophecies.[32]

Along similar lines, John 4 subtly reflects the gathering of "the nations" into the Father's house that results from the outpouring of God's Spirit/living water. That the "fields are white for harvest" is demonstrated throughout the chapter (4:35). First, Jesus ministers in Judea and baptizes his own people (4:1–3). Next, he offers living water to the Samaritans, many of whom believe (4:39–41). Finally, he heals the son of a nobleman, and the whole household places faith in Christ (4:46–53).

Whether the nobleman and his household are gentile or Jewish is impossible to know. However, as a royal official in Herod's court, the man may have been nearly as repellent as the Samaritan woman regardless of his heritage.[33] Therefore, just as Jesus breaks racial divides, he likewise destroys social divisions, a theme that is continued with the healing of the

---

32. For reaping: Isa 2:2; 24:13; 28:4; Hos 6:11; Gal 6:7–10; Rev 14:18–20; for gathering: Isa 11:11–12; 27:12; 56:1–8; 66:18; Ezek 47:22–23; Matt 24:14; 25:32; 28:19–20; Rev 21:24–26.

33. Keener, *John*, 1:630–31.

beggar in 5:1–15. As the OT prophets foretold, Jesus gathers the children of Israel *and* the nations to himself as he pours out the living water of God.

Third, John uses the uncommon verb *hallomai* to describe the welling up of living water, which is depicted as a vigorous spring (*pēgē hudatos hallomenou*, 4:14). Used only three times in the NT (John 4:14; Acts 3:8; 14:10), the term *hallomai* describes quick movement, typically with the nuance of shaking, jumping, or leaping. For example, when Paul performs a healing in Acts 14:10, the formerly lame man leaps (*hallomai*) to his feet. Similar usages are attested in the Greek OT, as in Isa 35:6 when, in the eschaton, the lame will leap (*hallomai*) like deer. Though it is tempting to make a connection between the eschatological healing prophesied in Isa 35:6 and the healing Jesus offers, *hallomai* is not used in the healing accounts of John 5 or 9. Instead, John uses the term to associate living water with the Holy Spirit. In the Greek OT, *hallomai* describes the Spirit of God coming upon Samson (Judg 14:6, 19; 15:14), Saul (1 Sam 10:10; 11:6), and David (1 Sam 16:13). Considering the uncommon nature of the term, in addition to John 4:14 being the only instance of *hallomai* applied to water, John seems to be making an intentional connection between the living water of Christ and the Spirit of God. Just as the Spirit of God rushed upon noteworthy leaders in the OT, the Spirit of Christ now wells up within those who accept his offer of living water.

While drawing a parallel, John also develops the OT imagery further. In the OT, God only granted his Spirit to certain men and women at certain moments. But through Christ, an astonishing new development takes place—the Spirit of God is now available to all people for all time. Even more shocking, as Christ's living water wells up within believers, it springs forth and begets life in others.[34]

The movement from living water in 4:14 to true worship in 4:23 is a logical progression. Greene explains, "Without the Spirit, the earthly cannot understand or enter into the heavenly realities that the Messiah inaugurates."[35] In the new eschatological age—the hour that is coming and now is (4:23)—Christ offers a new means of accessing God—the Spirit—who makes a new manner of worship possible. This true worship consists of a transformed life of loving obedience and sacrificial service—in other

---

34. Morris, *John*, 263; Osborne, *Revelation*, 738. In contrast, Beasley-Murray argues that only the individual's possession of the life that Jesus offers is in view, as opposed to the theory that believers share the life with others; Beasley-Murray, *John*, 61.

35. Greene, "Jesus as Heavenly Temple," 438. Cf. DeSilva, *New Testament*, 430.

words, "the total orientation of one's life and action toward the Father," which is impossible apart from the indwelling presence of the Spirit.[36]

The imagery of water and Spirit in John 4 is clarified further in John 7, which is set during the Feast of Tabernacles, or *Sukkot*. Though we discussed the festival in a prior chapter, essential concepts will be repeated for the sake of clarity. *Sukkot* was a sacred holiday that commemorated God's provision and protection in the wilderness. The festival also anticipated a future time of prosperity in which all nations would be gathered toward Jerusalem and experience Edenic blessings.[37] Such expectations were rooted in the belief that the temple was the center of the earth and the point of connection with heaven. Reubenstein explains, "Israelite myth viewed the temple as *axis mundi* and the foundation of cosmic order, as located above the subterranean waters and as the ultimate source of fertility. The cult actualized those powers through ritual, tapping the temple's resources and bringing blessing and fertility to the land itself."[38]

The water libation ceremony during *Sukkot* tapped into the power of the primordial waters under the temple. Each morning of the seven-day festival, priests proceeded to the pool of Siloam, from which they would draw water. Upon returning to the temple, the priest carrying the water would pour the water upon the altar "to recall God's miraculous provision in the wilderness, to ask God to provide rain for the year, and to anticipate God's final abundant provision in the eschaton."[39] More specifically, tradition held that "the libation descended through channels beneath the altar, stimulated the waters, and set in motion processes which led to the refertilization of nature."[40]

Numerous OT prophecies likewise drew upon the tradition of primordial waters beneath the temple and were, thus, closely associated with *Sukkot* and the end-time outpouring of the Spirit. Passages such as Ezek 47:1–12, discussed above, likely inform John's narrative in chapter 7. Ezek 47:1–12, which typifies many biblical and extra-biblical expectations, describes the eschatological river that flows *from the temple* and

---

36. Moloney, *John*, 129.

37. Zech 14:16–19; Isa 2:2–4; 56:6–8; cf. Brown, *John I–XII*, 326; Coloe, *God Dwells with Us*, 121; Hoskins, *Jesus as Fulfillment*, 163–64; Reubenstein, "Sukkot," 185–86.

38. Reubenstein, "Sukkot," 189. Cf. Barker, *Gate of Heaven*, 18.

39. Greene, "Jesus as Heavenly Temple," 440. Cf. m. Sukkah 4.9–10; Coloe, *God Dwells with Us*, 121; Charlesworth, "Dead Sea Scrolls," 76.

40. Reubenstein, "Sukkot," 183.

revivifies the barren land and the people that live upon it. Manning offers a thoughtful explanation:

> For Ezekiel, water used in the Temple cult came to symbolize moral and spiritual cleansing, and thus God's promise to give his Spirit. Water was also a symbol of God's abundant provision, and especially of his ability to re-create and heal, as in the river from the Temple. The image of the river from the Temple appears to combine these ideas: water comes from God's presence, purifying, healing, and bringing life to the land and its people. Like Ezekiel's other symbols, water communicates both outward physical restoration of the land as well as a spiritual transformation of the people.[41]

Such symbolism is the background upon which John overlays the words of Jesus in chapter 7. In 7:37–38, Jesus offers, "If anyone should thirst, let them come to me and drink. The one who believes in me, just as the Scripture says, rivers of living water will flow from within them." As the passage continues, John explains Jesus' words: "But this he spoke concerning the Spirit, whom those believing in him were to receive" (7:39a). Whereas the correlation of living water with the Spirit had only been implied in John 4, the link is made explicit in John 7. Similarly, whereas the eschatological elements of living water were only hinted at in John 4, the setting of John 7—during *Sukkot*—clarifies that Jesus' offer of living water includes the end-time outpouring of the Spirit.[42]

Thus, as Jesus replaces the temple as the source of living water, he likewise replaces the water rituals associated with the cult.[43] Through the Spirit, Jesus offers a cleansing more complete than any ritual; he offers life-giving nourishment more effective than any water libation ceremony could call forth; he offers access to God that quenches the deepest thirst of the human soul. Every source of earthly water is impotent compared to the live-giving water offered by Christ.[44] As such, living water—the Spirit of God—is effectual in the present, yet also mediates blessings of the age

---

41. Manning, *Echoes of a Prophet*, 182.

42. Keener, *John*, 1:722.

43. Biblical scholars commonly refer to the OT temple system as the "cult." Such usage is a convenient way to encapsulate the priestly duties and ritual practices of ancient Israel. It does not carry the modern nuance of religious fanatics who drink poisoned Kool-Aid.

44. Keener, *John*, 1:604; Michaels, *John*, 70; Moloney, *Signs and Shadows*, 86.

to come.⁴⁵ As the Spirit nourishes, cleanses, and heals those who believe into Christ, they begin to experience the blessings of the eschaton.⁴⁶ And those who are in Christ likewise become fountains of the Spirit, spreading God's life-giving presence to all creation.

After chapter 7, John's discussion of the Spirit recedes until the Farewell Discourse (John 14–17), and the water theme doesn't reappear until John 19. We will therefore conclude this section with Spirit and water in chapters 19–20, then deal with the Farewell Discourse in the following section.

In chapter 19, John narrates the crucifixion and death of Christ. As the Messiah suffers upon the cross, he utters the words "I am thirsty" (19:28). In a moment of the most extreme irony imaginable, the one who offers living water is unable or unwilling to quench his own thirst. Yet only by experiencing the weakness of humanity can Christ pour out living water upon those who would follow him.⁴⁷ As he suffers both physical and spiritual thirst, Christ bears the sins of his people upon the cross; as his body is torn, he tears away the veil that separates God's children from their Father. And as he enters the realm of death he "releases the living water that will become a spring welling up to eternal life."⁴⁸ And indeed, both water and blood pour from Christ—blood to atone for sin and water to provide new life (19:34).

As Jesus dies, he gives the Spirit of God to his people. However, the translation of John 19:30 somewhat obscures this momentous event. According to most translations, as Jesus died, he "gave up his spirit."⁴⁹ Other, less literal, translations indicate that "he gave up his life."⁵⁰ Indeed, the words are often understood as a reference to Jesus' death.

Though Jesus does, in fact, perish, two factors render this interpretation of 19:30 unlikely. First, in the Greek, Jesus does not give up *his* spirit. He gives up *the* Spirit. As Spirit (*pneuma*) is preceded by the definite article—the—rather than a third person pronoun—he—Jesus gives *the Spirit*, not his personal life force. Second, the act of *giving* the Spirit is not a euphemism for death. Rather, in using *paradidōmi*, John makes

---

45. Hoskins, *Jesus as Fulfillment*, 167.
46. Greene, "Jesus as Heavenly Temple," 438.
47. Culpepper, "Johannine Passion," 33.
48. Culpepper, "Reading Johannine Irony," 204.
49. See ASV, AMP, CSV, ESV, GNT, HCSB, NASB, NET, NIV, NLT, NRSV, RSV.
50. See CEB, CEV, GW, NLV.

a "deliberate choice" to use a verb that refers to handing over, entrusting, or bequeathing.[51] In other words, Jesus doesn't give up his life, he entrusts the Holy Spirit to his followers. Keener notes, "Jesus gives up his *pneuma* so that now his *pneuma* may be multiplied and available to his followers as he had promised."[52] In doing so he has perfectly completed (*tetelestai*) the task given to him by the Father as well as the entire plan of redemption. According to Malina and Rohrbaugh, "In this scene specifically, it is the spirit given by the glorified Jesus that was the outcome of Israel's Scripture, the reality it was intended to realize. Thus, what pious Pharisees sought in vain by their holiness concerns, and what devoted priestly ranks sought to no avail by their temple ceremonies and rituals, Jesus effects as he is lifted up and exalted."[53]

The final mention of the Holy Spirit occurs in John 20:22. In this chapter, the risen Jesus returns to his disciples, who, despite the comforting words Jesus offered prior to his departure (John 14–17), are hiding behind locked doors in fear (20:19). Though Jesus' appearance brings great joy, the Messiah hasn't returned simply to celebrate. As he breathes upon his disciples, the Lord says, "Receive the Holy Spirit" (John 20:22b).

The short phrase prompts two closely related points of discussion. First, Jesus' words should never be understood in isolation from the first nineteen chapters of John. When Jesus breathes the Holy Spirit upon his followers, John's audience should immediately recall the Spirit baptism offered in chapter 1, the new birth offered to Nicodemus, the living water offered to the Samaritans, and the Spirit-mediated blessings of the eschatological age offered during *Sukkot*. Whereas in John 7:39 "the Spirit was not yet *given*, because Jesus was not yet glorified," in 20:22 Jesus' work is complete.[54]

Though the gift of the Holy Spirit is personal in nature, John 20:22 should also recall the cosmic scope of God's life-giving Spirit. In Gen 1:2, God's Spirit hovers over the waters and imparts life to creation, and

---

51. Moloney, *Glory Not Dishonor*, 146. Cf. Friedrich Büschsel, "*Paradidōmi*," *TDNT*, 2:169–72; Coloe, *God Dwells with Us*, 189; Moloney, "Johannine Passion," 44; Moloney, *John*, 508–9.

52. Keener, *John*, 2:1149. Keener suggests that the phrase may be yet another instance of Johannine double meaning; i.e., the phrase indicates that Jesus dies *and* passes on his spirit. Cf. Brown, *John XIII–XXI*, 931; Culpepper, "Johannine Passion," 34.

53. Malina and Rohrbaugh, *John*, 271.

54. Domeris, "Paraclete," 20; Jobes, *John*, 290; Moloney, *John*, 532.

in Gen 2:7, God breathes life into humanity. Much later, Ezekiel relays a prophecy that God will one day breathe new life into his people, a prophecy that is fulfilled in Christ's resurrection and completed in the future resurrection of all God's people (Ezek 37:1–14). Manning explains, "John begins and ends with Jesus as the source of life, the agent of the first creation and the new creation."[55]

Second, Jesus' gift of the Spirit in 20:22 has a missional focus. As Jesus breathes into his followers, they are called to convey the Spirit of God to the ends of the earth. Such a focus is confirmed by the lines that bookend the giving of the Spirit. First, Jesus says, "As the Father has sent me, so also I am sending you" (20:21); and immediately after breathing upon the disciples, Jesus says, "If you forgive anyone's sins, their sins are forgiven; if you do not forgive them, they are not forgiven" (20:23). Through the power of the Spirit, the disciples are called to be to the world what Jesus was to them. As Jesus brought both forgiveness and judgment, the disciples will now do likewise. Just as the Spirit of God empowered Jesus during his earthly ministry, he empowers those who believe into Christ—those who will carry on his mission.[56]

The missional focus also explains why the giving of the Spirit is relayed twice—first in 19:30 and again in 20:22. Jesus first *gifts* the Spirit to his followers and, second, *commissions* them to reach beyond the community of faith into the world. Maloney clarifies,

> There are not two "gifts of the Spirit." As there is only one hour of Jesus, there is only one Spirit given to the members of the community (19:30) so that they might be witnesses to Jesus (20:22). At the hour of the cross and resurrection, Jesus pours down the Spirit into its members so that they might be in the world as he was in the world (20:22). The oneness of the hour and all that is achieved by and through it is nowhere clearer to the reader than in these two episodes that take place at the hour: the founding gift of the Spirit (19:30; see 14:16–17) and the commissioning of the disciples who have been with him from the beginning to be his witnesses empowered by the Spirit (20:22; see 15:26–27).[57]

In short, as Jesus *comes* to his disciples in the form of the Spirit, he simultaneously commissions them to *go* forth.

---

55. Manning, *Echoes of a Prophet*, 167. Cf. Jobes, *John*, 290.
56. Beale, *Union*, 11.
57. Moloney, *Glory Not Dishonor*, 172. Cf. Culpepper, "Johannine Passion," 23.

To conclude, imagery and dialogue throughout the Gospel have progressively equipped readers to understand the giving of the Spirit. The opening chapters of John all feature water in prominent dialogues. In chapter 1, John the Baptist baptizes with water, but Jesus baptizes with the Spirit (1:26–34). In chapter 3 Jesus tells Nicodemus that he must be born of water and Spirit to enter God's kingdom (3:3–5). In chapter 4, Jesus offers living water that grants eternal life while anticipating worship in Spirit and truth (4:13–24). By chapter 7, readers should be prepared to understand that Jesus' offer of living water actually points to the indwelling presence of the Spirit of God (7:37–39). Such an offer is fulfilled when Jesus gives up his Spirit upon the cross (19:30) and then rises again to breathe the Spirit into his disciples (20:22). The living water of Christ, poured out upon and welling up within the disciples, will be the channel through which blessings flow to all of creation.

Spirit and Paraclete in the Farewell Discourse

The teaching on the Spirit in John 14–16 is distinct from the rest of John and, in fact, distinct from the rest of the NT. The imagery of water fades into the background as a different facet of the Spirit comes to the fore. Rather than a breath, wind, or stream of water, the Spirit of God is introduced as a personal entity, an intimate counselor: the Paraclete.[58] Referenced only five times in Scripture, the "Paraclete" is unique to Johannine literature.[59]

Although the noun *paraklētos* is rare in the Bible, the verbal form is quite common; *parakaleō* can refer to the action of summoning, inviting, imploring, urging, exhorting, advocating, mediating, or comforting.[60] With such a broad range of meaning, determining the precise nature of the nominal form, *paraklētos*, depends heavily upon context.

In the first century, *paraklētos* often referred to "a person who came to one's aid in a situation of judgment, such as a court of law, either as counsel at law or as a friendly witness."[61] Yet, such a technical definition doesn't cohere with the context of John 14. As a result, different scholars suggest different aspects of the term are primary in the Farewell

---

58. Brown, "Paraclete," 124.
59. John 14:16, 26; 15:26; 16:7; 1 John 2:1.
60. Otto Schmitz, "*Parakaleō*," *TDNT*, 5:773–814.
61. Jobes, *John*, 229.

Discourse. For example, Jobes posits that the nuance of comfort is dominant, and Hoeck suggests mediation.[62] Brown, however, offers a different perspective. He writes, "The concept of the Paraclete, like love, is a many-splendoured thing: the Paraclete is a *witness* in defense of Jesus and a *spokesman* for him in the context of the trial of Jesus by his enemies; the Paraclete is a *consoler* of the disciples; more important, he is their teacher and guide and thus, in an extended sense, their *helper*. No one translation captures the complexity of these functions."[63] As no single word adequately translates the term, Brown suggests that the best option is to retain the transliteration "Paraclete" and remain mindful of the manifold functions it encompasses.[64]

In addition to a lexical explanation of *paraklētos*, a more thorough understanding of his role can be achieved through the identity of Christ. In fact, some scholars refer to the Paraclete as the "alter ego" of Jesus.[65] Hoeck explains, "The ministry of the Spirit in the life-giving mission of Jesus is so inextricable, that there exists a 'linking' or 'tandem' relationship between the two, even to the point where Christ at times appears to replace the Holy Spirit in key places within the Fourth Gospel, e.g. in the prologue: here the *logos* becomes the prime agent in creation as opposed to the Spirit of God, who hovers over the face of the abyss in Gen 1."[66]

In addition, both the Gospel of John and 1 John indicate that *Jesus* is the first Paraclete.[67] According to 1 John 2:1b, "If anyone should sin, we have a Paraclete before the Father, Jesus Christ the righteous one." In John 14:16, Jesus says, "I will ask the Father, and he will give you *another* Paraclete" (emphasis mine), implying that Jesus was the first. Hoeck, again, explains, "The Spirit should be seen as the continuing presence of Jesus with his disciples, empowering them to continue to do the same works as he did during his earthly ministry."[68]

Indeed, that which Jesus does during his earthly ministry the Paraclete does in, with, and through the disciples.[69] Just as Jesus abides with

---

62. Jobes, *John*, 230; Hoeck, "Johannine Paraclete," 25.
63. Brown, "Paraclete," 118 (emphasis original).
64. Brown, "Paraclete," 119.
65. Shillington, "Spirit-Paraclete," 31–39.
66. Hoeck, "Johannine Paraclete," 29–30, 30n17.
67. Shillington, "Spirit-Paraclete," 35; Domeris, "Paraclete," 21.
68. Hoeck, "Johannine Paraclete," 27. Cf. Pryor, "Jesus and Israel," 211–12.
69. Brown, "Paraclete," 126.

his followers, the Spirit likewise remains with them.[70] Just as the world does not know or accept Jesus, the world does not know or recognize the Spirit.[71] Just as Jesus teaches his followers, the Spirit teaches all things.[72] Just as Jesus reveals the truth, the Spirit testifies to all truth.[73] Just as Jesus bears witness about God, the Spirit bears witness about Christ.[74] Just as Jesus convicts the world of righteousness and judgment, the Spirit judges the world.[75] According to Brown, "This detailed parallelism between the ministry of the Paraclete and the ministry of Jesus is too exact to be coincidental. As 'another Paraclete', the Paraclete is, as it were, another Jesus. . . . Since the Paraclete can come only when Jesus departs, the Paraclete is the presence of Jesus when Jesus is absent."[76]

At the same time, the Paraclete carries on the ministry of Christ in distinct ways. Most significantly, he amplifies the work of Christ. Through the indwelling presence of the Spirit-Paraclete, believers are empowered to do even greater works than Christ himself (14:12). Just as the prophets of the OT were imbued with the Spirit of God to proclaim the word of God in their own culture, Christ followers now play a similar Spirit-filled role in the latter days.[77]

The theme of Jesus passing on the torch to his followers likewise reflects OT patterns. Brown points out that the relationship in which one leader dies and another carries on his work "is exemplified in the Moses/Joshua and the Elijah/Elisha pattern. The secondary figure in each case is closely patterned on the first so that Joshua is another Moses . . . and Elisha is another Elijah. . . . So also we shall see that the Paraclete is closely patterned on Jesus. The concept of the spirit is not divorced from this relationship: Deut xxxiv. 9 describes Joshua as filled with the *spirit* of wisdom when Moses lays hands upon him, and Elisha receives a double share of Elijah's *spirit* (II Kings ii. 9, 15)."[78] In a similar manner, Jesus passes his Spirit to the disciples, equipping them to carry forth his

---

70. John 1:37–39; 4:40; 14:20, 23; 15:4–5; 17:23, 26.
71. John 5:43; 8:14; 12:48; 16:3.
72. John 3:2; 6:59; 7:14; 14:25–26.
73. John 1:14; 14:6, 17; 16:13.
74. John 3:11; 5:36; 15:26.
75. John 7:23; 16:8–9; 20:22–23.
76. Brown, "Paraclete," 128. Cf. Hoeck, "Johannine Paraclete," 27.
77. Brown, "Paraclete," 120–21.
78. Brown, "Paraclete," 120.

mission and message. Yet, the OT pattern is amplified as Jesus passes on his Spirit not to a single successor, but whosoever should place faith in him. Along such lines, the Paraclete magnifies the teaching of Christ by helping believers internalize, apply, and share Jesus' message. Each generation is equipped afresh to interpret the events of their time in the light of Jesus and his mission (16:12–14).[79] As such, life in the Spirit is a reality that should lead to complete transformation and radical obedience. For believers, "Jesus is not a mere memory but a real presence for the performance of faith in the midst of adversity."[80]

Finally, to a greater magnitude than Christ himself, the Spirit-Paraclete confronts the world through those who bear God's presence. According to John 16:8–11, "When [the Paraclete] comes, he will convict the world concerning sin and righteousness and judgment; concerning sin, because they do not believe in me; and concerning righteousness, because I am going to the Father, and you will no longer see me; and concerning judgment, because the ruler of this world has been judged." The Spirit's abiding presence within *all* of God's people proves that the prince of the world has been defeated. As the Spirit-Paraclete leads God's people "into all truth" (16:13), he empowers them to see reality, both the truths of God and the lies of the devil.[81] In doing so, he protects the people of God from deception, strengthens them in the face of persecution, and empowers them to boldly speak the truth of the gospel. And, thus, through the saints, the Paraclete convicts the world of sin, righteousness, and judgment.

Spirit and Paraclete in John 14

John never describes the departure and death of Jesus in isolation, but rather "as a part of the total event which includes resurrection and ascension."[82] In 14:3, Jesus says, "And if I should go and prepare a place for you, I will come again and receive you to myself, that where I am also you will be," and in 16:7, he says, "But I tell you the truth, it is to your advantage that I go away; for if I do not go away, the Paraclete will not

---

79. Brown, "Paraclete," 129; Hoeck, "Johannine Paraclete," 35–37; Shillington, "Spirit-Paraclete," 36.

80. Shillington, "Spirit-Paraclete," 35. Cf. DeSilva, *New Testament*, 431.

81. Draper, "Sociological Function of the Spirit," 22–23.

82. Holwerda, *Holy Spirit*, 21.

come to you; but if I should go, I will send him to you." The references to the Paraclete in the Farewell Discourse thus emphasize that the departure of Christ is an essential precursor to his return in a manner that will empower his followers to a greater degree than before.[83] Brown affirms, "It is scarcely an accident that the Paraclete is mentioned in John only in the last discourse as part of Jesus' farewell to his disciples. This setting reinforces the connexion between the departure of Jesus and the coming of the Paraclete."[84]

The verb used to describe Jesus' return in John 14:3 is *erchomai*, one of the most common verbs in the NT.[85] McCaffrey argues that the term is used characteristically of the parousia—the second coming of Christ.[86] However, *erchomai* is such a common verb that his argument lacks firm textual support. While the "return" *may* refer to the parousia as McCaffrey and many others suggest,[87] some interpret the "return" as the coming of the Paraclete,[88] the coming of Jesus to the disciples at the time of their deaths,[89] or the recurring "coming" of Jesus' presence during worship "in the Spirit."[90] Jesus' return could also be viewed as his post-resurrection appearances, but few scholars favor this option. Westcott offers a way forward with his proposal that 14:3 predicts all forms of Jesus' return: the resurrection, the parousia, the coming of the Spirit, and Jesus' coming to believers at their time of death.[91] Nonetheless, Westcott's approach is a bit too broadsided. The eschatology of John allows for both a present and a future aspect but not necessarily everything in between.

Although the language used to describe Jesus' return, "I will come again" (*palin erchomai*), is in the present tense, the words express a future

83. Shillington, "Spirit-Paraclete," 34.

84. Brown, "Paraclete," 114.

85. The verb appears 634 times in the NT and around 1,200 times in the LXX; McCaffrey, *House*, 110n1.

86. McCaffrey, *House*, 40.

87. Beasley-Murray, *John*, 250; Blomberg, *Historical Reliability*, 198; Carson, *John*, 488; Jonge, *Jesus*, 173–74; Holwerda, *Holy Spirit and Eschatology*, 84; Köstenberger, *Encountering John*, 427; Michaels, *John*, 771–72; Moloney, *Glory Not Dishonor*, 34; Morris, *John*, 568; Whitacre, *John*, 348.

88. Becker, "Die Abschiedsreden Jesu," 222–28; Bultmann, *Theology of the New Testament*, 2:57; Dodd, *Interpretation*, 395; Keener, *John*, 1:299; Santos, "Jesus," 49–70; Schnackenburg, *John*, 59.

89. Lightfoot, *John*, 275–76.

90. Aune, *Cultic Setting*, 129.

91. Westcott, *John*, 2:168. Cf. Barrett, *John*, 381–82.

sense in both English and Greek.⁹² The future tense of the subsequent phrase, "I will receive you to myself," also reinforces the future sense of the verse. As a result, many scholars, as noted above, read in John 14:2–3 a promise of Jesus' end-time eschatological return. Studied in the wider context of John's Gospel, vv. 2–3 do *seem* to imply a future eschatological paradigm. Within the context of the Farewell Discourse, however, such an interpretation does not adequately consider the correlation between the departure of Christ and return of the Spirit-Paraclete.⁹³

Chapters 14 and 16 both indicate that the return of Christ is an imminent event that will impact the lives and ministries of the disciples, as well as Jesus' ongoing relationship with them. In chapter 14, the references to departure and return are closely related to the theme of believing in Jesus: the "going" and "coming" of vv. 2–9 are bookended by the exhortations to believe in vv. 1 and 10–11. In short, the discourse promises "Jesus' return to those, and only those, who believe in him."⁹⁴ When Jesus returns, he returns *to his followers* as the Spirit-Paraclete, whom he has given throughout the process of being crucified, glorified, and resurrected (19:30; 20:22).⁹⁵ Though his return was future-oriented when he first promised to "come again," the promise becomes a present reality for the disciples and for all who place faith in Christ post-Calvary.

Supporting the thesis that the return, or "coming," of Christ in 14:3 is accomplished through the Spirit is the proximate discussion of the Paraclete in 14:16–18. Those who have placed faith in Christ will not be abandoned as orphans (14:18) but rather will experience the continuing presence of God in Christ through the Spirit-Paraclete. Through the Paraclete "believers are already receiving the living, indwelling source of love and wisdom by which they recognize and accomplish the Father's will."⁹⁶ Even believers living in the centuries after Christ's death and resurrection are no further removed from Jesus' power and guidance "because the Paraclete dwells within [them] just as he dwelt within the first generation."⁹⁷ Therefore, Christ's promised "return" in John 14 (14:3, 18,

---

92. *Erchomai* in the present tense with a future sense is common in John; see 1:15, 30; 4:21, 23, 25, 28; 14:18, 28; 16:2, 13, 25; Beasley-Murray, *John*, 249–50.

93. Keener, *John*, 2:932; Brown, *John XIII–XXI*, 626; Schnackenburg, *John*, 62.

94. Segovia, "Structure," 478–79.

95. Brown, "Paraclete," 128.

96. Reese, "Literary Structure," 326.

97. Brown, "Paraclete," 129.

22–23) does not refer to an eschatological second coming, but an immediate experience for all who follow the risen Messiah.[98]

Spirit and Paraclete in John 16

The promises of chapter 16 are helpful in deciphering those of chapter 14. Whereas the message that Jesus conveys in 14 is a matter of debate, scholars generally agree that 16:5–14 describes the giving of the Spirit. Yet, the strikingly similar terminology of "knowing" (*ginōskō*; 14:7, 17; 16:3), "going" (*aperchomai, poreuomai*; 14:2–5, 12, 28; 16:7), "coming" (*erchomai*; 14:3, 6, 18, 23, 28; 16:7), "believing" (*pisteuō*; 14:1, 10–12; 16:9), and "seeing" (*theōreō*; 14:9, 17, 19; 16:16–19) creates an intertextual link that is difficult to deny. In language heavily reminiscent of chapter 14, John gives close attention to the presence of the Spirit among the followers of Christ.[99] In other words, chapter 16 clarifies that Jesus' promised return in chapter 14 is accomplished through the Spirit-Paraclete.

The most difficult nuance of interpreting the return of Christ as the Spirit-Paraclete is the "seeing" in 14:19 and 16:16–19. In both passages, Jesus indicates that in "a little while you will not see me, and then after a little while you will see me again." If Christ returns in the form of the Spirit-Paraclete, how precisely will believers be able to *see* him? Two avenues of interpretation offer an easy, yet contextually inconsistent, solution. First, Christ could be referring to his parousia, or second coming, when all peoples will see the Messiah return in glory. Unfortunately, such an interpretation disregards the immediate context in which Jesus was encouraging his disciples. The promise of a return in the eschaton would have been small comfort in the face of the inevitable persecution they would face for following an executed criminal. Keener explains that although the time frame Jesus describes—"in that day" (14:20; 16:23)—can carry eschatological connotations, the primary emphasis of the passage remains upon the immediate future in which Jesus imparts the Spirit.[100] Though the notion of seeing Christ at his second coming may be a subtle undercurrent of John 14 and 16, the disciples to whom Jesus spoke did not, in fact, "see" his second coming during their lifetime.

---

98. Malina and Rohrbaugh, *John*, 231–32.
99. Malina and Rohrbaugh, *John*, 241.
100. Keener, *John*, 2:974.

Second, Christ could have been referring to his immediate post-resurrection appearances. Yet, again, such a promise, even after being fulfilled, would offer little substantive encouragement or aid to the disciples since Jesus did not remain with them bodily. Instead, the promise not to leave them "as orphans" implies a long-term relationship of mutual fellowship.

Jesus himself provides a solution to the dilemma of "seeing." In John 16:25, he explains that he has been speaking *figuratively*. As such, interpreters should have no problem regarding the "seeing" as a figurative reference to experiencing the presence of the Spirit-Paraclete. Just as the ascent/descent of Christ isn't a spatial reference but a statement of Christ's divine identity and relationship with the Father, the "seeing" isn't a physical but a relational experience. In sum, upon resurrection Jesus returns to impart his Spirit to believers, effectively continuing his relationship with them.[101] The point John strives to make is that Jesus comes again to offer "an intimacy even greater in the Spirit than the one possible when Jesus was still physically among his earthly followers."[102]

Converging Streams

Our examination of the Farewell Discourse has revealed that in John 14, Jesus promises to return to his followers in the form of the Spirit-Paraclete. As Shillington points out, "In John there is little mention of a future apocalyptic return of Jesus to rescue his own from the judgment to fall on the world. Instead, Jesus comes back to his own in the form of the Spirit-Paraclete, enabling them to face the trials of life through which they must surely pass, as Jesus did during his lifetime."[103] Indeed, John never even narrates Jesus' ascension to heaven, emphasizing the presence of the Messiah with his people. Further, Jesus' return is actualized in the giving of the Spirit in 19:30 and 20:22.

Yet, considering the larger context of the Gospel, i.e., John's use of living water imagery and his propensity for double meaning, we should likely see an eschatological element in the text. Although the Spirit-Paraclete is primary in John 14–16, the recurring theme of living water throughout the Gospel points to the end-time outpouring of God's Spirit upon his people, an event which is accompanied by the eschatological blessings of

---

101. Bultmann, *Theology of the New Testament*, 2:57; Dodd, *Interpretation*, 395.
102. Köstenberger, *Encountering John*, 155.
103. Shillington, "Spirit-Paraclete," 35. Cf. Keener, *John*, 2:973–74.

a renewed creation filled with God's presence. More specifically, the sending of the Spirit in John 14 is the fulfillment of the Spirit baptism promised in 1:32–34 and "the realization of the 'new birth' by which fleshly human beings can enter into their new inheritance as children of God (John 1:12–13; 3:3–8)."[104] No longer would God's people be enslaved to the kingdom of the devil, and the Spirit-Paraclete would empower them to walk according to the ways of their new "place" of residence.

In addition, the return of Christ as Spirit-Paraclete sets the precedent for Jesus' future coming in the parousia.[105] As Holwerda emphasizes, John's eschatology demands a "final manifestation of Christ's victory over Satan."[106] Indeed, numerous verses identify the Spirit as a "promise." Second Cor 1:21–22 reads, "Now the one who establishes us with you in Christ and anointed us is God, who also sealed us and gave the promise (*arrabōn*) of the Spirit in our hearts."[107] Interestingly, the promissory term used by Paul (*arrabōn*) can be translated literally as "first installment," implying that believers are awaiting a second, or final, installment that is yet to come.[108] In other words, the first installment consists of the Paraclete, while the second installment, Christ's eschatological return, has yet to occur. Stagg sums up by explaining that "John's eschatology allows for present realization and future consummation."[109]

Ever since the prologue, John has been leading his readers down a road of redemption and resurrection that culminates in God's presence.[110] In 1:32 the Spirit comes to rest upon Jesus and abide with him, in chapters 14 and 16, the Messiah promises to return and abide with his disciples in the form of the Spirit-Paraclete, and in chapters 19 and 20 he fulfills such a promise. Pryor explains,

> The disciples were conscious of a new relationships with God by the presence of the Spirit in their lives, and this Spirit awareness was also felt to be the Spirit of Jesus, his ongoing presence with them. Yet at the same time there was an element of

---

104. DeSilva, *New Testament*, 431.

105. Segovia argues that the resurrection appearances of Christ are a temporary precedent for the more permanent indwelling of the spirit. Segovia, "Structure," 486n47.

106. Holwerda, *Holy Spirit and Eschatology*, 85.

107. Cf. 2 Cor 5:5; Eph 1:13; 4:30.

108. "*Arrabōn*," *L&N* 57.170.

109. Stagg, "Farewell Discourses," 465. Cf. McCaffrey, *House*, 40.

110. Wright, *Resurrection*, 447; Brown, "Paraclete," 127.

incompleteness and anticipation in it all—indeed the present experience only received its meaning in the light of the fulfilment yet to come. Thus, while the Father and the Son came to dwell (*menein*) with the disciples while they were still "in the world", this present dwelling is but an anticipation of the fuller, the perfected indwelling yet to be.[111]

In short, John's narrative doesn't lead to heaven, but to life in the presence of God. Initially, Jesus gives new Spirit-filled life to those who believe into him, and later, Christ will return bodily to resurrect his people. Though Jesus' promise to return is fulfilled in part through the Paraclete, the presence of the Spirit in the life of the believer is assurance that Jesus will return again and consummate the work that was begun at Calvary.

In the meantime, however, believers are called to partner with Christ in his cruciform mission. In his embodied, human form, Christ could not be with all of his people at all times. Thus, his departure is of benefit to his followers; Jesus explains, "But I tell you the truth, it is to your advantage that I go away; for if I do not go away, the Paraclete will not come to you; but if I should go, I will send him to you" (16:7). Through coming again as the Paraclete, Christ makes possible a more perfect co-abiding—one in which every believer can personally experience the presence of God and the empowering of the Spirit.[112]

Unfortunately, the identity and function of the Spirit has been diminished, if unintentionally, in many strands of Christian belief. It is, thus, no surprise that when Jesus promises to return in the form of the Spirit, his return is interpreted as something else—anything else. Replacing the embodied Christ with a disembodied babysitter seems like a considerable downgrade. Or, perhaps, some believers avoid a Spirit-led life because the Spirit seemingly manifests only as a bizarre supernatural force that induces verbal outbursts and physical expressions in charismatic church services. Certainly, the church, as a whole, needs to recover a more balanced, biblical understanding of God's Spirit. The point here, however, is that Jesus' promised return in the form of the Spirit-Paraclete should be an impetus for great joy, a stimulus for deeper abiding, and a motivation to take part in Christ's redemptive work in the world.

---

111. Pryor, "Jesus and Israel," 211–12.
112. DeSilva, *New Testament*, 431.

7.

The End of the Road

WE'VE ARRIVED AT THE end of the road. As our journey comes to a conclusion, I hope you've arrived with a new or renewed perspective on John 14 and the afterlife.

I have proposed that Christ's message in John 14 is one of exhortation, by which the Lord urges his followers to emulate his pattern of obedience to the Father. As Christ *walked* in obedience, he modeled a new *halakah*—one based on personal, relational faith. I've argued that specific themes throughout the Gospel support such an interpretation by providing an interpretive matrix for Jesus' teaching in John 14. These themes include mutual indwelling (or abiding), the law as embodied and modeled by Christ, Christ as sacrificial lamb and means of atonement, Christ as a new locus of sacred space, and the accessibility of sacred space through the work of Christ. Because Christ abides in the Father in perfect obedience, he opens the door for all people to enter the Father's household; and through his death and resurrection, Jesus returns in the form of the Spirit-Paraclete to empower God's children to follow a new *halakah*, thus spreading the life-giving presence of God throughout the earth.

In this brief concluding chapter we will return to where we started and examine several passages that inform our understanding of the afterlife while also supporting our interpretation of John 14. Along the way, I will summarize our conclusions from the entirety of the book and offer final thoughts.

Is Heaven for Real?

In chapter 1, we concluded that Christianity is and has always been a resurrection movement. From its birth out of Judaism and onward, the promise of life after death has consisted of an embodied existence in a restored creation in the presence of God. As such, John directs the attention of his readers not to the heavenly realm but to Jesus himself. The great hope in the Gospel of John, and the Christian faith, is not "heaven," but eternity in the presence of God.

Though an intermediate paradise does seem to exist, the exact relationship between paradise/heaven, earth, and the redeemed creation is not clearly outlined by the biblical authors.[1] Likely, our finite human minds simply can't comprehend the complex manner in which God's "space" overlaps with our own. Wright proposes, "What we are encouraged to grasp precisely through the ascension itself is that God's space and ours—heaven and earth, in other words—are, though very different, not far away from each other. . . . God's space and ours interlock and intersect in a whole variety of ways even while they retain, for the moment at least, their separate and distinct identities and roles."[2] As the first fruits of the resurrection (1 Cor 15:20–23), Jesus binds together heaven and earth; even when he is on earth he is in "heaven" because he bears the presence of God.[3] As a result, those who abide in Christ also have access to the Father. And though God's space is not completely separated from humanity, for the moment, it remains distinct until the future return of Christ fuses the two domains fully.

More than a spatial domain, "heaven" is a relational space in which God and his people mutually abide.[4] Allen suggests that "the language of 'heaven' speaks to God's special presence amidst creation. . . . It involves not only the divine life but also the eternal reality turned into the creaturely realm in grace and mercy."[5] The first portrait of such a "space" in the Bible is Gen 1–3, in which the Father dwells in his "very good" creation with his "very good" people (Gen 1:31).[6] Yet, even after the fall,

---

1. Luke 23:43; Acts 3:20–21; 2 Cor 5:8; 12:4.
2. Wright, *Surprised by Hope*, 116.
3. Black, "Johannine Rhetoric," 228–29; Stagg, "Farewell Discourses," 464.
4. Wright, *Surprised by Hope*, 151. Cf. 1 Pet 1; Matt 6:20; 19:21; Luke 12:21; 1 Tim 6:19.
5. Allen, *Grounded in Heaven*, 92.
6. McCaffrey, *House*, 55.

God's people are not directed toward a supernatural dwelling but the promised land:

> For the Lord your God is bringing you into a good land; a land with brooks of water, fountains and deep springs flowing into valleys and hills; a land of wheat and barley, of vines and fig trees and pomegranates, a land of olive oil and honey; a land in which you will eat of its provision without scarcity. You will not lack anything in it; a land whose stones are iron, and from its hills you will dig copper. (Deut 8:7–9)[7]

The depiction of the promised land bears distinctly paradisal imagery. The lush vegetation is reminiscent of a garden, the presence of water is evocative of the Spirit of God, and the unlimited supply of food parallels the abundant provision in Eden.

As time passed and Israel/Judah failed to take full possession of their inheritance, the hope of a future promised land, or prepared place, became a symbol of eschatological restoration.[8] As such, when Jesus promises that he has prepared a place, he doesn't point to a heavenly mansion but to the fulfillment of God's original plan: a good creation inhabited by a holy people who abide fully in his presence. In fact, when we envision heaven as a fancy city with lavish personal dwellings, we neglect the most meaningful aspect of the afterlife—direct access to God himself—and make an idol of worldly riches.

The ultimate goal of the believer is to be where Christ is, and John 14:1–3 explains how the lost fellowship with God is finally regained.[9] The place prepared in the presence of God is experienced through the union of the believer with Christ, a relational space that is prepared through the cruciform work of Jesus and will be fully consummated when he returns.[10] Though Jesus' act of "receiving" his people to himself initially takes place in the spiritual realm, such a union will later encompass a more physical expression.

Though popular interpretations of John 14 often teach that Christ will return to earth to gather believers and transport them to heaven, the Messiah never mentions heaven in chapter 14. Jesus doesn't promise

---

7. Cf. Exod 20:12; 23:22–26.

8. McCaffrey, *House*, 55. Cf. Hos 2:14–23; Isa 11:6–9; 51:3; 65:25; Ezek 36:35; 47:7–12; Joel 3:18.

9. Köstenberger, *Encountering John*; Jonge, *Jesus*, 173.

10. Whitacre, *John*, 349; McCaffrey, *House*, 58.

to prepare a place *in heaven*; he promises to prepare a *place*.[11] Wright explains, "It is simply assumed that the word *heaven* is the appropriate term for the ultimate destination, the final home, and that the language of resurrection, and of the new earth as well as the new heavens, must somehow be fitted into that."[12] Yet, the place, or *topos*, that Jesus prepares refers to the culmination of the Father's promises. More than a space delineated by a geographical boundary, the "place" is a space in which God's people receive the fullness of his provision, protection, and presence.

Along similar lines, rather than viewing the "Father's house" as a description of heaven, the biblical imagery points to Jesus as a new locus of sacred space and point of entry into God's family. Jesus is the new temple of God, and as such, the place where God's presence dwells. As Jesus makes preparation through his obedience, crucifixion, and resurrection, he renders the "place" accessible for believers. Rather than a room in heaven, those who place faith in Christ are granted an abode in the household of the Father that is permanent, indestructible, and unbroken by death.

The departure and death of Jesus is the preparatory act that makes mutual indwelling between God and believers possible. In his "going away" Jesus provides the perfect model of obedience, while at the same time reconciling believers to God. Jesus' departure, rather than creating separation, provides greater intimacy. As believers follow in the footsteps of Christ, they enter the prepared place—a new way of Spirit-empowered living—and take on his mission to prepare the way for others to experience life in God's family.

Downward Mobility

A brief examination of other relevant passages supports our interpretation of John 14:1–3. Rather than believers *ascending* to heaven upon death, Jesus *descends* to the earth in the eschaton. Though the language is metaphorical, the downward movement indicates that Christ returns to creation, as opposed to the common idea that believers depart.

One passage that inevitably emerges in discussions of the eschatological future is 1 Thess 4:16–17. Paul instructs,

---

11. McCaffrey, *House*, 38.
12. Wright, *Surprised by Hope*, 19.

> For the Lord Himself will descend from heaven with a shout, with the voice of *the* archangel and with the trumpet of God, and the dead in Christ will rise first. Then we who are alive and remain will be caught up together with them in the clouds to meet [*apantēsin*] the Lord in the air, and so we shall always be with the Lord. (NASB, emphasis original)

According to this familiar passage, Paul seems to imply that believers will join Christ in the air, i.e., heaven. Yet, Paul says nothing about transporting believers *to heaven*, especially upon closer examination of the original text.[13]

An understanding of the key term *apantēsis* equips modern readers to better interpret the verse. According to most translations, Paul says, "[We will] meet (*apantēsin*) the Lord in the air." However, a translation that adheres more closely to the Greek syntax and grammar would indicate that we are caught up "for a reception (*apantēsin*) of the Lord in the air." Gene Green defines the noun as an "almost technical term that described the custom of sending a delegate outside the city to receive a dignitary who was on the way to town."[14] Thus, believers greet Jesus and welcome him back to creation; they don't fly away into the sky.

The noun is used only three times in the NT: Matt 25:6, Acts 28:15, and here in 1 Thess 4:17.[15] In all three references, the verb is used similarly. In Matthew's parable of the bridegroom, the bridesmaids *apantēsin* the bridegroom to welcome him to the wedding banquet. In Acts, Roman believers *apantēsin* Paul to welcome him into their city.

In the Greek OT the term is attested more frequently. In 1 Sam 13:10, Saul meets (*apantēsin*) Samuel to welcome him to the battlefield, and in 1 Chr 12:17, David welcomes (*apantēsin*) leaders of the tribes of Israel who have come to parley with him. In fact, of thirty-four usages, nearly every occurrence adheres to such a pattern.[16] Outside the biblical

---

13. First, *apantēsis* is typically translated as a verbal infinitive, "to meet," when it is actually a noun that is better rendered "a reception." Second, most translations ignore the genitival quality of *tou kyriou*, translating the term as a direct object in the accusative ("to meet the Lord") rather than the genitive ("a reception *of* the Lord").

14. Green, *Letters to the Thessalonians*, 226. Cf. Erik Peterson, "*Apantēsis*," *TDNT*, 1:380–81.

15. The term is also attested in a textual variant of Matt 27:32.

16. See 1 Sam 6:13; 9:14; 13:10, 15; 16:4; 21:1; 25:32, 34; 30:21; 2 Sam 6:20; 19:25; 1 Chr 12:17; 14:8; 19:5; 2 Chr 12:11; 15:2; 19:2; 28:9; Jdt 5:4; 10:4; Jer 28:31; 34:2; 48:6. The term is used with the nuance of confrontation in 1 Sam 4:1; 15:12; 2 Chr 20:17; 1 Esd 1:23–25; Sir 19:29; 36:1; Esth E:9 LXX; 1 Macc 12:41. The term is used with the

texts, Josephus provides an instructive use of the term to describe the reception of the emperor Vespasian into Rome:

> Amidst such feelings of universal goodwill, those of higher rank, impatient of awaiting him, hastened to a great distance from Rome to be the first to greet [*apantōn*] him. Nor, indeed, could any of the rest endure the delay of meeting, but all poured forth in such crowds—for to all it seems simpler and easier to go than to remain—that the very city then for the first time experienced with satisfaction the paucity of inhabitants; for those who went outnumbered those who remained. But when he was reported to be approaching and those who had gone ahead were telling of the affability of his reception of each party, the whole remaining population, with wives and children, were by now waiting at the road-sides to receive him; and each group as he passed, in their delight at the spectacle and moved by the blandness of his appearance, gave vent to all manner of cries, hailing him as "benefactor," "savior," and "only worthy emperor of Rome." The whole city, moreover, was filled, like a temple, with garlands and incense.[17]

Josephus's imagery provides a vivid description of the manner in which believers will one day welcome the Lord Jesus Christ back to his earthly realm. And the day when Jesus returns will be an even greater occasion for exultation.[18] To interpret *apantēsin* any other way simply violates overwhelming textual evidence.

Philippians 3:20–21 also describes a downward rather than an upward movement of Christ in the last days.

> For our citizenship is in heaven, from which we also await a deliverer, Lord Jesus Christ; who will reshape our lowly body into the same form as his glorified body by the working of his ability to subject all things to himself.

In this passage Jesus is described as coming *from* heaven, at which time he will complete the transformation begun at Calvary. Just as he received a new resurrection body, those who follow him will likewise receive their redeemed form.

---

nuance of a spoken response in 2 Macc 12:30; 14:30; 15:12.

The verbal form of *apantēsin*, *apantaō*, is used twice in the NT (Mark 14:13 and Luke 17:12), as well as forty times in the LXX, nearly always as "to meet" or "to encounter."

17. Josephus, *J.W.* 7.4.1.

18. Wright, *Resurrection*, 217–18.

The historical context of the verse also proves informative. Citizenship, *politeuma*, parallels the ideas of home and dwelling, and thus citizenship in heaven appears to imply a residence there. Middleton points out, "It is worth noting that Philippi was a Roman colony and that many in the Philippian church would have been Roman citizens. In drawing on the analogy between Roman citizenship and citizenship in heaven, Paul . . . was designating Jesus as the true 'Savior' and 'Lord' in contrast to Caesar."[19] Indeed, Paul isn't promising a house in heaven but citizenship in God's kingdom—a place in the household of God.

The notions of residence and homeland are also present in Heb 11:13–16:

> All these died in faith, without having received the promises, but having seen and welcomed them from afar, and having confessed that they were strangers and exiles on the earth. For those who say such things clarify that they are seeking after a homeland. And indeed if they were thinking of that place from which they went out, they would have had opportunity to return. But now, they desire a better place, that is, a heavenly one. Therefore God is not ashamed to be called their God; for He prepared a city for them.

The anticipated homeland in these verses is another way of picturing inheritance, salvation, and heritage, i.e., the Father's house. In addition, the "heavenly place" should be interpreted as the kingdom of God rather than a supernatural realm in the sky. As in the gospels, the kingdom of heaven refers to the community of faith and new way of life inaugurated by Christ as opposed to the systems of this world. Further, the mention of the "city" as a prepared place evokes familiar imagery of the eschatological fulfillment of God's promises to his people.

Along such lines, in Rev 21:1–3 the "city," which is prepared, descends to earth:

> And I saw a new heaven and a new earth; for the first heaven and the first earth passed away, and the sea was no more.[20] And I saw

---

19. Middleton, *New Heaven*, 218.

20. Water imagery is often associated with the forces of chaos in biblical and ancient Near Eastern literature. In Gen 1:2 God gives form and structure to the void as he "hovers over the face of the waters." Note also the destructive power of the flood waters in Gen 6–9 as an act of de-creation. Cf. Amos 5:8; 9:6; Job 9:8; et al. Rev 21:1 and 22:1 reveal that in the eschaton the chaotic forces of the sea have been replaced by the life-giving waters that flow from God's throne.

the holy city, the new Jerusalem coming down from heaven, out of God, having been prepared as a bride adorned for her husband. And I heard a great voice from the throne saying: Behold the tabernacle of God with men, and he will dwell with them, and they will be his people, and God himself will be with them.

Astute readers will notice several familiar themes in this passage. First, the verses indicate God himself *prepares* the new heaven and earth, a process that is completed upon Christ's second coming.[21] In the new heaven and earth, the true promised land and ultimate prepared place, all of God's promises come to fruition.

Second, the most noteworthy aspect of the "city" is not the city itself, but the one who abides within it. In the larger context of Revelation, cities symbolize the people who dwell in them. Thus, John isn't describing the eternal dwelling place of the saints, but rather the union of believers with God.[22] In short, being in the heavenly city means dwelling with God.[23] Sandra Richter stresses that "heaven is . . . where God is. More specifically, heaven is the place where the people of God dwell in the place of God with full access to the presence of God."[24]

The dwelling/tabernacling of God with his people, available in the beginning, lost due to sin, promised through Israel, and initiated by Christ is now made manifest on the earth. In Rev 21:22, God and Christ have replaced the temple: "And I did not see a temple in it, for the Lord, the Almighty God and the Lamb are its temple." Such imagery reinforces our preceding conclusions about Christ as a new temple—a sacred space in which God dwells among his people as they abide in his presence. The return of Christ will be a blissful event in which the dwelling of the believer with God will have its fullest and final manifestation in the new heavens and earth.[25]

United Nations

The inception of the eschatological temple-city was expected to usher in an age of peace and prosperity for all humanity. The bringing together

21. Middleton, *New Heaven*, 219–20.
22. Gundry, *Old Is Better*, 400–408.
23. Middleton, *New Heaven*, 219–20.
24. Richter, *Epic of Eden*, 129.
25. Collins, *Studies on the Fourth Gospel*, 201; Santos, "Jesus," 49.

of God's children through the work of Christ is, for John, the inception of the eschatological unity of God's people.[26] McCaffrey emphasizes that "the blessings of salvation reserved for the eschatological age are also inseparably linked with the Jerusalem temple as the *gathering-place of the nations*" (emphasis mine).[27] Through portraying Christ as the temple, John reveals that Jesus himself prepares the eschatological temple, i.e., his own body, in order to draw all the peoples of the earth to the Father.[28]

The people of Israel were never able to take full possession of the place God prepared for them because of sin. Even when they inhabited a portion of the land God had promised, the recurring threat of destruction and expulsion became a reality due to disobedience.[29] In truth, perfect obedience was impossible because God's people were enslaved to sin and trapped in the kingdom of Satan. To ever claim the promises of God and be restored to the "land," they would need to be freed from bondage and transformed from the inside out.

Only Jesus is able to effect such a transformation. As one who is fully God and fully human, he is able to live a sinless life. As such, he is able to die as a perfect sacrifice and atone for the sin of his people. Moreover, by bearing the sin of humanity, rising to new life, and nullifying the power of death, Jesus overthrows the rule of Satan and transfers people into God's kingdom. In John, as in Rev 11:15, "The kingdom of the world has become the kingdom of the Lord." Middleton explains, "Through the life, teaching, death, and resurrection of Jesus, God has done battle with, and vanquished, the powers of evil and death that have held humanity and the world in bondage, thus bringing atonement for our sin, deliverance from its multifaceted power, and the restoration of our relationships with God, one another, and the created order."[30]

Jesus is both a second Moses who leads his people out of captivity and a second Adam who leads humanity into its true mission. Jesus perfectly accomplishes image-bearing as he interacts with the natural world and human society. And in turn, he calls his people to follow in his footsteps—to do even greater works than himself (John 14:12). Following Jesus, thus, entails living sacrificially by carrying out the original commission to steward

26. Jonge, *Jesus*, 174.
27. McCaffrey, *House*, 60. Cf. Collins, *Studies on the Fourth Gospel*, 200.
28. Aalen, "'Reign' and 'House,'" 227–28.
29. Hoskins, *Jesus as Fulfillment*, 84–87.
30. Middleton, *New Heaven*, 67.

God's creation as well as leading God's people out of slavery. Indeed, one's understanding of God's overarching plan is inseparable from one's ethics. In John, ethics and eschatology are not about *getting to heaven*, but about *getting to God* and carrying out his mission in the world.[31]

As such, an inherent aspect of being part of God's family is following Christ and walking in radical obedience to the Father and in sacrificial love for others. According to such a *halakah*, those who believe into Christ reveal him to the world and begin the process of redemption that will be completed when he returns.[32] Through his followers, Jesus doesn't simply gather the scattered tribes of Israel to himself, but all peoples.

The availability of "many rooms" in the Father's house indicates that God's presence is expansive enough for every person, indeed, "whosoever might believe" (John 3:16). As Jesus ministered to people from various cultures and socioeconomic standings, he embodied the fulfillment of OT prophecies in which the gentiles would stream toward the Jerusalem temple.[33] As Hag 2:6–9 prophetically promises, the glory of the latter temple surpasses that of the former because the nations come to the house of the Lord, i.e., to the Father's house made available through the temple of Jesus' body.

Walking with Jesus

Just as Jesus renders the sacred space of God available to his followers, he commissions them to follow in his footsteps and make his presence available to every tribe, people, and nation.[34] Whereas God sent his son, Jesus now sends forth all who believe into him. And he doesn't send them out ill-equipped or unprepared, he goes with them as the Spirit-Paraclete (14:12, 18).

Prior to Christ, the Spirit was available only to certain men and women at certain moments for specific feats of faith. In Christ, God's Spirit donned human form and walked among his people. As the first Paraclete, Jesus himself was the locus of God's presence and activity in the world. Yet, through his departure and return, Christ makes the presence

---

31. Middleton, *New Heaven*, 68; Moloney, "God," 197–217.

32. Rensberger, *Johannine Faith*, 148.

33. Brown, *John I–XII*, 443; Hoskins, *Jesus as Fulfillment*. See Isa 2:3; 11:11–12; 27:12; 56:1–8; 60:5–7; 66:18; Ezek 47:22–23; Zech 14:16; Matt 24:14; 25:32; 28:19–20; Rev 5:9–10; 7:9; 21:24–26.

34. John 3:16; 17:18; 20:21.

of God available to every person who places faith in him. According to Hoskins, "Clearly, the Spirit is the key gift that flows out from Jesus, the true Temple. It is the means by which believers experience the unique communion with Jesus and the Father that is the foretaste and guarantee of eternal life. The communion both fulfills and anticipates the ultimate fulfillment of the role of the temple as the locus of God's provision for his people in the new age."[35]

Through the indwelling and empowering of the Spirit-Paraclete, the true people of God would be able to spread his presence throughout the earth. As such, God's people begin to fulfill the OT promises that the earth would be renewed and filled with the presence of the Lord in the eschaton.[36] As such, the Spirit-Paraclete isn't a subpar replacement for the physical presence of Christ, but an epoch-changing development in salvation history in which every single member of the Father's household receives access to the direct presence and power of God.

Although John offers scant explicit teaching on eschatology, the new creation, or the second coming of Christ, the recurring narrative pattern in which OT institutions are brought to fruition indicates that Christ has inaugurated the beginning of the end. With his life, death, and resurrection, Christ begins a new era of history and prefigures an even better age to come. Beale explains that "Christ's resurrected body was the first newly created body to pass to the other side into the new creation. The coming new creation penetrated back into this world through the resurrected, new-creational body of Jesus."[37] By juxtaposing the present with the future, John communicates both delight in the present world and hope for the future.[38]

In sum, to read John 14 as a monologue about departing this life and transporting to an otherworldly heaven is to lose sight of the Johannine context, as well as the overarching narrative of Scripture. In John 14, Jesus offers a profound statement on the goal and purpose of the Christian life. That which was broken "in the beginning" is now healed as humanity can again enter the presence of their creator, thanks to the indwelling presence of the Spirit-Paraclete and the cruciform work of our Savior Jesus, in whose footsteps, or *halakah*, we are called to walk.

---

35. Hoskins, *Jesus as Fulfillment*, 167.
36. Hab 2:14; Jer 31:34; Heb 8:11.
37. Beale, *Union*, 70.
38. Moloney, "God," 209; Pryor, "Jesus and Israel," 211.

Bibliography

Aalen, Sverre. "'Reign' and 'House' in the Kingdom of God in the Gospels." *NTS* 8 (1962) 215–40.
Allen, Michael. *Grounded in Heaven: Recentering Christian Hope and Life on God.* Grand Rapids: Eerdmans, 2018.
Allison, Dale C., Jr. "The Living Water (John 4:10–14, 6:35c, 7:37–39)." *SVTQ* 30 (1986) 143–57.
Arndt, William, et al. *A Greek-English Lexicon of the New Testament and Other Early Christian Literature.* 3rd ed. Chicago: University of Chicago Press, 2000.
Aquinas. *Summa Theologica.* Translated by the Fathers of the English Dominican Province. New York: Benzinger Brothers, 1947.
Augustine. *Tractates on the Gospel of John 55–111.* Translated by W. Rettig. Washington, DC: Catholic University of America Press, 2014.
Aune, David Edward. *The Cultic Setting of Realized Eschatology in Early Christianity.* Leiden: Brill, 1972.
Barker, Margaret. *The Gate of Heaven: The History and Symbolism of the Temple in Jerusalem.* Sheffield: Sheffield Phoenix, 2008.
Barrett, C. K. *The Gospel according to St. John: An Introduction with Commentary and Notes on the Greek Text.* 2nd ed. Philadelphia: Westminster, 1978.
Bauckham, Richard. *Gospel of Glory: Major Themes in Johannine Theology.* Grand Rapids: Baker Academic, 2015.
———. "John for Readers of Mark." In *The Gospels for All Christians: Rethinking the Gospel Audiences,* edited by Richard Bauckham, 153–61. Grand Rapids: Eerdmans, 1998.
———. *The Testimony of the Beloved Disciple: Narrative, History, and Theology in the Gospel of John.* Grand Rapids: Baker Academic, 2007.
Bauckham, Richard, and Trevor Hart. *Hope against Hope: Christian Eschatology at the Turn of the Millennium.* Grand Rapids: Eerdmans, 1999.
Bavinck, Herman. *Reformed Dogmatics.* Grand Rapids: Baker Academic, 2011.
Beale, G. K. *The Book of Revelation.* NIGTC. Grand Rapids: Eerdmans, 1999.
———. *The Temple and the Church's Mission: A Biblical Theology of the Dwelling Place of God.* Downers Grove, IL: InterVarsity, 2004.
———. *Union with the Resurrected Christ: Eschatological New Creation and New Testament Biblical Theology.* Grand Rapids: Baker Academic, 2023.
Beasley-Murray, G. R. *John.* WBC 36. 2nd ed. Nashville: Thomas Nelson, 1999.

Becker, Jürgen. "Die Abschiedsreden Jesu im Johannesevangelium." *ZNW* 61 (1970) 215–46.

Bernard, J. H. *A Critical and Exegetical Commentary on the Gospel according to St. John.* ICC. Edinburgh: T & T Clark, 1928.

Black, C. Clifton. "'The Words That You Gave to Me I Have Given to Them': The Grandeur of Johannine Rhetoric." In *Exploring the Gospel of John: In Honor of D. Moody Smith*, edited by R. Alan Culpepper and C. Clifton Black, 220–39. Louisville: Westminster John Knox, 1996.

Blomberg, Craig L. *The Historical Reliability of John's Gospel: Issues and Commentary.* Downers Grove, IL: InterVarsity, 2001.

Brown, Colin, ed. *New International Dictionary of New Testament Theology.* 4 vols. Grand Rapids: Zondervan, 1975–78.

Brown, Raymond. *The Gospel according to John I–XII.* AB 29. New York: Doubleday, 1966.

———. *The Gospel according to John XIII–XXI.* AB 29A. New York: Doubleday, 1970.

———. "The Paraclete in the Fourth Gospel." *NTS* 13 (1967) 113–32.

Brown, Sherri. "Believing in the Gospel of John: The Ethical Imperative to Becoming Children of God." In *Johannine Ethics: The Moral World of the Gospel and Epistles of John*, edited by Sherri Brown and Christopher W. Skinner, 3–24. Minneapolis: Fortress, 2017.

Bryan, Steven M. "The Eschatological Temple in John 14." *BBR* 15 (2005) 187–98.

Bultmann, Rudolf. *The Gospel of John: A Commentary.* Translated by G. R. Beasley-Murray. Philadelphia: Westminster, 1971.

———. *Theology of the New Testament.* Translated by Kendrick Grobel. 2 vols. New York: Scribner, 1951.

Burns, J. Lanier. "John 14:1–27: The Comfort of God's Presence." *BibSac* 172 (2015) 299–315.

Bynum, Caroline Walker. *The Resurrection of the Body in Western Christianity, 200–1336.* New York: Columbia University Press, 1995.

Calvin, John. *Institutes of the Christian Religion.* Vol. 1. Translated by Henry Beveridge. Edinburgh: The Calvin Translation Society, 1845. Accessed using Logos Bible Software.

Carey, George L. "The Lamb of God and Atonement Theories." *TynBul* 32 (1981) 97–122.

Carson, D. A. *The Gospel according to John.* PNTC. Grand Rapids: Eerdmans, 1991.

Carter, Warren. "The Prologue and John's Gospel: Function, Symbol and the Definitive Word." *JSNT* 39 (1990) 35–58.

Charles, Robert Henry, ed. *Pseudepigrapha of the Old Testament.* Oxford: Clarendon, 1913.

Charlesworth, James H. "The Dead Sea Scrolls and the Gospel according to John." In *Exploring the Gospel of John: In Honor of D. Moody Smith*, edited by R. Alan Culpepper and C. Clifton Black, 65–97. Louisville: Westminster John Knox, 1996.

Collins, Raymond F. "'Follow Me': A Life-Giving Ethical Imperative." In *Johannine Ethics: The Moral World of the Gospel and Epistles of John*, edited by Sherri Brown and Christopher W. Skinner, 43–63. Minneapolis: Fortress, 2017.

———. *These Things Have Been Written: Studies on the Fourth Gospel.* Grand Rapids: Eerdmans, 1990.

Coloe, Mary L. *Dwelling in the Household of God: Johannine Eschatology and Spirituality.* Collegeville, MN: Liturgical Press, 1989.

———. *God Dwells with Us: Temple Symbolism in the Fourth Gospel*. Collegeville, MN: Liturgical Press, 2001.

———. *John*. WisC 44. 2 bks. Collegeville, MN: Liturgical Press, 2021.

———. "Temple Imagery in John." *Int* 63 (2009) 368–81.

Cross, F. L., and Elizabeth A. Livingstone, eds. *The Oxford Dictionary of the Christian Church*. 3rd ed. Oxford: Oxford University Press, 2005.

Culpepper, R. Alan. "The Creation Ethics of the Gospel of John." In *Johannine Ethics: The Moral World of the Gospel and Epistles of John*, edited by Sherri Brown and Christopher W. Skinner, 67–90. Minneapolis: Fortress, 2017.

———. "The Johannine *Hypodeigma*: A Reading of John 13." *Semeia* 53 (1991) 133–52.

———. "Reading Johannine Irony." In *Exploring the Gospel of John: In Honor of D. Moody Smith*, edited by R. Alan Culpepper and C. Clifton Black, 194–207. Louisville: Westminster John Knox, 1996.

———. "The Theology of the Johannine Passion Narrative: John 19:16b–30." *Neot* 31 (1997).

Daube, David. "Jesus and the Samaritan Woman: The Meaning of *Sungcharomai*." *JBL* 69 (1950) 137–47.

Davies, W. D. *The Gospel and the Land: Early Christianity and Jewish Territorial Doctrine*. Berkeley: University of California Press, 1974.

———. "Torah and Dogma: A Comment." *HTR* 61 (1968) 87–105.

DeSilva, David. *An Introduction to the New Testament: Contexts, Methods and Ministry Formation*. Downers Grove, IL: IVP Academic, 2004.

Dodd, C. H. *The Founder of Christianity*. New York: Macmillan, 1970.

———. *The Interpretation of the Fourth Gospel*. Cambridge: Cambridge University Press, 1953.

Domeris, Bill. "The Paraclete as an Ideological Construct: A Study in the Farewell Discourses." *JTSA* 67 (1989) 17–23.

Draper, J. A. "The Sociological Function of the Spirit/Paraclete in the Farewell Discourses in the Fourth Gospel." *Neot* 26 (1992) 13–29.

Evans, Craig A. *Word and Glory: On the Exegetical and Theological Background of John's Prologue*. LNTS. Sheffield: Sheffield Academic Press, 1993.

Ferguson, Everett. *Backgrounds of Early Christianity*. 3rd ed. Grand Rapids: Eerdmans, 2003.

Fischer, G. *Die himmlischen Wohnungen: Untersuchungen zu Joh. 14,2f*. Bern: Herbert Lang, 1975.

Fortna, Robert T. "Theological Use of Locale in the Fourth Gospel." *AThRSup* 3 (1974) 58–95.

Gibbs, Jeffrey. "Already Dwelling in the Father's House: Reading John 14:2–3 in Context." *ConcJ* 49 (2023) 13–34.

Green, Gene L. *The Letters to the Thessalonians*. PNTC. Grand Rapids: Eerdmans, 2002.

Greene, Joseph R. "Jesus as the Heavenly Temple in the Fourth Gospel." *BBR* 28 (2018) 426–46.

Gundry, Robert H. "In My Father's House are many *Monai* (John 14:2)." *ZNW* 58 (1967) 68–72.

———. *The Old Is Better: New Testament Essays in Support of Traditional Interpretations*. WUNT 178. Tübingen: Mohr Siebeck, 2005.

Harris, R. Laird, et al., eds. *Theological Wordbook of the Old Testament*. Chicago: Moody, 1999.

Harstine, Stanley. *Moses as a Character in the Fourth Gospel: A Study of Ancient Reading Techniques*. JSNTSS 229. London: Sheffield Academic Press, 2002.

Hart, Addison Hodges. *The Woman, the Hour, and the Garden: A Study of Imagery in the Gospel of John*. Grand Rapids: Eerdmans, 2016.

Hayes, Richard B. *Echoes of Scripture in the Letters of Paul*. New Haven: Yale University Press, 1993.

Himmelfarb, Martha. "Afterlife and Resurrection." In *The Jewish Annotated New Testament*, edited by Amy-Jill Levine and Mark Zvi Brettler, 549–51. Oxford: Oxford University Press, 2011.

Hoeck, Andreas. "The Johannine Paraclete—Herald of the Eschaton." *JBPR* 4 (2012) 23–37.

Holwerda, David Earl. *The Holy Spirit and Eschatology in the Gospel of John: A Critique of Rudolf Bultmann's Present Eschatology*. Grand Rapids: Eerdmans, 1959.

Homer. *The Iliad*. Translated by Caroline Alexander. New York: Ecco, 2015.

———. *The Odyssey*. Translated by Emily Wilson. New York: Norton, 2020.

Hoskins, Paul M. "Deliverance from Death by the True Passover Lamb: A Significant Aspect of the Fulfillment of the Passover in the Gospel of John." *JETS* 52 (2009) 285–99.

———. "Freedom from Slavery to Sin and the Devil: John 8:31–47 and the Passion Theme of the Gospel of John." *TJ* 31 (2010) 47–63.

———. *Jesus as the Fulfillment of the Temple in the Gospel of John*. PBM. Eugene, OR: Wipf & Stock, 2006.

Howard, J. K. "Passover and Eucharist in the Fourth Gospel." *SJT* 20 (1967) 329–37.

Jobes, Karen. *John through Old Testament Eyes*. Grand Rapids: Kregel Academic, 2021.

Jonge, Marinus de. *Jesus: Stranger from Heaven and Son of God*. Translated by John E. Steely. Missoula, MT: Scholars Press, 1977.

Josephus, Flavius. *The Works of Josephus: Complete and Unabridged*. Translated by William Whiston. Peabody, MA: Hendrickson, 1987.

Kanagaraj, Jey J. "The Implied Ethics of the Fourth Gospel: A Reinterpretation of the Decalogue." *TynBul* 52 (2001) 33–60.

Keener, Craig S. *The Gospel of John: A Commentary*. 2 vols. Grand Rapids: Baker Academic, 2003.

Kittel, Gerhard, et al., eds. *Theological Dictionary of the New Testament*. Grand Rapids: Eerdmans, 1964.

Klink, E. W., III. *The Sheep of the Fold: The Audience and Origin of the Gospel of John*. SNTSMS 141. Cambridge: Cambridge University Press, 2007.

Koester, Craig. "Hearing, Seeing, and Believing in the Gospel of John." *Bib* 70 (1989) 327–48.

Köstenberger, Andreas J. *Encountering John: The Gospel in Historical, Literary, and Theological Perspective*. Grand Rapids: Baker, 1999.

Lee, Dorothy A. "Paschal Imagery in the Gospel of John: A Narrative and Symbolic Reading." *Pacifica* 24 (2011) 13–28.

———. *The Symbolic Narratives of the Fourth Gospel: The Interplay of Form and Meaning*. Sheffield: Sheffield Academic Press, 1994.

Levenson, Jon. "The Temple and the World." *JR* 64 (1984) 275–98.

Lightfoot, R. H. *St. John's Gospel: A Commentary*. Oxford: Clarendon, 1956.

Longenecker, Richard N. *The Christology of Early Jewish Christianity*. Vancouver, BC: Regent College Publishing, 1994.

Louw, Johannes P., and Eugene Albert Nida. *Greek-English Lexicon of the New Testament: Based on Semantic Domains*. New York: United Bible Societies, 1996.
Lund, Glen. "The Joys and Dangers of Ethics in John's Gospel." In *Rethinking the Ethics of John: 'Implicit Ethics' in the Johannine Writings*, edited by Jan G. Van der Watt and Reuben Zimmerman, 264–89. Tübingen: Mohr Siebeck, 2012.
Lundquist, John M. "Temple, Covenant, and Law in the Ancient Near East and in the Old Testament." In *Israel's Apostasy and Restoration*, edited by Avraham Gileadi, 293–305. Grand Rapids: Baker, 1988.
Malina, Bruce J. *The New Testament World: Insights from Cultural Anthropology*. 3rd ed. Louisville: Westminster John Knox, 2001.
Malina, Bruce J., and Richard L. Rohrbaugh. *Social-Science Commentary on the Gospel of John*. Minneapolis: Fortress, 1998.
Manning, Gary T., Jr. *Echoes of a Prophet: The Use of Ezekiel in the Gospel of John and in Literature of the Second Temple Period*. London: T & T Clark, 2004.
Martin-Achard, Robert. "Resurrection: Old Testament." Translated by Terrence Prendergast. In *AYBD*, edited by David Noel Freedman, 680–84. New York: Doubleday, 1992.
McCaffrey, James. *The House with Many Rooms: The Temple Theme of Jn. 14,2–3*. Rome: Pontifical Biblical Institute, 1988.
McDannell, Colleen, and Bernhard Lang. *Heaven: A History*. 2nd ed. New Haven: Yale University Press, 1988.
McKelvey, R. J. *The New Temple: The Church in the New Testament*. Oxford: Oxford University Press, 1969.
Michaels, J. Ramsey. *The Gospel of John*. NICNT. Grand Rapids: Eerdmans, 2010.
Middleton, J. Richard. *The Liberating Image: The Imago Dei in Genesis 1*. Grand Rapids: Brazos, 2005.
———. *A New Heaven and a New Earth: Reclaiming Biblical Eschatology*. Grand Rapids: Baker Academic, 2014.
Milgrom, Jacob. *Leviticus 17–22*. AB. New York: Doubleday, 2000.
Miller, Stephen R. *Daniel: An Exegetical and Theological Exposition of Holy Scripture*. NAC 18. Nashville: Broadman & Holman, 1994.
Moloney, Francis J. *Belief in the Word, Reading the Fourth Gospel: John 1–4*. Minneapolis: Fortress, 1993.
———. *Glory Not Dishonor: Reading John 13–21*. Eugene, OR: Wipf & Stock, 1998.
———. "God, Eschatology, and 'This World': Ethics in the Gospel of John." In *Johannine Ethics. The Moral World of the Gospel and Epistles of John*, edited by Sherri Brown and Christopher W. Skinner, 197–217. Minneapolis: Fortress, 2017.
———. *The Gospel of John*. SP 4. Collegeville, MN: Liturgical Press, 2005.
———. "The Johannine Passion and the Christian Community." *Sal* 57 (1995) 26–61.
———. *Love in the Gospel of John: An Exegetical, Theological, and Literary Study*. Grand Rapids: Baker, 2013.
———. *Signs and Shadows: Reading John 5–12*. Minneapolis: Fortress, 1996.
Montgomery, James A. "'The Place' as an Appellation of Deity." *JBL* 24 (1905) 17–26.
Morgan, Richard. "Fulfillment in the Fourth Gospel: Old Testament Foundations." *Int* 11 (1957) 155–65.
Morris, Leon. *The Gospel according to John*. NICNT. Rev. ed. Grand Rapids: Eerdmans, 1995.
Mounce, Robert H. *The Book of Revelation*. Rev. ed. Grand Rapids: Eerdmans, 1998.

Mouton, Elna. "Torah Reimag(in)ed between *Sarx* and *Doxa*? Implied Household Ethos in the Fourth Gospel." *Neot* 50 (2016) 93–112.

Murphy, Frederick James. *The Structure and Meaning of Second Baruch*. Atlanta: Scholars Press, 1985.

Neusner, Jacob. "The Jacob Allusions in John 1:51." *CBQ* 44 (1982) 586–605.

———. *Mekhilta Attributed to Rabbi Ishmael: Part 1*. Vol. 8 of *The Components of the Rabbinic Documents: From the Whole to the Parts*. Atlanta: Scholars Press, 1997.

———. "Money-Changers in the Temple: The Mishnah's Explanation." *NTS* 35 (1989) 287–90.

———. *Sifre to Numbers and Sifre to Deuteronomy*. Vol. 8 of *A Theological Commentary to the Midrash*. Lanham, MD: University Press of America, 2001.

Neyrey, Jerome H. *The Gospel of John in Cultural and Rhetorical Perspective*. Grand Rapids: Eerdmans, 2009.

———. "Jacob Traditions and the Interpretation of John 4:10–26." *CBQ* 41 (1979) 419–37.

Nock, Arthur Darby. "Gnosticism." *HTR* (1964) 255–79.

Nylund, Jan H. "Court of the Gentiles." In *The Lexham Bible Dictionary*, edited by John D. Barry et al. Bellingham, WA: Lexham, 2016. Accessed using Logos Bible Software.

Olson, Dennis T. "Sacred Time: The Sabbath and Christian Worship." In *Touching the Altar: The Old Testament for Christian Worship*, edited by Carol M. Bechtel, 1–34. Grand Rapids: Eerdmans, 2008.

Origen. *De Principiis*. In *Fathers of the Third Century: Tertullian, Part Fourth; Minucius Felix; Commodian; Origen, Parts First and Second*, edited by Alexander Roberts et al., 239–382. Translated by Frederick Crombie. Vol. 4 of The Ante-Nicene Fathers. Buffalo, NY: Christian Literature Company, 1885.

Osborne, Grant R. *Revelation*. BECNT. Grand Rapids: Baker Academic, 2002.

Osiek, Carolyn. "Dwellings." *TBT* 53 (2015) 34–39.

Pancaro, Severino. "The Relationship of the Church to Israel in the Gospel of St. John." *NTS* 21 (1974) 396–405.

Patte, Daniel. *Early Jewish Hermeneutic in Palestine*. Missoula, MT: Scholars Press, 1975.

Peterson, Robert A. "Union with Christ in the Gospel of John." *Presb* 39 (2013) 9–29.

Philo. *The Works of Philo: Complete and Unabridged*. Translated by Charles Duke Yonge. Peabody, MA: Hendrickson, 1995.

Plato. *Euthyphro. Apology. Crito. Phaedo. Phaedrus*. Translated by Harold North Fowler. LCL 36. Cambridge, MA: Harvard University Press, 1914.

———. *Theaetetus. Sophist*. Translated by Harold North Fowler. LCL 123. Cambridge, MA: Harvard University Press, 1921.

———. *Timaeus. Critias. Cleitophon. Menexenus. Epistles*. Translated by R. G. Bury. LCL 234. Cambridge, MA: Harvard University Press, 1989.

Porter, Stanley E. "Can Traditional Exegesis Enlighten Literary Analysis of the Fourth Gospel? An Examination of the Old Testament Fulfillment Motif and the Passover Theme." In *The Gospels and the Scriptures of Israel*, edited by Craig A. Evans and W. Richard Stegner, 396–428. JSNTSS 104. Sheffield: Sheffield Academic Press, 1994.

———. *John, His Gospel, and Jesus: In Pursuit of the Johannine Voice*. Grand Rapids: Eerdmans, 2015.

———. *Sacred Tradition in the New Testament: Tracing Old Testament Themes in the Gospels and Epistles*. Grand Rapids: Baker Academic, 2016.

Pryor, John W. "Jesus and Israel in the Fourth Gospel—John 1:11." *NT* 32 (1990) 201-18.

Rad, Gerhard von. *Genesis: A Commentary*. OTL. Philadelphia: Westminster, 1972.

Rahlfs, Alfred. *Septuaginta: Morphologically Tagged Edition*. Stuttgart: Deutsche Bibelgesellschaft, 1996. Accessed using Logos Bible Software.

Reddish, Mitchell G. "Heaven." In *The Anchor Yale Bible Dictionary*, edited by David Noel Freedman, 90–91. New York: Doubleday, 1992.

Reese, James M. "Literary Structure of Jn 13:31—14:31, 16:5–6, 16:33." *CBQ* 34 (1972) 321–31.

Rensberger, David K. *Johannine Faith and Liberating Community*. Philadelphia: Westminster, 1988.

Reubenstein, Jeffrey L. "*Sukkot*, Eschatology, and Zechariah 14." *RB* 103 (1996) 161–95.

Richter, Sandra. *The Epic of Eden: A Christian Entry into the Old Testament*. Downers Grove: IVP Academic, 2008.

Robinson, Andrea. "Heaven or *Halakah*: John 14:1–3 Reexamined." *JBTM* 19 (2022) 303–25.

———. *Temple of Presence: The Christological Fulfillment of Ezekiel 40–48 in Revelation 21:1—22:5*. Eugene, OR: Wipf & Stock, 2019.

Santos, João Alves, II. "Jesus e as Moradas na Casa do Pai: Interpretando Monai em João 14." *Fides Reformata* 16 (2011) 49–70.

Schaefer, O. "Der Sinn der Rede Jesu von den vielen Wohnungen in seines Vaters Haause und von dem Weg zu ihm (Joh 14, 1–7)." *ZNW* 32 (1933) 210–17.

Schnackenburg, Rudolf. *The Gospel according to St. John*. Translated by David Smith and G. A. Kon. London: Burns & Oats, 1982.

Segal, Peretz. "The Penalty of the Warning Inscription from the Temple of Jerusalem." *IEJ* 39 (1989) 79–84.

Segovia, Fernando F. "The Structure, *Tendenz*, and *Sitz im Leben* of John 13:31—14:31." *JBL* 104 (1985) 471–93.

Seneca the Elder. *Controversiae*. Vol. 1 of *Declamations*. Translated by Michael Winterbottom. LCL 463. Cambridge, MA: Harvard University Press, 1974.

Shillington, V. George. "The Spirit-Paraclete as Jesus' Alter Ego in the Fourth Gospel (John 14–16)." *Vision* 13 (2012) 31–39.

Siliezar, Carlos Raúl Soza. *Creation Imagery in the Gospel of John*. London: T & T Clark.

Skinner, Christopher W. "Another Look at the 'Lamb of God.'" *BSac* 161 (2004) 89–104.

———. "Introduction: (How) Can We Talk about Johannine Ethics? Looking Back and Moving Forward." In *Johannine Ethics: The Moral World of the Gospel and Epistles of John*, edited by Sherri Brown and Christopher W. Skinner, xvii–xxxvi. Minneapolis: Fortress, 2017.

———. "Love One Another: The Johannine Love Command in the Farewell Discourse." In *Johannine Ethics: The Moral World of the Gospel and Epistles of John*, edited by Sherri Brown and Christopher W. Skinner, 25–42. Minneapolis: Fortress, 2017.

Stagg, Frank. "Farewell Discourses: John 13–17." *RevExp* (1965) 459–72.

Stone, Michael Edward. *Fourth Ezra*. Hermeneia. Minneapolis: Fortress, 1990.

Tabor, James D. "Heaven, Ascent to." In *The Anchor Yale Bible Dictionary*, edited by David Noel Freedman, 91–94. New York: Doubleday, 1992.

The Talmud of Babylonia: An American Translation, XIV.C: Tractate Ketubot, Chapters 8–13. Translated by Jacob Neusner. BJS 260. Atlanta: Scholars Press, 1992.

Telushkin, Joseph. *Jewish Literacy*. Rev. ed. New York: HarperCollins, 2001.

Tenney, Merrill C. "The Old Testament in the Fourth Gospel." *BSac* 120 (1963) 300–308.

Thiessen, Matthew. *Jesus and the Forces of Death*. Grand Rapids: Baker Academic, 2020.

Thompson, Marianne Meye. *The Humanity of Jesus in the Fourth Gospel*. Philadelphia: Fortress, 1988.

Van der Watt, Jan G. "Ethics and Ethos in the Gospel according to John." *ZNW* 97 (2006) 147–76.

———. "Ethics of/and the Opponents of Jesus in John's Gospel." In *Rethinking the Ethics of John: 'Implicit Ethics' in the Johannine Writings*, edited by Jan G. van der Watt and Reuben Zimmerman, 175–91. Tübingen: Mohr Siebeck, 2012.

Vermes, Geza. *The Complete Dead Sea Scrolls in English*. New York: Penguin Books, 1997.

Walton, John. *The Lost World of Adam and Eve: Genesis 2–3 and the Human Origins Debate*. Downers Grove, IL: IVP Academic, 2015.

Westcott, Brooke Foss. *The Gospel according to St. John: The Greek Text with Introduction and Notes*. Grand Rapids: Baker Book House, 1980.

Whitacre, Rodney A. *John*. IVPNTC. Downers Grove, IL: InterVarsity, 1999.

Witherington, Ben, III. "The Waters of Birth: John 3.5 and 1 John 5.6–8." *NTS* 35 (1989) 155–60.

Wright, N. T. *The Resurrection of the Son of God*. Minneapolis: Fortress, 2003.

———. *Surprised by Hope: Rethinking Heaven, the Resurrection, and the Mission of the Church*. New York: HarperOne, 2008.

Subject Index

Abiding, x, xxii, xxv, 3, 34–35, 44–54, 64–65, 68, 75, 77, 79–83, 86–87, 91, 99, 102–3, 106, 113, 116–18, 120, 123, 135, 137, 142–47, 151
Abraham, 4, 37, 61, 69, 114, 116
Adam, 4, 37–38, 57, 59, 63, 152
Aquinas, Thomas, 20–21
Afterlife, xviii, xx, xxvii, 1–33, 35, 37, 55, 144, 146
Aristotle, 10, 11, 22
Ascent, 24, 65, 125, 137, 141, 145, 147
Atonement, 67, 90, 94–108, 112, 116–17, 131, 144, 152,
Augustine, 20, 23, 116
Belief. *See* Faith.
Bethel, 65–66, 97, 115
Blood, 47, 58, 72, 83, 93, 95–96, 98–99, 104–5, 117, 121, 131
Body, 104–6, 108, 112, 114, 117, 125, 131, 149, 152–54
Calvin, John, 21
Cleansing, 21, 66–68, 90, 94, 97, 102–6, 117, 121–24, 130–31
Coming (of Christ), xxvi–xxvii, 11, 15–16, 21, 26, 28, 30, 33–34, 39, 43–44, 46, 51, 53, 59, 63–64, 70, 73–74, 77, 86, 88–91, 120, 125–27, 119–28, 130–54
Command, xxi, 43, 77–83, 87, 89–90, 98–99, 102, 104, 123
Commission. *See* Mission.
Consecration, 72, 100
Cosmos, 2, 20, 56, 57
Creation Narrative, 4, 37–38, 57, 63, 80–81, 109, 133, 135, 145, 150

Creation, xix–xx, xxvii, 2, 4–5, 11, 17–18, 20–21, 23–32, 37–38, 40, 42, 45, 57–59, 63, 69, 72, 75, 80–82, 92, 109, 120, 122–23, 125–26, 131–35, 142, 145–48, 150, 153–54
Cross, the, xxv–xxvi, 27, 44, 66, 72, 77, 87–92, 101, 104–5, 113, 116–17, 131, 133–34
Darkness, 16, 39, 81, 84–85, 88, 92
Dead Sea Sect. *See* Qumran Sect.
Death, xxviii, xxv–xxvii, 1–24, 27–32, 40–42, 51, 55, 72–74, 77, 86–107, 111–12, 116–18, 120, 125, 131, 137–39, 144–45, 147, 152, 154
Descent, 14, 46, 64–65, 108–9, 125, 141, 147–50
Dwelling. *See* Tabernacling.
Eden, 2, 4, 21, 37–38, 57, 59, 70, 122, 129, 146,
Elysium, 8–9, 11
Embodied, xx, 4–5, 8, 11, 14–15, 18, 20–24, 26, 31–32, 35, 38, 42–43, 55, 64, 66, 68, 71, 81–83, 85, 88, 103, 108–9, 112, 125, 143–45, 153
Epictetus, 18
Eschatology, xx, 4–6, 11, 18, 20, 26, 32, 60, 62, 64, 69, 70, 105, 114–15, 118, 121–22, 126–32, 138–42, 146–54
Eternal Life, xxviii, 6, 13, 18, 22, 24, 31, 38, 47, 49, 84, 95, 98, 105, 112, 125–26, 131, 134, 154
Ethics, xx–xxi, 80, 153

SUBJECT INDEX

Exodus, the, xix, xxvi, 36, 43, 45, 47, 64, 80, 84, 90, 94–100, 104
Expiation, 67, 96, 102,
Faith, xviii, xix–xxii, xxvi–xxvii, 4–5, 7, 28–29, 32, 35, 39, 41–46, 54, 59, 62, 66, 70, 73, 76–79, 83, 85, 88, 90, 102, 110, 111, 114, 117, 127, 133, 137, 139, 143–45, 147, 150, 153–54
Father's House. *See* House.
Firstborn, 37–38, 96–97, 100
First Fruits, 24, 26, 59, 145
Following, xviii–xix, xxii, xxvi, 29, 34, 42, 46–48, 53, 71, 77, 80, 82–92, 94, 103, 118, 131, 140, 144, 147, 149, 152–53
Foot Washing, 76, 85–86, 88, 101–3, 106
Gerizim, Mount, 68–69
Glory, 17, 21, 29, 30, 38, 45, 64, 82, 89, 116–17, 123, 140, 153
Gnosticism, 18–20, 23, 29, 31, 124
Going, xviii, xxvi, 1, 8, 13, 19, 23, 25, 28–30, 38, 41, 47, 50, 53, 73, 75, 77, 85, 88–91, 113, 116–18, 120, 124, 127, 133, 137–40, 143, 147, 149
Great Commission, 37–38, 92
Hades. *See* Sheol.
Halakah, xix, xxvi, 77–92, 94, 102, 110, 144, 153–54
Hannukah, 71–72
Harvest, 126–27
Healing, xx, 31, 92, 98, 110–11, 123–30
Heaven(s), xviii–xx, xxiv–xxvii, 1–33, 35, 38, 42, 44, 47–50, 55–58, 60, 65, 74–75, 84, 86, 88–89, 117, 118, 120, 122, 125, 129, 141, 143, 145–54
Holiness, xxv, 25, 56–70, 75, 78, 85, 94, 97, 106–7, 112, 114, 117, 127, 132, 146, 151
Holy of Holies, 90, 107
Holy Spirit. *See* Spirit.
House, ix–x, xviii–xix, xxv–xxvi, 35, 44, 49, 51, 53–56, 59–62, 65, 70, 73–75, 89, 94, 97, 100, 112–13, 115–18, 127, 147, 150, 153

Household, x, xix, xxv–xxvi, 50, 61, 72–75, 86, 91, 94, 97, 100, 102, 106, 118, 127, 144, 147, 150, 154
Hyssop, 104,
Ignatius of Antioch, 19
Inheritance, 14, 86, 113, 142, 146 150
Intermediate State, xix, 17, 26–28, 145
Irenaeus, 19
Israel(ite), xxiv, xxvi, 3–5, 15, 36–40, 42, 45, 48, 56–71, 79, 80–81, 84, 86, 90, 92, 94–101, 104–7, 112–15, 117–18, 127–30, 132, 135, 143, 146, 148, 151–54
Jacob, 40, 65–69, 115, 126
Kingdom of God/Heaven, xx–xxi, 20, 23, 30, 39–40, 42, 61–62, 82–83, 99, 104, 106, 109, 113, 117–18, 124–25, 134, 150, 152
Kingdom of the World/Devil, xxi, 99, 106, 117, 125, 142, 152
Knowledge, 18–19, 21, 35, 37, 41–45, 47, 49, 53–54, 68–69, 74, 83, 85, 88, 91, 111, 116, 136, 140
Lamb, xix, xxvi, 36, 39, 94–106, 108, 111–12, 117, 144, 151
Law, xix, xxi, 7, 17, 34, 36, 38–39, 43–44, 76–85, 90–91, 94, 102, 110, 112, 114, 121–22, 134, 144
Light, 16, 26, 36–37, 42, 50, 70–72, 81, 84–85, 88, 95, 109
Living Water, xxvii, 68–70, 120–34, 141
Love, xviii, xxi–xxii, xxvi, 3, 41, 43, 61, 74, 80, 83, 86, 92, 94, 102, 109, 113, 115–17, 135, 139, 153
Luther, Martin, 21
Manna, 84, 95, 98, 105
Mission, xx, xxiv, xxvi, 35, 37–42, 48–49, 77, 90–92, 118, 133, 135–37, 143, 147, 152–53
Moses, 3–4, 39, 41, 43, 78, 81–82, 84–85, 90, 95, 98, 105, 107, 111, 136, 152
Mutual Indwelling. *See* Abiding.
Nations, 37, 64, 70, 104, 114, 126–29, 151–53
Neoplatonism. *See* Platonism.
Neopythagoreanism. *See* Pythagoreanism.

Noah, 37–38
Obedience, xviii–xix, xxi, xxv–xxvi, 13, 38, 42, 44, 47–48, 77–78, 83, 87–91, 102, 114, 117, 128, 137, 144, 147, 152–53
Oral Torah, 78,
Origen of Alexandria, 20, 23
Orphism, 9, 11
Papias, 19
Paraclete, xx, xxvi–xxvii, 51, 120, 134–44, 153–54
Paradise, xviii–xx, xxvi, 2, 4, 11, 17–18, 21, 27–28, 118, 122, 145
Parousia. See Second Coming.
Passover, xviii–xix, xxvi, 36–37, 79–80, 83–84, 90, 94–108, 112
Pharisees, 14–16, 22, 85, 111, 132
Philo, 13–14, 22
Plato, 10–13, 17–18, 22, 52
Platonism, 10–14, 18–23, 29, 32
Plotinus, 19–20
Polycarp, 19
Prepared Place, xviii–xix, xxvi, 60, 90, 94, 98, 106, 113–18, 146–47, 150–52
Presence (of God), ix, xviii–xx, xxiii–xxvii, 13–14, 21, 26–27, 30–32, 34–35, 40, 44, 47, 49, 51–53, 55–75, 77, 79, 82, 84, 89–91, 94–95, 103, 106–18, 122–23, 129–31, 134–47, 151, 153–54
Prologue, John's, 31, 45, 80–82, 109, 135, 142
Promised Land, xix, xxvi, 4, 37, 41, 86, 90–92, 94–95, 98, 104, 113, 117, 146, 151
Purity, 25, 85, 96–97, 102–3, 106–7, 111, 117, 121, 130
Pythagoreanism, 9–10, 13, 18
Qumran Sect, 15–16, 22, 31, 60–61, 84
Resurrection, xix, xxvi–xxvii, 2, 4–7, 11–17, 19–24, 26–32, 47, 51, 66, 72–73, 90, 112, 114, 117, 120, 125, 133, 137–49, 152, 154
Returning. See Coming.
Sabbath, 79, 110–11

Sacred Space, xxv, 56–59, 63–75, 80, 91, 94, 106–12, 116–18, 144, 147, 151, 153
Sacrifice, xxvi, 36, 66, 85, 90, 94–101, 105–6, 108, 112, 116, 152
Sadducees, 14–16, 22
Samaritans, 46, 67–69, 109–11, 125, 127
Second Coming, 138–42, 151, 154
Sheol, 2–3, 6–8, 10–12, 14, 17, 22, 25
Shepherd, 47
Sky, 3, 25–30, 58, 125, 148, 150
Sleep, 6, 12, 26–28
Socrates, 10, 18
Soul, 6–27, 32–33, 42, 50, 124–25, 130
Spirit/spirit, xx–xxi, xxvi–xxvii, 8, 17, 19, 32, 42, 44, 46, 59, 62–63, 68, 75, 79, 90, 99, 110, 111, 114, 119–47, 153–54
Suffering Servant, 96
Sukkot, 69–71, 79, 84, 129, 130, 132
Synoptic Gospels, xx, 29, 30, 35, 44, 46, 67, 79, 97, 103–4, 109, 123
Tabernacle, xxvi, 37, 57–58, 63–64, 66, 71–72, 74, 106–7, 112, 115, 151
Tabernacles, Feast of. See *Sukkot*.
Tabernacling, 45, 95, 108, 151
Temple, ix–x, xix, xxv–xxvi, 5, 15–17, 23, 25, 34, 36–37, 45, 56–75, 82, 85, 90, 94, 97–98, 100–118, 122–24, 126, 129, 130, 132, 147, 149, 151–54
Temple, Heavenly, 3, 15, 56, 60–61, 75, 78–81, 85, 87–88, 121, 123
Tertullian, 19
Torah, 13, 62–63
Truth, xxv, 35, 40–44, 46, 48–49, 53, 63, 66, 68, 71, 74, 79, 81–83, 85, 87, 90–92, 98, 100, 103, 110–11, 113, 125–26, 134, 136–37, 143, 152
Underworld. See Sheol.
Vine, 48, 53, 102
Walk(ing), xix–xxi, xxvi, 44, 68, 77–92, 121, 142, 144, 153–54
Water, xxvi–xxvii, 7, 18, 57, 68–72, 82, 95, 98–99, 104–5, 109–10, 120–34, 141, 146, 150

Way, the, xvii, xix–xx, xxiii–xxvi, 14, 17, 23, 30, 34, 40–41, 47–48, 50, 53, 66, 71, 74, 77–92, 98, 106, 110, 113, 116, 121, 142, 147

Well, 68–69, 109, 116, 126

Wisdom, 13–14, 16, 19, 31, 62, 66, 80–81, 121, 123, 136, 139

Worship, 36, 58, 60, 62–64, 67–68, 70, 79, 109–11, 116, 121, 126, 128, 134, 138

Yom Kippur, 58, 90, 107

Zoroastrians, 4

Greek and Hebrew Terms Index

Airō, 103
Alēthia, 42
Amnos, 95–96
Apantaō, 149
Apantēsin, 148–49
Apantēsis, 148
Apantōn], 149
Aperchomai, 140
Aphēsō, 74
Arrabon, 142
Aulē, 71
Bayit, 59
Beth-El, 65
Dabar YHWH, 81
Doxa, 45, 64
Ean mē, 83
Eis, 46
Emet, 42
Entolē, 87
Erchomai, 90, 138–40
Ginōskō, 140
Gnosis, 18
Hagiazō, 72, 100
Halak, 77–78, 89–90
Halakah, xix, xxvi, 77–80, 85, 88–89, 91, 94, 102, 110, 144, 153–54
Hallomai, 128
Hekal, 59
Heortē, 95
Hetoimazō, 113–16
Hodos, 91, 113
Hydōr zōn, 121
Ioudaios, 38–39
Israēl, 39
Israēlitē, 38–39
Kardia, 41
Kathairō, 103
Kyriou, 148
Lamad, 52
Logos, 19, 32, 81, 135
Menō, 44–51, 64
Meros, 86
Monē, 49–51, 53
Oikia, 56, 73–74
Oikon, 73
Oikos, 73–74
Ouranos, 3, 25, 28–30
Paradeisos, 27
Paradidōmi, 131–32
Paradidous, 52
Parakaleō, 134
Paraklētos, 120, 134–35
Paralambanō, 51–53
Pascha, 95
Pēgē hudatos hallomenou, 128
Pisteuō, 140
Pleura, 105
Pneuma, 131–32
Politeuma, 150
Poreuomai, 89–90, 140
Pros, 45–46
Psychē, 10
Shamayim, 25
Skēnē, 64
Skenoō, 43, 45, 64
Sōma, 10
Talmidim, 52
Tamid, 67
Tarassō, 41–42
Tē oikia tou patros, 56, 73

Teknia, 74
Tetelestai, 132
Theōreō, 140
Topos, 115–16, 147

Ancient Document Index

**OLD TESTAMENT/
HEBREW BIBLE**

Genesis

1–3	57, 145
1–2	4, 57, 135
1:1	63
1:2	132, 150
1:6–8	3
1:26–28	37, 80, 92
1:31	145
2:7	133
2:10	122
5:1–3	37
6–9	150
7:11	3
11	25
12:1	61
16:5	45
17:1–8	37
17:6–8	113
18:1–2	57
18:23–27	61
22:3–14	116
26:19	121
26:24	41
28	115
28:11	115
28:12–19	57, 65, 115
29	68
32:23–32	57, 65
33:19	69
34:19	61
34:30	61
48:22	69
49	40
49:25	3
50:4–22	61

Exodus

3:2–10	57
3:5	115
3:14	47
4:22	37
6:4–7	113
9:22–35	3
12	96–97, 112
12:7–8	99
12:10, 22, 46	104
13:21–22	70, 84
14:11–12	100
15:17	114
15:24	100
16	84
16:2–8	100
16:19–20	84
17:1–2	70
19:5–6	37
20:12	146
23:20	113
23:22–26	146
25:8	74
25:9	64
25:31–40	57
26:30	64
27:9	64

Exodus (cont.)

29:36	72
29:43	72
29:45	74
30:17–23	82, 85
33:21	115
34:5–7	43, 82
35:11	64
40:2	64
40:30–32	85
40:34	57, 64

Leviticus

6:16	71
8:10	64
8:11	72
10:1–3	106–7
11	84
14:4–7	104, 121
14:50–52	121
15:13	121
15:19–33	109
16	58, 90
16:2	107
17:10–14	99
18:28–29	114
19:2	114
19:17	80
19:18	xxi, 87
25:23	114
26:11–12	74

Numbers

1:2–45	61
1:50	64
7:1	72
9:12	104
11:12	45
19:6	104
19:12	111
19:17	80, 121
19:18	104
20:5	113
21:4–9	98
22:22–35	57
28:19	96, 115
28:22	96
32:1	113
35:34	114

Deuteronomy

1:21	41
1:29–33	41, 113
1:30	90
4:40	114
5:33	77
6:4–5	48
8:7–9	146
12:11, 21	115
13:6	45
14:24	115
20:1–3	41
21:4	121
30	4
31–33	40
31:6	41
33:13	3
34:9	136

Joshua

1:3	113
1:9	41
5:13–15	57, 115
10:11	3
22:29	64

Judges

14:6, 19	128
15:14	128
18:10	113

1 Samuel

1:7	60, 73
4:1	148
6:13	148
9:14	148
10:10	128
11:6	128
13:10, 15	148
15:12	148
16:4	148

16:13	128	8:16	114
21:1	148	12:11	148
25:32–34	148	15:2	148
30:21	148	15:18	60, 73
		19:2	148
		20:17	148
2 Samuel		28:9	148
6:20	148	31:11	114
7:24	114		
19:25	148	**Job**	
		9:8	150
1 Kings		24:13	78
3:20	45	26:11	3
6:5–16	105	28:15–28	80
6:6–49	115	37:9	3
6:29–35	37	38:22	3
6:31–36	57		
7:18–20	37	**Psalms**	
8:32–34	60	1:1	78
8:64	72	11:4	60
9:3	72	13:3	27
11:36	115	18:15	122
14:21	115	19:8	81
17:19	45	20:2–6	60
		23:6	60, 73
2 Kings		27:4	60, 73
2:9–15	136	28:2	71
21:4–7	115	29:10	122
25:24	41	33:6	81
		36:8–9	122
1 Chronicles		46:4	122
12:17	148	51:7	104
14:8	148	75:3	115
15:1–3	114	76:2–8	60
17	62	80:1–14	60
17:7–14	61	80:8–16	48
19:5	148	90:5	27
25:8	52	92:12	57
		102:18	3
2 Chronicles		106:9	122
1:4	114	107:20	81
3:1	114	118:30	78
5:11–14	64	119:105	81
6:21	60	122:1	60, 73
7:7–20	72	123:1	60
7:16	57	135:7	3

Proverbs

8	80
13:14	121
16:22	121
18:4	121
21:16	78
30:5–6	81

Ecclesiastes

5:2	60

Isaiah

1:12	71
2:2–4	70, 129
2:2	114, 127
2:3	153
4:5	115
5:1–7	48
6:1–6	60
10:24	41
11:6–9	4, 146
11:9	121
11:11–12	127, 153
12:3–4	70
24:13	127
25–26	5
26:7	78
27:2–6	48
27:12	127, 153
28:4	127
30:23–26	121
32:1–15	122
33:21	115
35:1–6	122
35:6	128
35:8	78
40:3	113
40:22	3
41:17–20	121
42:6	37
43:19–21	121
44:3	70, 121–22
44:3–4	121
44:27	122
46:3	61
48:21	121
49:10	121
50:2	122
51:3	4, 146
51:10	122
53:7	96
55:1	70, 121
55:10	3, 121
55:11	81, 121
56:1–8	127, 153
56:6–8	70, 129
56:7	73
57:14–15	62
58:11	70
60:5–7	153
60:7	73
63:15	60
65:25	4, 146
66:1	60, 115
66:18	127

Jeremiah

1:8	41
2:21	48
10:30	3
23	47
23:29	81
25:30	60
28:31	148
31:31–34	62
31:34	154
34:2	148
48:6	148
51:15–16	121
51:36	122
51:39	27

Ezekiel

10:4	71
10:18	64
12:1	81
15:2–6	48
17:5–10	48
19:10–14	48
20:6	113
28:13–17	37
34	47

36:24–28	62, 121–22
36:35	4, 146
37	5
37:1–14	133
37:25	126
37:26–28	74
40–48	62
40:20	71
41:5–26	105
42:13	115
43:4–5	64
45:4	113
45:21–25	96
46:1	71
46:19–20	115
47:1–12	4, 37, 70, 121–23, 129, 146
47:22–23	127, 153

Daniel
8:11	115
12	31
12:2–3	6, 27

Hosea
2:14–23	4, 146
6:11	127

Joel
2:28–29	122
3:11–18	126–27
3:18	4, 121–22, 146

Amos
1:3	81
5:8	150
8:11–12	121
9:6	150

Micah
1:2–3	60
4:1	114
6:6–8	62

Nahum
1:4	122

Habakkuk
2:14	121, 154
2:20	60

Zechariah
4:6	81
10:11	122
13:1	115, 121
14:8	121–22
14:16–19	70, 129, 153

APOCRYPHA

Tobit
3:10	6
4:19	6

Judith
3:3	113
5:4	148
10:4	148

Wisdom of Solomon
1:14—2:3	13
3:1–4	13
4:7	13
4:18–20	13
5:1, 3	13
5:15–16	13
7:21–30	62
8:21	62
9:8	60, 114

Sirach
14:16–19	6
15:3	121
17:25–32	6
19:29	148
24	62
24:23–29	121
24:23	80–81, 121

Sirach (cont.)

24:25–30	121
36:1	148
38:16–23	6
41:3–4	6
47:13	114
49:12	114
48:4–5	6
51:5–6	6

Baruch

2:16	60
2:26	60–61, 73
3:24	61, 113
4:1–3	80–81, 114, 122, 127

1 Maccabees

4:48	72
7:38	49–50
12:41	148

2 Maccabees

5:20	115
7	13
7:20–23	7
7:36	7
10:5–8	71
12:30	149
14:30	149
15:12	149

2 Esdras

1:33–35	61

4 Maccabees

7:18–20	13
9:8–22	13
10:15	13
14:5	13
16:13–25	13
17:5–18	13
18:3–23	13

PSEUDEPIGRAPHA

2 Baruch

4:3–7	60
21:19–25	17
21:23–24	17
30:1–5	17
32:4–6	17
44:9–10	17
44:15	17
49:2—51:3	17
51:11	17
54:13–14	81

3 Baruch

4:3–6	18
10:1–10	18

1 Enoch

14:8–23	60
14:10–15	60
21–22	7, 60
41:2	60
90:2–4	40, 99
90:28–36	114
90:33–36	122
91:13	60
92:2	40

Jubilees

22:23	40

Pseudo-Philo (LAB)

11:1	85
32:7	80

Letter of Aristeas

89–91	122

Sibylline Oracles

5:158–59	122
5:447–48	122

Testament of Levi

4:1	122
14:4	81
18:5–8	122

Testament of Zebulun

10:1–2	40

NEW TESTAMENT

Matthew

1:20, 24	52
2:13–21	52
3:2	30
3:3	113
4:5, 8	52
4:17	30
5:3–20	30
5:12	29
6:9–13	30
6:20, 29	145
7:21	30
8:11	30
8:22–23	52
9:24	27
10:7–12	30
10:37	52
12:45	52
13:11–52	30
16:19	30
17:1	52
18:1–23	30, 52
19:12–23	29, 30, 145
19:28–29	29
20:1	30
20:17	52
22:2	30
22:16	78
22:36–40	xxi
23:13	30
24:14	127, 153
24:40–41	52
25:1	30
25:6	148
25:32	127, 153
25:34	113
26:37	52
26:58, 69	71
27:24	121
27:27	52
27:32	148
27:51–53	24, 26–27, 29
28:1–10	29
28:2–7	24
28:19–20	92, 127, 153

Mark

1:3	113
2:26	73
4:36	52
5:39	27
5:40	52
7:4	52
9:2	52
9:42–48	24
10:21	29
10:32	52
12:14	78
12:25–27	29
14:13	149
14:33	52
14:54, 66	71
16:1–8	29
16:5–19	24

Luke

1:6	89
1:17, 76	114
2:31	113
2:49	72
6:33	29
8:52	27
9:10, 28	52
9:60–62	52
11:26	52
11:51	73
12:21	145
12:33	29
14:14	30
14:26	52
16:19–31	27
16:22–23	45
17:12	149

Luke (cont.)

17:34–35	52
18:22	29
18:31	52
20:21	78
20:34–38	29
22:28–30	29
22:55	71
23:43, 27	145
24:1–44	29
24:6–7, 38–40	24

John

1	36, 52, 66, 82, 88, 97, 112, 132, 134
1:1–18	82
1:1–3	65
1:1	45–46, 109
1:2	65
1:4–9	81, 85, 88
1:9	109
1:10–14	42–43
1:11–12	52
1:12–18	40
1:12–13	142
1:12	46, 72, 74
1:14	31, 45, 63–64, 95, 126, 136
1:15	139
1:16–18	36, 43, 45–46, 65, 82, 90, 95
1:19–28	39
1:19	82
1:23	82, 113
1:26–34	134
1:26–30	124
1:26–28	92
1:29–36	95
1:29	36, 96–97, 103, 105
1:30	139
1:31	39
1:32–34	45–46, 123–24, 142
1:35	46
1:36	96, 105
1:37–39	136
1:38–43	82
1:38–39	45, 46
1:43	77, 88
1:45	95
1:46	43
1:47–51	39, 65
1:51	64–65, 75, 97, 115
2	62, 73–74, 82–83, 112
2:1–10	124
2:6	82
2:12	45
2:13–25	95, 97, 103
2:16–17	73–74
2:19–21	43, 66, 73, 97
2:23	95
2:25	97
3	83, 112, 124–25, 134
3:1–10	109
3:2	136
3:3	83
3:3–8	142
3:3–5	124, 134
3:10	39
3:11	136
3:12	125
3:14–15	95, 98, 105
3:15	47
3:16–21	88
3:16–17	40, 109
3:16	xxi, xxiii, 47, 83, 153
3:19–21	xxi, 83, 125
3:31	125
3:35	xxi
3:36	44, 47, 99
4	105, 112, 125, 134
4:1–42	68
4:1–3	127
4:5	69

4:12	69	6:27	44–45, 47–48
4:13–24	134	6:31–59	95
4:14	47, 125, 128	6:35	47
4:20–24	43, 66	6:39–54	24, 31
4:21–28	139	6:40	47–48
4:22	95	6:42	43
4:23–26	68	6:44	31
4:23	110, 126, 128	6:47–48	84
4:24	68–69, 126	6:47	47
4:35	126–27	6:49	84
4:36	47	6:51–58	43
4:39–45	126	6:51–56	99
4:39–42	46, 127	6:51	36, 98
4:40	45, 136	6:53	83, 99
4:41	81	6:54	31, 47
4:42	110	6:56	44, 47
4:44	108	6:59	136
4:45	95	6:63	99
4:46–53	127	6:68	47
5	110, 112	7	69–70, 105, 129–31, 134
5:1–15	128		
5:1–9	31	7:9	45
5:1	95	7:14–19	90
5:8–9	83	7:14	85, 136
5:13	115	7:19, 22–23	85, 95
5:16	110	7:23	136
5:19–30	110	7:27	43
5:20	xxi	7:28	43
5:24–28	24, 31	7:37–39	70, 95, 99, 130, 132, 134
5:24	47, 81		
5:36	136	7:40	81
5:38	44, 81	7:41	43
5:39–47	43	7:52	43
5:39	47	8	70
5:42	xxi	8:5	95
5:43	136	8:12	36, 43, 47, 71, 85, 88, 95
5:45–46	95		
6	47	8:14	136
6:1–14	98	8:21–51	99
6:1–12	31	8:23–44	xxi
6:4–14	90	8:31	44, 81
6:4	95	8:32–34	99
6:5–6	83–84	8:33–34	95
6:7	84	8:35	45, 62
6:10	115	8:37	81
6:23	115	8:41	48
6:26–58	90, 98	8:42–55	43
6:27–30	43	8:42	xxi

John (cont.)

8:44	99
8:51–52	81
8:51	99
8:55	81
9	110–12
9:1–7	31
9:6–7	83
9:12	111
9:16	111
9:24–34	111
9:28–29	95
9:34–38	111
9:36	111
9:41	43–44
10	47–48, 71
10:1–18	47
10:1	71
10:7	47
10:15	72
10:16	48, 71
10:17	xxi
10:18	87
10:25–27	48
10:27	82
10:28	47
10:30	48
10:36	72, 100
10:38	48
10:40	45, 115
11	100, 111–12
11:3, 5	xxi
11:6	45, 115
11:9	85, 88
11:11–12	27
11:25–26	24, 31
11:25	47
11:30	115
11:31	74
11:36	xxi
11:38–41	31
11:43–44	83
11:47—12:8	100, 102
11:47–57	100–101, 105
11:48	101, 116
11:50	48, 101
11:52	48
11:54	45
11:55	95, 100
11:56	95
11:57	87
12–13	88
12	100–101
12:1–8	100
12:1	95, 100
12:3	74, 85
12:3–8	85
12:12	95
12:13	39
12:23–26	24
12:24–26	31, 87
12:24	44, 83
12:25	xxi, 47
12:26	53, 82
12:27	42
12:31	42
12:32	53
12:34	44
12:35–36	85
12:43	xxi
12:46	44
12:47–50	99
12:48	136
12:49	87
12:50	47, 87
13	89, 101–2
13:1–16	86
13:1–2	86
13:1	xxi, 87, 95, 101–3
13:3–4	86
13:8	83, 86
13:10–11	102–3
13:12–20	87
13:21–30	89
13:23	xxi
13:25	45
13:29	95
13:33	74
13:34	xxi, 87
13:35	xxi
13:36–38	89
14–17	40, 88, 131–32
14–16	134, 141
14–15	87

14	ix, xviii–xix, xxiv–xxvii, 33, 35, 40–41, 44, 48–50, 52, 55–56, 72–75, 77, 88–90, 92, 113, 116–17, 120, 134, 139–42, 144, 146, 154	14:31	87, 116
		15	48, 87, 102, 106
		15:1–17	53
		15:1–10	102
		15:1	47
		15:2	103
		15:3	103
		15:4–5	136
14:1–6	35	15:4	44, 83
14:1–3	ix, xviii, 87–88, 92, 146–47	15:5	44
		15:6	44, 103
14:1–2	49	15:7	44
14:1	41–44, 140	15:9	xxi, 44, 87
14:2–5	140	15:10–17	88
14:2–3	40, 73, 88, 115–16, 139	15:10	xxi, 44, 48, 83, 87
		15:12	xxi, 83, 87
14:2	xxv, 49–51, 53, 74, 89, 113	15:13	xxi, 83, 89, 100
		15:14	83, 87
14:3	xxvi, 51–53, 116, 120, 137–40	15:15–16	103
		15:15	95
14:4–6	53, 78, 91	15:16	44, 48
14:6	47, 53, 74, 92, 116, 136, 140	15:17	xxi, 83, 87
		15:19	xxi
14:7	47, 74, 116, 140	15:20	95
14:9	116, 140	15:26–27	133
14:10–12	116, 140	15:26	68, 134, 136
14:10	44	16	139–40, 142
14:12	90, 116, 136, 140, 152–53	16:2	139
		16:3	136, 140
14:14–15	90	16:5–14	140
14:15	xxi, 83, 87, 116	16:7	68, 134, 140, 143
14:16–18	120, 139	16:8–11	137
14:16–17	68, 133	16:8–9	136
14:16	134–35	16:9	140
14:17	44, 116, 136, 140	16:12–14	136–37, 139
14:18	74–75, 139–40, 153	16:14–15	68
		16:16–19	140
14:19	31, 140	16:17–18	90
14:20	116, 136, 140	16:23	140
14:21–24	xxi	16:25	139, 141
14:21	87, 116	16:27	xxi
14:22–23	139–40	16:33	42
14:23–24	81, 116	17	48, 117
14:23	49, 74, 136, 140	17:2–3	47, 49
14:25	44, 113, 116–17, 136	17:7–8	49
		17:11	48–49
14:26	134, 136	17:17–19	100, 153
14:28	116, 139–40	17:21	49

John (*cont.*)

17:22–23	48
17:23	xxi, 136
17:24–26	116
17:24	xxi, 53
17:26	xxi, 136
18–19	103, 112
18:2	115
18:14	48
18:15	71
18:28—19:42	103
18:28	95, 103
18:33–38	40
18:33	39
18:36	xxi, 39
18:38	42
18:39	95, 103
19–20	131
19	36, 39, 131, 142
19:13–20	116
19:14	95, 103–4
19:16	52
19:26–27	xxi, 72
19:28	131
19:29	104
19:30–34	99
19:30	123, 131, 133–34, 139, 141
19:31	45, 103–4
19:33	104
19:34	105, 123, 131
19:42	103–4
20	132, 142
20:1–31	31
20:2	xxi
20:7	115
20:17	72
20:19	132
20:11–18	83
20:21	133, 153
20:22–23	132–34, 136, 139, 141
20:33	123
21:7, 15–17	xxi
21:19–22	77, 82, 88
21:20	xxi
21:22–23	45, 50

Acts

3:8	128
3:20–21	145
8:32	96
9:1	79
9:31	89
14:10	128
18:25–26	78
19:9, 23	79
22:4	79
24:14	79
24:22	79
28:15	148

Romans

5:12–21	37
5:14	38
6:8–23	24, 29
8:18–25	24, 29
8:20–23	29
8:29	38

1 Corinthians

3:16–17	59
4:17	78
6:14	29
6:19–20	59
11:23	52
12:31	78
15:1, 3	52
15:18–20	27
15:20–23	24, 29, 145
15:45–47	38

2 Corinthians

1:21–22	142
4:7–11	28
5:1–5	28–29, 142
5:8	27, 145
12:2–10	27–28, 145

Galatians

1:9, 12	52
5:15	99
6:7–10	127

Ephesians

1:10	29
1:13	142
2:19, 21	61, 62
4:30	142
5:14	27

Philippians

1:21–24	27
3:10–11	29
3:20–21	149
4:9	52

Colossians

1:15–23	29, 38
2:6	52
4:17	52

1 Thessalonians

2:13	52
4:1	52
4:13–18	24, 27, 29
4:16–17	28, 147, 148
5:10	27

2 Thessalonians

3:6	52

1 Timothy

3:15	62
6:19	145

Hebrews

8	59
8:5	60
8:11	154
9:19–22	104
10:22	121
11	24
11:13–16	150
12:28	52

1 Peter

1	145
1:3	24
1:19	96
4:3	89
4:17	62

2 Peter

2:10	89
2:21	78
3:3	89

1 John

2:1	134, 135
2:28	26
3:2	26

Jude

11:16, 18	89

Revelation

1:5–6	24
2:7	27
5:9–10	153
6:9–11	27
7:9–17	24, 153
11:2	71
11:15	152
11:19	3
14:18–20	127
21:1—22:5	24
21:1–3	122, 150
21:22	114, 151
21:24–26	127, 153
22:1–2	122

DEAD SEA SCROLLS

Damascus Document (CD)

I, 19	61
III, 16	121
III, 19	61
VI, 3–5	121

Thanksgiving Hymns (1QH)

V, 13–16	124
XVI, 5–26	15

War Scroll (1QM)

I, 5–13	16
XVIII	16

Community Rule (1QS)

IV, 9–11	85
VIII, 5–10	15, 61
IX, 5–8	61

Songs of the Sabbath Sacrifice (4Q ShirŠabb)

	15

Temple Scroll (11QT)

XLIV	60

RABBINIC WRITINGS

b. Ketubbot

111.17A	114
111.5C–D	114

b. Šabbat

88a	80

Genesis Rabbah

1.1, 4	80
65.23	69

m. 'Abot

1.4, 11–12	121
2.8	121
3.1	124

m. Baba Meṣi'a

2.11	52

m. Kelim

1.6–9	107

m. Middot

3.3	105
5.3–4	60

m. Miqwa'ot

1.4–8	121

m. Niddah

4.1	109

m. Sanhedrin

10.1–6	15

m. Sukkah

4.9–10	129
5.2	71

Mekilta Pisha

I:III.3B	114

Midrash on the Psalms

78.6	69

Pesiqta Rabbati

30.3	69
17.2	69

Sifre Numbers

119	69

Targum Neofit

Gen 28:10	69

Targum Yerušalmi I

Gen 29:1	69
Num 23:17–31	69

GRECO-ROMAN WRITINGS

Homer

Iliad

1.1–3	8
3.320–22	8
6.486–89	8
23.99–107	8

Odyssey

3.409	8
4.562–69	8
11.205–9	8
11.208–22	8
11.219–25	8
11.475–77	8

Josephus

Antiquities of the Jews

2.14.6	96
3.7.7	58
8.13.7	49
13.2.1	49, 50
15.11.5	107
18.1.3	15
18.1.4	15
18.1.5	15

Jewish War

5.5.2	107
7.4.1	149

Plato

Phaedo

64c–69a	10

Theaetetus

198b	52

Timaeus

29e–31b	10

Philo

On the Giants

13–15	14

Seneca

Controversiae

1.8.16	99

EARLY CHRISTIAN WRITINGS

Aquinas, Thomas

Summa Theologica

1.102	21

Calvin, John

Institutes of the Christian Religion

3.25.6	21
3.25.8	21
3.25.10	21

Origen

First Principles

2.3.7	20

www.ingramcontent.com/pod-product-compliance
Lightning Source LLC
Chambersburg PA
CBHW060609230426
43670CB00011B/2045